GENDER AND MIGRATION

About the Editors

Ingrid Palmary is an associate professor in the Forced Migration Studies Progamme at the University of the Witwatersrand, Johannesburg. She has written on a range of topics including gender-based violence in times of armed conflict and the gendered nature of displacement. She is the co-editor of the forthcoming book *International Feminisms*.

Erica Burman is professor of psychology and women's studies at Manchester Metropolitan University. As a feminist developmental psychologist, critical social researcher and group analyst, she has written extensively on gender, culture and mental health issues. Her most recent books are *Deconstructing Developmental Psychology* and *Developments: Child, Image, Nation*.

Khatidja Chantler is a lecturer and researcher in social work at the University of Manchester. She has undertaken a range of research projects, including on forced marriage and domestic and sexual violence in male, black, lesbian, gay and transgendered communities. She is co-author of *Attempted Suicide and Self-harm: South Asian Women* and *Domestic Violence and Minoritisation*.

Peace Kiguwa lectures in psychology and currently gender and human rights at the University of the Witwatersrand, Johannesburg. She is co-editor of *Critical Psychology* and *The Gender of Psychology*. Her research interests include critical studies in race and gender issues.

GENDER AND MIGRATION

Feminist Interventions

Edited by

INGRID PALMARY
ERICA BURMAN
KHATIDJA CHANTLER
PEACE KIGUWA

Zed Books
London & New York

Gender and Migration: Feminist Interventions was first published in 2010 by Zed Books Ltd, 7 Cynthia Street, London N1 9JF, UK and Room 400, 175 Fifth Avenue, New York, NY 10010, USA

www.zedbooks.co.uk

Typeset in Sabon by Free Range Book Design & Production
Index: Rohan Bolton, Rohan.Indexing@gmail.com
Cover designed by www.alice-marwick.co.uk
Printed and bound in Great Britain by CPI Antony Rowe, Chippenham and Eastbourne

Distributed in the USA exclusively by Palgrave Macmillan, a division of St Martin's Press, LLC, 175 Fifth Avenue, New York, NY 10010, USA

A catalogue record for this book is available from the British Library
Library of Congress Cataloging in Publication Data available

ISBN 978 1 84813 410 2 hb
ISBN 978 1 84813 411 9 pb
ISBN 978 1 84813 412 6 eb

Contents

CHAPTER 1

Gender and migration: feminist interventions

Ingrid Palmary, Erica Burman, Khatidja Chantler
and Peace Kiguwa

Interrogating the 'and' in gender and migration

Gender has increasingly appeared as a specific preoccupation in research and writing on migration (see for example Chant 1992, Anthias 1992, Anthias and Lazaridis 2000, Jolly 2005). Whilst many have lamented the lack of attention to gender (see Indra 1999), a basic search of the literature now indicates much and frequent attention to 'gender and migration' (perhaps most clearly evidenced by the number of titles that attempt to 'engender' migration), although the nature of the 'and', the connection or articulation, has been little interrogated. It would seem, then, that the question should be less about why gender has not been (as yet) 'mainstreamed' into migration, than about how and why it figures in conceptualisations of mobility, and with what effects. Hence, in this collection, we aim not so much to 'add' gender to the existing migration research taking place globally, but rather to reflect upon *how* gender has become a preoccupation when thinking about migration. As such, we comment on the absences, silences and exclusions of understandings of gender that have become part of the production of knowledge about migration whilst also offering new analytic starting points for thinking through the connections. In this book, we are concerned with the meanings attached to different kinds of migrants, different kinds of movements and

1

different motivations for moving, and how these meanings shape the kinds of support, or alternatively (symbolic or literal) violence – including non-response – assigned to their 'mobility'. The terms that circulate often reflect these classifications of migration, with 'mobility' evoking a specific register – of class mobility – so importing the spectre of economic issues that so much of state immigration policy proscribes or pathologises in order to frame forced migration. The term 'mobility' not only involves notions of movement to and from places (including assumptions about the unidirectional character of contemporary migration that are often unfounded), but also has notions of difference coded into distance. This implicit feature of spatio-temporal distancing is part of what allows racialised, gendered and classed assumptions to be covertly reproduced within migration discourses (Frello 2008). Thus the act of pathologising that is enacted within migration discourses is often only able to function or exist in decontextualised, essentialist and organic categories of 'the migrant'. Whilst much discussion on gender and migration, both here and elsewhere, focuses on the movement of women and the meanings assigned to this, the chapters presented here also interrogate the contested meanings of more broadly gendered constructs of home, nation, the political and the domestic and how these impact on both embodied migrants, and symbolic understandings of home and away.

Our rationale in composing this volume, therefore, arose from our view that, whilst the current focus in existing literature on women is not necessarily inappropriate, a further analytic shift is needed to interrogate the concept of gender at play. In other words, rather than understanding gender as a synonym of 'women' we seek to analyse gendered positionings within normative discourses (of state policies and practices) as our topic. Here gender represents a topic of inquiry rather than an assumed identity or even relationship. In spite of this, moving away entirely from constructed gender binaries is difficult, and potentially problematic, given that they shape so much of the response to migrants. As Calavita (2006) notes, the law (which structures much of the state response to migration) takes the male/female binary to be a fact. Therefore, the different chapters in this book address gender as subject position rather than identity or attribute. In particular the chapters by Julie Middleton and Sajida Ismail, addressing the South African and United Kingdom asylum systems respectively, consider how implicitly masculine forms of violence are privileged in state responses to violence, as well as challenging the heteronormativity of the law that draws on this binary. Even as we may wish to challenge the male/female binary of legal responses to migration we cannot avoid its implications for those deemed less worthy migrants. In this sense, in its masculine presumptions, migration has, of course, always been gendered (see also Indra 1999). This has had deleterious consequences for both women and men, but in different ways. Thus while in this book we have taken up the focus on gender mainly in relation to consequences for women, this does not mean that gendered issues should be assumed or normalised in relation to men. It has long been recognised that migrant masculinity, including male migrant bodies, have been portrayed (following longstanding themes of hypersexual 'alien' men) as posing a threat to the host nation, often through an assumed threat to 'its' women (see also Bhattacharrya 2008). In this book Stavros Psaroudakis' chapter focusing on young male migrants in Greece specifically highlights the different, if equivalently problematic, positions accorded to these young men and their (attributed and proscribed) sexualised positionings. Recognising this requires us to challenge the aggressive claims to neutrality of so much state attention to migration – a task taken up in the chapter by Erica Burman (see also Spivak 1993).

In a related critique, Loescher and Scanlan (1986) refer to the double standards and calculated kindnesses of US refugee policy. This expression neatly captures the often benevolent discourse of state protection that functions to obscure its violence against migrants. States are increasingly drawing their boundaries ever more tightly in an attempt to dissuade people from entering – including those most typically identified as 'forced migrants'. The resultant policies are frequently harsh and punitive and, given this context, some may question or challenge the focus on gender that this book takes. It could be argued that all migrants are treated punitively and that the focus on gender detracts from the overall positioning of migrants. By contrast, however, we argue that although the overall context is the same for men and women, a focus on gender illuminates accounts and positions (of both women and men) that would otherwise remain invisible and highlights the significance of gender (whether visible or not) in the responses that are made to migrants. More than this, we propose that gender is not merely an additional (discretionary or supplementary) variable that qualifies an already existent gender-neutral category of 'migrant' but rather structures that category (as male or female) in the first place, with the prototypical (presumed economic) migrant characterised as the single male and the woman positioned as dependent or victim. Developing Butler's (1990) analysis we should note that, once so founded, other related categories of identity that prompt or warrant migration – such as sexuality – are then elaborated. In this sense, we could say – following Shepherd (2008) – that migration discourses participate within the wider international relations debates that do not simply reflect but perform, and so often violently reproduce, gender.

The subtitle of this book, feminist interventions, is reflected in the conceptual and methodological tools drawn upon to evaluate representations of migrants and their gendered consequences. Key political consequences follow from the ways in which migrants are gendered. In the case of women migrants, these range from the level of the intimate and interpersonal realm of family to the nation-state, and indeed one of the central contributions of this collection is to recognise the interrelatedness of what Silvey (2006) terms scales of analysis. The tendency in writings on migration to perpetuate an imagined separation of state and family – of the household and labour market, for example – reflects the way that gender categorisations have been treated as 'ontologically given' (Silvey 2006: 68). Challenging the assumed distinctness between the political and the domestic, the state and the family is a longstanding but still necessary feminist intervention (see also Anthias and Yuval-Davis 1989, Palmary 2006). This is a concern central to many of the chapters in this book that focus on the state's regulation of intimate relationships in ways that highlight the myth of the public/private dichotomy. Further interventions include reflections on humanitarianism, state interventions and those more rooted in advocacy. As such, they are interventions both into the ways that gender is conceptualised and (under)theorised as well as reflecting critically on interventions with and for migrants.

But this book does not only draw on feminist politics as an interpretive frame. It also offers significant challenges to feminist theory and practice. A key assumption guiding contributions to this book is that attention to the gendered nature of the meanings we give to migration necessarily requires a rethinking and reassertion of themes central to the feminist project. This includes reconceptualising the relationship between state and domestic violence, including highlighting what kinds of violence get cast as political and what as domestic. These themes are elaborated in the chapters by Julie Middleton, Sajida Ismail and Khatidja Chantler, who – writing from the diverse contexts of South Africa and the UK – analyse the role that the asylum systems in both national contexts play in creating and perpetuating these categorisations and what might be at stake in undoing them.

This interpretive move also involves challenging the assumed distinction between economic and political migration alongside exploring consequences of the gendered division between the body and the nation.

Fekete (2006), as well as contributors to this book (in particular see chapters by Chandré Gould and Ingrid Palmary), have raised concerns about the increasing alliances between right-wing politics and a (proclaimed) feminist movement. Practices such as loyalty testing and attitude testing, on the increase in many European countries, are frequently justified as a means of protecting the imagined gender equality of the host country from migrants from 'less progressive' countries. These developments require greater and more critical attention and intervention. There has been a long feminist tradition of engagement with and critique of the project of the nation-state (see Yuval-Davis and Anthias 1989, Gouws 2005, Ueno 2004) and the new ways that the nation is re-created through discourses of migration requires attention for the way it equally legitimates practices of racism and exclusion in the name of protecting the 'womenandchildren' (Enloe 1990; Sylvester 1999). Thus, for example, denying family reunification on the basis that a marriage was not freely entered into has been justified in the name of protecting the woman in that relationship. The need to be able to analyse exploitative conditions of marriage in host and migrant communities without lapsing into racist assumptions about whether, for example, arranged marriages (set up in hierarchical comparison to an idealised and mythical notion of Western marriages) are ever freely entered into is central for a new feminist politics of migration. The growing concern in the West about the need to protect women and men from forced marriage has resulted in the state taking up feminist concerns (e.g. of forced marriage) and introducing immigration policies such as the increase in the age at which one can sponsor or reside with a non-European Union spouse to 21 in the UK and 24 in Denmark. Hence feminists need to be alert to the dangers of co-option in the current nation-state project of protecting borders (Chantler *et al.* 2009, Razack 2004). Fekete (2006) quotes Azizah Y. Al-Hibri, president and founder of Muslim women lawyers for Human Rights as saying: 'If Western women are now vying for the control of the lives of immigrant women by justifying coercive state action, then these women have not learned the lessons of history, be it colonialism, imperialism, or even fascism' (cited in Fekete 2006: 13).

In similar ways, debates in France over the ban on the hijab have often set racism and sexism up as competing concerns in unhelpful ways that return us to the single-issue politics that has been so thoroughly critiqued in, for example, post-colonial feminist writing (see Mohanty 1993). Examples of questioning the legitimacy of marriages and the preoccupation with migrant women's sexual transgressions is just one example of how sexuality and racialised gender norms are disciplined by social institutions, assumptions and practices that normalise (racialised) heterosexuality and subject different migrants to different kinds of gendered stereotypes. Attention to the sexual lives of migrants has been extensive and almost entirely problem focused – through a preoccupation with HIV infection, sex work, trafficking, forced marriage and so on. The inseparability of these practices and their role in sustaining the myth of the 'free world' figure as an important undercurrent in this book.

Equally evident in this kind of approach to protecting migrant women is the assumption that the threat posed to migrant women is from migrant men. This excludes the hierarchies set up between citizens and migrants that make violence against non-citizens tolerated, a topic clearly taken up in Monica Kiwanuka's chapter, and it occludes the ways that the state renders migrants more vulnerable to abuse and indeed perpetrates much of this abuse; for example, through extended detention periods for migrants. In this way, the history of racism, sexism and colonialism of Western societies is erased at the same time as, and by virtue of, migrants being positioned as those who are bringing intolerance to host societies. This theme is central to Alexandra Zavos' analysis of the anti-racist movement in Greece, which explores the risks and challenges of different political standpoints for social movements and activists, as well as state protagonists. Similarly, subtle forms of this representation of the state as neutral and rational are challenged by Erica Burman's chapter in her analysis of formal institutional responses to questions about the functioning of the asylum system.

The authors of these chapters draw from a range of diverse national contexts and arenas of practice. As such, the arguments may appear divergent, but read together these diverse contexts raise some questions about the spatial distribution of power, with each country context negotiating its own forms of recognition and exclusion in the context of an increasingly globalised and Anglo-US dominated discourse on migration. Furthermore, an obvious but significant point to note is that the *meaning* of different places affects who migrates and with what consequences – consequences that are (over)determined by 'race', class, religion and country of origin. A third area of differentiation is the range of research frameworks and analytic methods drawn upon by the authors, which include critical reflection on academic research, cross-national research, and programme analysis. Articulating the tensions between and across such conceptual and topical arenas is important if we are to understand local manifestations of the global project of migration control and its particular forms of marginalisation and exclusion.

Nevertheless, whilst the contributions in this book draw from different disciplinary perspectives, some shared methodological as well as political presuppositions guide the analyses presented here. In particular, in part overdetermined by the longstanding cultural connections between women, emotions and the private sphere, there is an engagement with theoretical frameworks that emphasise their constructed character alongside the real, material effects of contingent constructions. Hence – contrary to some readings of 'discourse analysis' as relativist – a clear political commitment to using our analysis as the basis of critique and engagement informs the work collected here (Parker 2003, Van Leeuwen and Wodak 1999). In spite of these differences, there are three strong common themes that tie these chapters together, namely visibility, vulnerability and credibility.

Visibility, vulnerability, credibility

Three pervasive themes resonate across this collection. Together, its contributors focus attention on how visible different groups of migrants may be and may desire to be. Whilst one cannot argue that women have been visible as migrants, it is the nature of this visibility that needs to be contested. In particular, the chapters making up Part One of this collection – with the title *Visibility and Vulnerability* – consider how vulnerability gets constructed through representations of female suffering and the consequences of naming certain groups as vulnerable. The labelling of vulnerable groups and the slide between vulnerability and pathology are concerns that have been common to feminist writing for some time (Allen 1981). Each of the contributors to this section continues this critique to consider the costs of being rendered part of a vulnerable group and who is excluded from such classifications. Ingrid Palmary and Chandré Gould problematise the notion of women as trafficking victims and how this might in fact render it more difficult to address the ongoing exploitation of migrant women and the domestic, and sexualised, nature of their work. Taking this theme further, Alexandra Zavos equally asks fundamental questions about who claims to represent the vulnerable, showing how, in the emotive debates posed by a benevolent desire to assist migrants on the part of Greek anti-racist activists, migrant perspectives are themselves silenced.

Continuing the critical reflection on who is rendered visible and how vulnerability is constructed in the process, Part Two of the book, called *Asylum*, concentrates on the visibility of women within the asylum system. While the chapters in this Part focus on the British and South African asylum system, they highlight important concerns for how this system globally has shaped notions of vulnerability. In this section of the book the notion of credibility comes most strongly to the fore, with chapters here considering how narrow interpretations of vulnerability work to minimise women's access to assistance by insisting on a pre-existing and feminised notion of vulnerability. Both Khatidja Chantler and Sajida Ismail note how this renders the claims of some women less credible than others in the UK. This theme is developed by Julie Middleton who, from her analysis of the South African systems, also points to how bureaucratic procedures can be used to render women's asylum claims incredible whilst retaining a myth of objectivity. Finally, organisational rationality is challenged in Erica Burman's analysis of responses by the British Home Office to questions about the asylum claims of Pakistani women. Collectively, each of the chapters highlights the ambivalent position of women and the forms of violence they encounter even within international frameworks for protection. In particular, these chapters identify how covertly gendered but explicitly gender-free notions of culture, domestic violence, and 'race' work to exclude women's experiences. The authors consider the ways in which discourses of 'race' and culture are mobilised to legitimate exclusion in spite of (and precisely because of) claims to bureaucratic and administrative objectivity. Each of these chapters evaluates the consequences of the narrow recognition of women's positions within the asylum system focused on exclusion, and ultimately functions to depoliticise and render their persecution 'domestic' or 'cultural'. At a wider level, such analyses graphically highlight key consequences that follow from the differentiation and classification of forms of violence, setting up hierarchies of suffering such that different kinds of interventions are deemed necessary depending on whether the violence is rendered political or domestic within official discourse.

This depoliticisation of violence against women through discourses of the cultural and domestic is continued and further elaborated in Part Three of the book, called *Depoliticising Migration*. In dealing with the depoliticisation of certain kinds of violence, this part of the book takes the questions about the credibility of different kinds of migrants further. In particular, the chapter by Monica Kiwanuka, discussing Southern African migrant women in South Africa, focuses on the role of the state and how it facilitates the perpetuation and sanctioning of supposedly 'domestic' violence, bringing to the fore the double nuance of 'domestic' as within-state as well as interpersonal and private. In particular, this chapter reminds us of how state violence shapes and renders possible intimate family violence. In contrast, Isabel Rodríguez Mora, in her chapter about the impact of the floods in Venezuela, adopts a different analytical position to consider the risks of being visible and who is rendered visible. She points out how it is the poor – and in particular poor women – who are most subjected to the scrutiny and evaluation that comes with humanitarian interventions and, through these, they are rendered visible to the state and the public in ways that the middle class are not – highlighting Hogan and Marandola's (2005) notion of 'multiple vulnerability', whereby vulnerability in one domain (class) will influence vulnerability in another domain (mobility). However, she goes beyond this to also critique the emphasis on the mothering and familial practices of women within aid interventions, which further lends itself to a depoliticisation of such interventions. Her chapter strikingly illustrates the slide between assistance and surveillance of 'proper' family relations, practices of motherhood and childcare, and sexuality. By such means, humanitarian aid can turn into the control and regulation of socially marginalised groups. Similarly, albeit in a very different (South African) context, Caroline Kihato considers migrant women's desire to stay invisible – from the state and others – and the risks of making oneself too visible. As development theorists have long been pointing out (Scott 1997, Parpart 1995), visibility may bring resources but it also imports surveillance and the possibilities of other forms of regulation, and even threatens to expose and so render impossible subaltern survival strategies. While Caroline Kihato's photographic project highlights the value for some migrants of remaining outside of the mainstream systems of migration surveillance, it also goes beyond this to consider how migrants represent themselves and their migration experiences to family 'back home'. This analysis prompts a rethinking of romanticised notions of home as a taken-for-granted space of women's protection, to consider instead the politics of being 'away from home'. This analysis underscores the politics of migrant representations, and the selective and contested processes of memory at work in how migrants are made (in the dual senses of both being rendered and allowed to be) visible. As Alexandra Zavos' account in Part One indicated, this is, of course equally true of how researchers represent migrants and so, also, the silences in migrants' own accounts of their experiences are of key significance. As such, Stavros Psaroudakis' chapter dealing with what kinds of relationships, and indeed visual representations, are rendered inadmissible or impossible for young male migrants in Greece offers new insights into this contested area of work.

Each of the issues raised above are contested illustrations of how, and by whom, claims to vulnerability and visibility are made, and each underpin a concern for naming some groups as more credible migrants than others. In particular, credibility is created by the range of gendered performances required in the process of migration. As such, migrants navigate and contest the varied constructs of 'vulnerability' that are ascribed to them. Thus 'vulnerability' may also be taken on by migrants as a marker of credibility in order to persuade, for example, border agencies that their experiences in countries of origin are 'real'. To counter the 'culture of disbelief' that is endemic in the North, vulnerability as a gendered performance is often vital, as to appear strong and resilient may well cast one's testimony in doubt.

Our aim in producing this book is to bring a critical engagement to 'gender and migration' by teasing out some commonalities and differences across different contexts and by bringing an explicitly feminist and interdisciplinary lens to the topic. In challenging the terms on which the gender and migration debate has been framed, we hope this book will contribute to more critically engaged practices for planning, conceptualising and evaluating work with migrants.

PART 1

Visibility and Vulnerability

In this Part the contributors open up for analysis the visibility of gender in studies of migration. The chapters by Ingrid Palmary and Chandré Gould specifically address counter-trafficking interventions to highlight the selective ways in which women are visible as migrants. They draw on critiques about the focus on the sexuality of people from marginalised groups and the consequences thereof, but equally show how contested claims to represent 'vulnerable' groups have significant implications for how resources are distributed, how one makes claim to be or is labelled a victim or perpetrator, and the kind of migrant one can claim to be. The chapter by Alexandra Zavos reinforces this theme of representation and its impact on the nature of the interventions that are thereby rendered possible.

The violence, pathologisation and exclusions created and sustained by gendered representations of vulnerability are topicalised most explicitly in this Part of the book. The risks of co-opting feminist concerns, such as those over the sexual exploitation of women or the ways that their work is rendered domestic, are introduced and these themes continue in the Parts that follow. Each of these chapters raises questions about the risks of seemingly benevolent interventions that might create and sustain the gendered ways that migrants are marginalised and stigmatised.

CHAPTER 2

Gender, migration and anti-racist politics in the continued project of the nation[1]

Alexandra Zavos

Introduction

This chapter addresses gendered aspects of anti-racist migration discourses in Greece and their implication in the re/production of anti-racist politics as a national, rather than transnational, space and ethnocentric practice. In spite of universalist references to social justice and anti-statist claims of freedom of movement for all, I argue that the gendered political representation of migrants in the context of the anti-racist movement is coded and regulated by an implicit investment in reproducing the nation-state as a dominant socio-political figuration. This is because, paradoxically, such anti-racist migration discourses reiterate assumptions of the nation-state and national identity as natural, self-evident and unambiguous ontologies. In so doing they thereby maintain and regulate hierarchies of entitlement and political participation within the anti-racist movement itself.

Feminist theorists have elaborated gender as a constitutive relation in the symbolic construction of the nation-state as a natural form of societal organisation based on the sexualised division of roles between women and men in the family (Halkias 2004, Pettman 1996, Yuval-Davis 1997). A two-way substantiation occurs: on the one hand sexualised gender roles – such as 'mother' or 'father'

– gain content and meaning in the context of the nation-state; on the other hand, the nation-state itself is defined as a natural, enclosing entity – much like a family – within which gendered subjects manifest their natural vocations. In the imaginary social space of the 'national family', the gender divide is articulated to the public/private and political/cultural divide and fixes men and women, natives and migrants in different structural positions (Anthias and Yuval-Davis 1992). These positions are approached from the perspective of gender and intersectionality.

A gendered approach to migration, understood from the perspective of intersectionality, elaborates the interrelationships between different social divisions, such as 'race', class, nationality (Yuval-Davis 2006a: 193). Against essentialising and homogenising tendencies inherent in identity discourses, intersectionality allows us to highlight and claim the complexity, situatedness and openness of social positionings (Phoenix and Pattynama 2006). Feminist research on migration looks in particular at the positions of both exclusion and agency that migrant women occupy (e.g. Andall 2003, Anthias and Lazaridis 2000, Morokvasic 2007).

Tracing the discursive construction of migrant subjectivities and social positionings in Greece, we observe notable overlap and continuity of discourses regarding women's migration in the media, in mainstream politics and in the anti-racist movement that draw on the same conceptual repertoire ranging between victimisation and criminalisation. Moreover, the same stereotypical representations occur in migrants' and migrant women's talk as well. In this sense, as I will show, representations of women migrants function as hegemonic discourses that overdetermine the available subject positions across disparate and even conflicting political practices (Howarth and Stavrakakis 2000). Nevertheless, the reiteration of these discourses in migrant women's public narratives displaces them and thereby opens up possibilities for new political subjectivities to emerge.

Genealogies of struggle: introducing 'support action'

With the influx of migrants after 1989 from countries of Eastern Europe and, significantly for Greece, Albania, the leftist anti-racist movement took upon itself and gradually targeted and monopolised the political formulation and representation of migrants' rights *vis-à-vis* formal political institutions of the Greek nation-state (Glarnetatzis 2001). 'Support Action', one of the oldest anti-racist groups in Greece, was formed as a designated collectivity in 1995 with the objective of becoming the political vanguard in the migration movement. Constituting itself as a solidarity organisation for migrants and refugees, represented as 'persecuted victims of neoliberal globalisation', it staged mass mobilisations, political interventions and social support actions, becoming a protagonist in the politicisation of migration. Spearheading the group's actions over the past ten years has been an ongoing campaign for the unconditional legalisation of migrants in Greece; at the same time it has been organising an annual Anti-Racist Festival in Athens, running a migrants' liaison and legal support office and a Greek-language school, and promoting the development of migrant networks and leaderships.

In spite of these efforts, the politicisation of migration is established in terms that very often exclude the subjects of migration from substantial and equal participation in the anti-racist movement, both at the level of narratives (non-existence of their 'voice') and at the level of practices (circumscribed and undervalued contribution), and is transformed into a relationship of representation-patronage. In this political milieu, anti-racist discourses on migration exemplify three interlinked characteristics: (a) the totalisation of social antagonisms in terms of the assumed dominant conflict between state–capital–labour, (b) the essentialisation of political subjects in terms of 'Greeks', 'migrants' and 'workers', and (c) the hegemonic and reductive signification of all social and political antagonisms in the above terms.

In relation to gender, in the broad gamut of activities undertaken by the anti-racist movement, the invoked and (occasionally) speaking subject of migration is, as a rule, male. Women migrants' issues remain marginal both in terms of political representation and in terms of subject matter. To the extent that women migrants become the object of political demands, this occurs uniformly through evoking representations of victimhood. The normative dimension of gendered discourses that determine the possible subject positions/roles for migrant women is so powerful that, even when migrant women themselves appear as speaking subjects in public contexts, they adopt stereotypical and commonly accepted/recognised female roles and subject positions, e.g. as mothers. However, as we shall see further, this is not an unambiguous practice. In fact the performative reiteration of common discourses can imply doubled or subversive meanings.

The development of anti-racist discourses on 'the problem' of migration

Drawing on written material produced by 'Support Action' over a period of ten-odd years (1995–2006), I explore how anti-racist discourses construct migration as a 'problem' through gendered and racialised representations of victimhood, exploitation and 'otherness'. I have chosen to focus on the periodic pamphlets titled *Open Borders*, which represent the group's official information bulletin.

Anti-racist movement and migration

In contrast to the 1980s, when issues of racism/anti-racism were discussed in relation to the rights of ethnic and religious minorities in Greece, from the 1990s onwards, the problem of migration became central to anti-racist discourses. This shift coincides with the presence of larger numbers of migrants in Greece; however, it also indicates a significant orientation: the externalisation of the phenomenon of racism. Racism, considered to be a product of neoliberal globalisation, is recognised/represented as a relation of power and discrimination, or in fact, violence, that affects 'others', foreigners, not 'us', Greeks. Of course, racism is understood to have an impact on native Greeks as well: 'Racism is not only hurting those suffering it but it is also offending those tolerating it', a 'Support Action' poster informs us (*Open Borders*, 2000, issue 7, p. 6, English original). The negative effects of racism are located either in the fracture of the invoked (and axiomatic) working-class unity, or in the production of feelings of intolerance and xenophobia.

As another poster states: 'Racism is an illness that afflicts whites and kills blacks' (my translation), where, we assume, 'whites' metonymically refers to 'Greeks' and 'blacks' to 'migrants'. The poignant doubling of Greeks as whites, and migrants as blacks, implies that racialised privilege is linked to national identity. However, the signifier 'illness' – a medical term identifying a problematic condition of the body/mind – points to the signification of racism as something out of the ordinary that assails, by analogy, the (national) 'social body'. In other words, racism is signified as an unnatural and abnormal condition, in contrast to an imagined 'healthy' one where no racism exists. In this way, racism is not represented as a foundational relation of the nation-state and its assumed unitary social body. Instead it is signalled as something that comes to assail the original well-being of this body. The externalisation of racism, seen as a result of the entrance of 'foreigners' in Greek territory, prevents us from recognising its complexity and historical continuity in the nation-state, constructed on the foundational distinction between insiders and outsiders, 'us' and 'them', as well as the evocation of an imagined (and required) unity against multiple internal and external enemies.

However, it is evident that the racialisation of Greek national identity is inscribed in the very institutional – and not only imaginary – construction of the Greek nation, which is defined in racial terms based on the (patrilineal) 'blood line' (Christopoulos 2004). The identification 'Greek' posits the *a priori* racial (and not only national) exclusion of 'foreigners', even in radical anti-racist discourses, which, in their invocation of 'Greeks' and 'migrants', inadvertently perhaps, reproduce national identifications as naturalised and essentialised identities.

Anti-racist discourses reify and homogenise migrants into, on the one hand, a particular, and on the other, a unitary category of people, who wear the clothes, not of the criminal, but, of the victim. We read in one of the pamphlets:

> Economic and political refugees: The homeless and vagrants of globalization, of neoliberal, capitalist, imperialist globalization. The human beings who are forced to take the road of exile in order not to have the fate of millions of their compatriots who cannot leave ... Victims of neoliberal, capitalist, imperialist globalization. Because they are forced to abandon their countries in order to survive, because on the road to the West and the North they suffer, are humiliated and often die, because when they manage to finally arrive in ... heaven they face the uninsured and badly paid labour, the fear of deportation, the bondage of a temporary residence permit, the contempt and suspicion of natives, social exclusion and state repression. (*Open Borders*, issue 9, 2003, my translation)

Here, in an attempt perhaps to provoke sympathy and solidarity according to common terms of misery, all elements of subjectivity and agency are reduced from the subjects of migration, who appear as an amorphous mass of wretched beings moving about without purpose, plan or other resources, simply struggling for survival. This image has very little connection to reality since it is often precisely the danger of undertaking the journey of migration that requires the development of well-organised migration networks, as well as strong personal motivation. On the contrary, the image of ultimate wretchedness justifies on the side of the anti-racist movement a protective-paternalistic relationship that on the one hand sanctifies its own superior 'heroic' position, and on the other integrates migrants in the already-shaped hierarchies in a subordinate position. It is indicative that in none of the anti-racist publications does one come across the voice of the subjects of migration themselves. The people, then, whom anti-racist discourse endeavours to render more visible and respected in Greek society, have been rendered voiceless within it.

In leftist anti-racist discourses the political conflict which inscribes migration is outlined in the social antagonism between state and bourgeois power on the one hand and wage labour on the other. The polarity is drawn between the 'savageness of the state', 'the overexploitation of employers', 'the introversion and conservatism of Greek society' and the (heroic and lonely we assume) anti-racist movement together with 'wretched' migrants. The political alignment between Greeks and migrants is announced on the basis of an assumed common 'worker identity'. Unity is axiomatically claimed, as a precondition, rather than the negotiated outcome of actions and objectives formed on the basis of specific alliances between different social and political actors. Feminist critiques have drawn attention to the need to move away from such authoritarian, top-down political organising towards more horizontal and collaborative 'alliance' building (Haraway 1991) or 'transversal politics' (Yuval-Davis 2006b). Critiques of the failure of leftist politics to encompass diverse political subjects and social struggles have been also voiced by feminists in the context of 'Support Action' (Dousia 1999). In fact, leftist feminists have elaborated the need for alternative political organising that takes gender as well as other social divisions into account (Vovou 2001). However, as I shall discuss further, these pronouncements are not easily deployed in action.

Female migration in anti-racist discourse: gender as an add-on

It is obvious at first sight that gender is added on through reference to the special category 'women migrants' rather than recognised as an intersecting relation of power through which different hierarchies are consolidated. Thus, the generalised subject of migration is represented as genderless, and by extension assumed masculine. The first explicit discussion of women migrants' situation occurs in a 1996 pamphlet, under the section: 'Women migrants: Overexploitation, racism and sexism', which sets the tone for all subsequent references to women migrants.

> Migrant women constitute the most oppressed category of our society. They are paid less, they are hired with more difficulty and fired more easily, they are dependent not only on their employer, but on their husband or father as well – who usually secure their residence permit.

> Foreign women are usually tragically isolated and excluded since they are subjected not only to the racism and the prejudices of the country they live in, but also the backward (anachronistic) mores and the conservatism of their country of origin. (*Open Borders*, 1996, issue 3, page 9, my translation)

The victimisation of migrant women is attributed not only to racism and the exploitation they suffer in host countries, but also to the patriarchal social relations they carry with them from their countries of origin. They are represented as more insecure, exploited, oppressed, vulnerable and victimised than their male counterparts who, together with Greek employers or pimps, keep them locked up and in conditions of dependency and incarceration.

> Migrant women ... suffer ... also many prohibitions and discriminations in the family, in the community, at work etc. from men of the same national origin as them. (*Open Borders*, 1996, issue 3, page 9, my translation)

> Moreover, they experience all the sufferings that are procured by the conservative norms of the societies they come from, as well as the insufferable isolation that being locked inside

a house offers, whether in the form of domestic labour or because of their dependence on their family. (*Open Borders*, 2000, issue 7, page 7, English original)

The insistent and repeated representation of migrant women exclusively as victims (of racism, sexism, neo-imperialism, patriarchy, slave-trade), together with the absence of any reference either to existing differences between them, or their agency and contributions to Greek society, fixes them in a subject position of almost fatalistic subjection, which seems inescapable and predestined. The gendered subject of migration, then, is only female, and is, moreover, uniform and unidimensional.

This schematisation appears to conform more to the ideological-political preoccupations of the authors rather than to migrant women's lived reality, since this kind of positioning ignores and obscures the initiatives and agencies that women migrants exhibit, both in planning the migration move and adjusting in host societies, and in undertaking crucial family responsibilities (e.g. Morokvasic *et al.* 2003, Parrenas 2001).

References to women migrants' isolation and family dependence, or to their oppression from male compatriots, always identify them in relation to men, or masculine power (the patriarchal family, the pimp, the state), and never in their own right. They are positioned as appendages. Telling examples occur most frequently in descriptions of female migrant sex workers as victims of trafficking to be used, bought and sold at will, without any resistance.

Thousands of desperate young women come to Greece – *it's not particularly significant if they do so of their own free will or not, since the deprivation they suffer does not leave much room for free choice* – to be abused, humiliated and often sold to buyers at the price of 500,000 or 1,000.000 drachmas. (Undated pamphlet 'Solidarity to migrants', my translation, my emphasis)

At the climax of this portrayal are references that signify a telling metonymic projection: in the place of the violated female body are positioned not only specific women working in prostitution, but the whole countries where they come from.

The organized slave-trade of women – lucrative as much as the illegal gun trade – flourishes on the ground of sordid poverty, wretchedness, and disintegration of whole societies, on the active role of diplomats, policemen and judges and, of course, the 'demand' on behalf of thousands of customers.

(*Open Borders*, 2005, issue 11, page 10, my translation)

Here, the reproduction of gendered and racialised stereotypes underscores the hegemonic imaginary of the nation-state: if the women of a country are violated, it is assumed that the whole country is violated as well, as if, in the end, women were – as feminist theorists have pointed out – the bearers of a country's (territorial, moral and social) integrity and wholeness.

At this point emerges the polarity of 'the West and the Rest'. On the one hand, Greek society is attributed with sexism, which, in the absence of any other qualification, we assume is located in the exploitation of migrant women as workers, therefore associated with the development of capitalist relations of production in the context of modernity and progress. On the other hand, migrant women's countries of origin are attributed with patriarchy and 'anachronistic and conservative social norms', conditions associated with the social organisation of pre-modern familial and community (or even tribal) relations that signal a repository of tradition, backwardness and fundamentalism. What is achieved is the fundamental and reductive division between two supposedly uniform, radically different and hierarchically ordered socio-political complexes: on the one hand we have the host societies that belong to the 'capitalist and neo-imperialist, yet also 'developed' West, and, on the other, we have sending societies that are massed as 'the Rest', the underdeveloped and inferior antipode of the West. It thus becomes impossible to differentiate between and within 'Western' countries as much as it is precluded to relativise the position of other, non-Western countries in, what Herzfeld (2007) has called, the 'global hierarchy of value'.

The anti-racist discourse I have been analysing, which focuses on the victimisation of migrant women, rather than empowering, remains external to the subjects it refers to. By claiming the position of just and progressive deputy of rights and at the same time speaking on behalf of/in the name of some 'other' – rendered voiceless – women, who moreover are implicitly signalled as backward since they do not speak out against their own oppression, this discourse becomes authoritarian/repressive. The inscribed relationship – in spite of evoking equality – bears elements of a racialising colonisation. As constructed in anti-racist discourse, migrant women, the subjects of migration, are infantilised and alienated as victims, against an assumed (national and paternalistic) 'us' that lurks in the background of this narrative.

Gendered anti-racist politics in practice

Further, drawing on my experience of organising a gender and migration initiative in 'Support Action', I explore some of the tensions and contradictions that emerge in anti-racist mobilisations in relation to two critical issues of migration politics: gender and domestic labour. Specifically, I consider migrant women's own self-presentation in the context of the anti-racist movement, as it was recorded on the occasion of a public discussion on 'Migration, Gender and Domestic Labour' organised at the 11th Anti-Racist Festival in Athens.

Why gender?

Mobilising around gender and migration offered a singular vantage point from which to question the politics of public representation in the anti-racist movement in relation to the premises of national sovereignty. In our political work we encountered two separate yet related practices where gender and migration combine to regulate the production of political discourses and subjectivities (Zavos 2008. On the one hand we encountered the marginalisation of gender in the anti-racist migration movement. As Dimitra Malliou, a migrant woman from Albania, noted: 'Because usually when we talk about migrants in general we mean only men ... And I want to tell you that we migrant women have particular problems indeed.'

Migrants in general and female migrants in particular, who as non-citizens and women cannot achieve public status, are constructed not as political but as 'feminized' subjects (Kambouri 2007). As such, only certain positions are available to them and they cannot enter the political field as autonomous actors but as protected and dependent members. For example, domestic labour relations between Greeks and migrants fall outside the scope of valid political issues; belonging to the private domain they are signified as 'feminine' and a-political, and therefore are not included in anti-racist repertoires. Moreover, women migrants are usually considered passive and politically inarticulate subjects who cannot participate in political processes or produce political discourses. Their assumed incapacity for political participation is premised on their double exclusion as migrants and women. In the words of a leading male migrant representative: 'Women migrants can only talk about their experience, they cannot understand the political issues at hand. You will have to instruct them in articulating their experience in political terms.' Unless they adopt the available, masculinist discourses or become the objects of these discourses, they cannot be recognised as valid political subjects. Thus, when migrant women do appear in public they mainly perform a combination of victim and/or mother roles. As Venelina Marinova, a Bulgarian migrant woman claims:

> Most of the, most of the Bulgarians here in Greece migrants are ... women. In the age around 40 and after. These women had to leave their professions in Bulgaria, their homes, their children in order to be able to raise their children, to help their parents in Bulgaria. You yourselves can understand how difficult it is [for] a woman who had another life to change and become the lowest rung [on the ladder] in another country, not knowing either the language, or the life, or nothing, in a strange family, in a strange house.

However, adoption of these subject positions should not be understood as a simple reproduction of dominant gender/ migration discourses. It can also signify a tactical move to gain foothold in public debates as well as strategically form alliances with Greek women on the basis of invoked common, universal gender experiences, as the following words of Dimitra Malliou, an Albanian woman activist, show:

> And I close with a question, in every conference and in every assembly meeting when I have in front of me friends, eh Greek women, I say, think that this [woman] too is a mother, when she crosses the limits of tiredness she doesn't have the strength to smile at the child which is waiting for her when she returns home.

On the other hand, we noted a similarly circumscribed understanding of female migration in the leftist feminist movement, which reproduces dominant representations of women migrants solely as victims of exploitation and sexual abuse. Discourses of victimisation ostensibly pathologise migrant women as backward, traditional, underdeveloped, disempowered, imprisoned in the family or as objects of male desire. Implicit in these discourses are normative Western, middle-class assumptions about the independent and self-directed individual as a political agent of progress and emancipation. Positions of advocacy and moral superiority are thus secured for Greek feminists, leaving classed, racialised and ethnocentric relations of power between women unquestioned. Particularly vocal and demanding women migrants who clearly fall outside the victim stereotype are considered a nuisance and disruptive. What is of interest in the case of migrant women's 'pathologized presence/normalized absence' (Phoenix 1987) is precisely the construction of their racialised and minoritised 'otherness' as an aspect of national identity, to which essentialist assumptions of cultural and moral inferiority are attached, obscuring class or other social divisions. Nationality is homogenised and reified for natives and foreigners alike. The space of politics, whether anti-racist or feminist, is guarded from the entrance of new political subjects, and is reproduced, in practice, by engendering particular hierarchies, entitlements and exclusions, as a national space. Integrating migrants into the nation means 'domesticating' them as one of 'us', rather than reconceptualising the politics of representation and citizenship, in favour of a diffusion of boundaries between public and private, male and female, Greek and migrant.

Why domestic labour?

Domestic labour articulates most poignantly the intersections between gender, migration and nation, as it not only constitutes a gendered area of employment and the *par excellence* area of migrant female employment, but also breaches the boundaries of the public/private divide and the political economies of the reproduction of the nation (Anderson and Phizacklea 1997).

In Greece, domestic labour has always been an area of female employment (Psarra 2009). Today it is mainly carried out by migrant women (Sakellis and Spyropoulou 2007). In fact the majority of migrant women are employed as domestic workers (Parsanoglou and Tsiamoglou 2008. In this sense, ironically, the reproduction of the nation – at least in terms of care labour – is in the hands of migrant women. The conflation of public/private and gender divisions renders domestic labour as a category of employment invisible, unregulated and feminised (Stiliou 2007). Labour relations in the domestic sphere, both in terms of legislation and in terms of union organising, remain practically uncontrollable and open to exploitation and abuse (Tastsoglou and Hadjiconstandi 2003). As Teresita Torevillas, a Filipina migrant woman speaker, points out: '... the work we are doing is largely left unrecognized. It is as if we are invisible ... working as *oikiaki voithos* [a domestic helper] means you are isolated from the rest of society ... and from other workers.'

For many migrant women this situation is exacerbated by the fact that they cannot obtain legal residence status in Greece and therefore cannot claim any kind of state protection, in fact have to live in hiding. As different analyses have shown, this cannot be explained only as administrative failure but needs to be understood in relation to the development and tolerance – if not direct promotion – of an informal, black-market migrant economy (Pavlou 2007). These issues are raised by a number of migrant women panel speakers, who, moreover, point out that their position in the Greek labour market is much more precarious and disadvantaged than that of their Greek counterparts, even though both suffer from gendered exploitation.

> The problems are many. Eh, but there are some that are particularly for the migrant women. When we talk about labour, the migrant [man] works in a more open space and ... his exploitation can be controlled in some way, and all the other things. The migrant woman who enters a house, who nobody knows about, where there is no agreement, can't prove, can't prove, let's say, the biggest exploitation, the way how she spends her hours. (Loretta Macaulay, Sierra Leone)

At the same time, this area of work offers possibilities for financial independence, social mobility, emancipation and creative expression (Kambouri 2008). In this respect, feminist research on migration has been instrumental in highlighting ways that women migrants wield power, even under such adverse circumstances, and use available opportunities to their maximum advantage (Kasimati and Mousourou 2007). In migrant women's talk, migration and domestic labour are often represented as situations in which gender stereotypes and roles are transformed. The women become the main breadwinners of the family, and assume the responsibility of raising children, even at a distance, without male help.

> I would like to say that what makes us happy is when we see our children which we once abandoned in Bulgaria ... and became both mother and father to them ... for their future, when we see that indeed they finish the Universities, they finish their high-schools, and are well. (Venelina Marinova, Bulgaria)

In the context of domestic labour the relationship between gender and migration becomes particularly important and subversive, not only in terms of the renegotiation of gendered power relations by migrant women, but also as it transforms reproductive labour from unpaid to paid work, albeit racialised, and imbues the hitherto private sphere of the family and the household with attributes of the public domain, thus displacing the set boundaries between them. Moreover, gendered identities such as that of the domestic worker, when transferred through the articulation of political demands from the private to the public domain, subvert the strict gender dichotomies that organise both.

Negotiations, subversions, resistances

Discrimination against migrant women functions selectively; it does not completely exclude them from public discourse, but rather includes them conditionally in subordinate, feminised positions. One question that emerges is to what extent migrant women can (and do) re-signify, negotiate, resist or challenge these prescribed positions and how this affects masculinist and ethnocentric political practices permeating the public sphere.

Unquestionably, the desire of migrant women to enter public discourse is pervasive. This was evident in their willingness to participate in the panel, in the intense preparation for it and in their choice of issues and language for their talks. Their anxiety about adopting the 'proper' political and linguistic forms is indicative of their wish to inhabit recognised and legitimised positions. One of the women asked us Greek participants to write up her speech for her, because she did not want to 'say something wrong': to use the 'wrong' language or make the 'wrong' political statements.

However the actual enactment of these accounts occasioned various distortions and digressions from normative positions. Even though migrant women themselves did not claim them as such, their performances can nevertheless be seen as engendering disruptive moments that elude and subvert dominant political practices, even as they remain within their explicit symbolic remit. For example, a participant from the United African Women's Organisation appeared in traditional African dress and read a very sophisticated academic text prepared for her by a Greek university researcher, thereby producing a clash between her 'traditional', 'exotic' appearance and the articulated intellectual discourse. Another participant from the Philippine Organisation KASAPI, who demanded domestic labour unionising by migrant women, delivered her presentation in English, thereby imposing a situation of unfamiliarity and comprehensive strain on the Greek audience. And at the very least, the use of broken or faulty Greek by several speakers, disrupted the expected flow and mastery of language and hindered the audience from immediate recognition and appropriation of the performed discourses precluding any kind of simple identification with the expressed positions. In other words the Greek audience could reconstruct itself unproblematically in the apparently common and well-rehearsed narratives.

Conclusion

This chapter has illustrated how migrant women are neither backward nor passive subjects, due to their identity or background, but rather structurally excluded and subordinated. The function of this is in direct relation to the gendered, classed and 'racialized' reproduction of the nation through both mainstream and anti-racist politics. Moreover I have tried to show how the inclusion of migrant women as political actors and subjects of knowledge can subvert dominant ethnocentric practices and transform the whole political stage, not only in terms of gender but also in terms of national sovereignty. Finally, I have tried to indicate how migrant women, even in the positions/roles cast *for* them, subvert and dislodge dominant imaginaries and create much-needed fissures in the seamless fabric of national political discourses.

Note

1   This analysis is based on research (September 2005–July 2006) carried out for my PhD on 'Gender, Migration and the Anti-racist Movement in Athens'. As part of my fieldwork I helped develop, in the context of a leftist anti-racist group, here anonymised as 'Support Action', and in collaboration with other Greek and migrant women, a 'gender and migration' initiative. I thank them dearly for the engaging moments we shared.

CHAPTER 3

The problem of trafficking[1]

Chandré Gould

Introduction

As a topic of debate and as the subject of research, human trafficking has, over the past ten years at least, drawn a tremendous amount of attention. This is reflected in the vast literature dealing with the issue, from books to advocacy materials; academic journal articles to government reports, and includes reports from the three most prominent intergovernmental organisations with an interest in the issue: the United Nations Office on Drugs and Crime (UNODC), the International Organization for Migration (IOM), and the International Labour Organization (ILO). Reports reflecting the extent of the problem and drawing attention to the need for urgent action are countered by an almost equal number of reports that call into question the numbers quoted and the methods employed.

This chapter therefore considers four key issues in relation to human trafficking. First, it discusses the problems and contradictions that the internationally accepted definition of trafficking poses and its contested nature. Second, it reflects on the debates about methods to study the problem, illustrates why the scale of the problem might be exaggerated and offers examples of more robust methods to assess the prevalence of human trafficking. Third, it illustrates the ways in which trafficking discourse is inextricably linked to issues of prostitution and how it seldom focuses on issues of forced labour. Fourth, the chapter looks at how concerns of securitisation have coalesced issues of immigration control, the 'War on Terror' and organised crime and eschew issues of human rights, social justice and individual autonomy. Lastly, the chapter highlights how a more informed debate about trafficking is essential to shift towards a more critical understanding of the issue. As will become clear in this discussion of the discourse on human trafficking, the debate is polarised and highly emotive.

Overall, if there is one thing that becomes clear from a scan of the vast body of writing about the problem of human trafficking, it is this. Trafficking is a highly contested concept that is as much a description of a particular set of activities as it is a term used to garner support for particular ideological agendas. It is also clear that it is impossible to separate concerns about human trafficking from discussions about prostitution. Historically, and currently, the focus of discussion, research and indeed national and international legislation is on countering, and preventing, the trafficking of 'women and children' for the purposes of sexual exploitation. While lip service is paid to other forms of trafficking, it is trafficking for prostitution that has grabbed the attention of policy makers, researchers, advocacy organisations and the media.

The problem of defining trafficking

The *Protocol to Prevent, Suppress and Punish Trafficking in Persons, Especially Women and Children, Supplementing the United Nations Convention Against Transnational Organised Crime* (hereafter referred to as the Palermo Protocol) of 2000, exists (as its name suggests) within the context of the effort to curb and prosecute organised crime. The definition of human trafficking contained in the Protocol is extremely broad, and purposefully so. It seeks to inform the formulation of domestic legislation in order to provide states with legal ammunition to prosecute all those involved in the process of recruiting individuals and transferring them into situations of extreme exploitation. Yet, ironically, in the effort to cast the net widely enough to capture all the perpetrators in the chain of deception and abuse, the definition of trafficking becomes cumbersome and difficult to work with.

On the other hand, the intention of anti-trafficking legislation (both national and international) is very specific. It seeks to apprehend organised groups involved in the recruitment, transport and exploitation of individuals, and to provide a framework for victim support and assistance (which appears at this stage to be based upon the return of the victim to their place of origin). As such, several contradictions arise in real-life situations. Let us consider an example based on the research conducted by the Institute for Security Studies (ISS) and the Sex Worker Education and Advocacy Taskforce (SWEAT) to determine the number of women (and children) who could be said to have been trafficked into the sex work industry in Cape Town.[2]

We found that of 118 sex workers surveyed,[3] none said they had been forced into the industry by a third party. They all knew what they would be doing when they entered the industry, but there were cases in which women were unable to leave a brothel where they were working because they were threatened by a manager or owner with exposure to their families. Most worked long hours, had to pay at least 50 per cent of their earnings to a brothel, and in some cases sex workers did not feel free to refuse clients. Arguably, these women were subjected to at least coercive, but probably exploitative working conditions. Yet, the definition of trafficking excludes such women from assistance, or from recourse against their exploiters. Why? Because they were not moved from one location to another, nor were they forced or deceived into entering the industry. In addition, few saw themselves as victims of anything more than their financial circumstances and would likely have resisted any assistance to get out of the industry unless it was accompanied by equivalent remuneration to what they could earn there.

Arguably, counter-trafficking legislation is not meant to address situations such as these, but since sex work is criminalised in South Africa, the effect of any future trafficking legislation will be to discriminate against those local women who are exploited while offering recourse to foreign women who find themselves in the same situation. This raises the very difficult question of what exactly it is that the trafficking discourse seeks to define as the problem that needs to be addressed and what countries adopting counter-trafficking legislation seek to stop. It also raises the question of whether the internationally accepted notion of trafficking matches the lived experience of individuals.

Throughout the literature on trafficking there is reference to the difficulty of adequately defining trafficking. Certainly the media frequently conflate trafficking and smuggling, often reporting cases of smuggling as cases of trafficking (but seldom the other way around). This definitional problem is complicated by the fact that an individual can both have been smuggled and trafficked if they paid a third party to assist them to enter a country (smuggling) and the third party later benefits from their exploitation (trafficking). The confusion between smuggling and trafficking flows over into the confusion around numbers of victims, with the former frequently being included in the estimation of the number of trafficked persons.

For the purpose of this chapter it is necessary to consider the definition provided in the Palermo Protocol:

(a) 'Trafficking in persons' shall mean the recruitment, transportation, transfer, harbouring or receipt of persons, by means of the threat or use of force or other forms of coercion, of abduction, of fraud, of deception, of the abuse of power or of a position of vulnerability or of the giving or receiving of benefits to achieve the consent of a person having control over another person, for the purpose of exploitation. Exploitation shall include, at a minimum, the exploitation of the prostitution of others or other forms of sexual exploitation, forced labour or services, slavery or practices similar to slavery, servitude or the removal of organs;

(b) The consent of a victim of trafficking in person to the intended exploitation set forth in subparagraph (a) of this article shall be irrelevant where any of the means set forth in subparagraph (a) have been used.[4]

Anderson and O'Connell Davidson (2003) question the utility of this definition if the intention of countering trafficking is to combat forced labour and slavery. They argue that if this is the motive behind anti-trafficking activities and legislation 'there is no moral or analytical reason to distinguish between forced labour involving "illegal immigrants", "smuggled persons" or "victims of trafficking"'. They argue that 'the distinction between trafficking and smuggling may be clear to those who attach political priority to issues of border control and national sovereignty, but it is far from obvious to those who are primarily concerned with the promotion and protection of the rights of migrant workers' (Anderson and O'Connell Davidson 2003: 7).

Yet, it is far from clear that the shared international agenda is indeed merely to combat forced labour and slavery. If this were the case the international agreement on countering trafficking may not have been located within the efforts to counter organised crime. Indeed, it is perhaps the multitude of intentions (including countering organised crime and abolishing prostitution) behind the movement to counter trafficking that to a large extent bedevils efforts to arrive at a workable definition.

Another criticism of the definition relates to the way in which the definition deals with the consent of victims. By making consent, or agency, irrelevant in the process of trafficking, the Protocol relegates the actions taken by 'victims' that in some way contributed to the eventual exploitation as irrelevant to their rescue or assistance. In other words it disregards individual agency. The intention of the wording may have been to ensure that traffickers could not defend their actions by arguing that an individual had agreed to their own exploitation. Nevertheless, through ignoring the agency and intentions of trafficked persons, their specific needs, which may *not* be to be rescued and returned home, are also ignored. Indeed the focus on rescuing and returning or rehabilitating victims has been criticised for being both paternalistic and ineffective. There is abundant evidence (as discussed below) that victims will allow themselves to be trafficked a second time, if they did not wish to be returned to where they came from.

One of the most salient problems with a confused definition is that, as Kauko Aromaa (2005: 3) notes, there are enormous difficulties associated with quantifying something that is difficult to define: '[T]he situation where a crime is characterized by an absence of the unity of time, place, perpetrator and activity makes the counting exercise particularly demanding.' Not only do these factors hinder quantification of the problem of trafficking, they also hinder law enforcement. Aromaa notes that law-enforcement officials have great difficulty applying anti-trafficking provisions. In one telling interview with Aromaa, a law-enforcement official expressed frustration that victims of trafficking often do not wish to be regarded as such, saying that:

> [I]t is very hard to identify a victim who does not co-operate, or as often happens, denies his/her victim status, does not accept our view of him/her as a potential or real victim. Then he/she has no reason to co-operate, on the contrary, he/she will try to escape us who are trying to help him/her. It is also not clear that if the victim's role is not beneficial to

the presumed victim he/she will have no reason to come to us – all we can do is send him/her back and he/she knows this. The only way to improve this situation could be if we would adopt a solution where the victim status is accompanied by some significant benefits – such as a permit to stay in the country, witness protection schemes, etc. (Aromaa 2005: 5)

What is not clear is why, when so-called victims do not wish to be defined as such, there is an insistence that they should be. This kind of thinking is pervasive in the anti-trafficking movement and appears to be a consequence of the view that no woman would choose to do sex work and that all sex workers are, by definition, exploited. Aromaa goes further, suggesting that some inducement should be offered to supposed victims to define themselves as such, so that a prosecution can follow. In other words, the needs of the state to be seen to be acting against human trafficking seem to trump those of individuals who find themselves in a trafficking-like situation.

It is this kind of thinking that sex workers and sex worker rights organisations have opposed. Doezema (1998: 42) argues that

[T]he campaigning efforts of anti-trafficking groups have been instrumental in creating a climate wherein the great majority of sex work, and practically all sex work involving young men and women in developing countries is seen as abuse. Forced prostitution, child prostitution and sex tourism are linked together and made indistinguishable.

Sharing this view, sex workers rights groups hold that it is in fact the criminalisation of prostitution and the barriers to travel that 'attract organized crime and create the possibilities for large profits, as well as creating the prostitute's need for protection and assistance' (Murray 1998: 60).

The enormous gulf between the views of those such as Doezema and Murray and those feminists who view sex work as necessarily exploitative and demeaning to women and who support the abolition of prostitution is clear from the following definition of trafficking which is put forward by Donna Hughes (2001: 9):

Trafficking is any practice that involves moving people within and across local or national borders for the purpose of sexual exploitation. Trafficking may be the result of force, coercion, manipulation, deception, abuse of authority, initial consent, family pressure, past and present family and community violence, economic deprivation, or others conditions of inequality for women and children.

By defining trafficking as such, Hughes essentially defines all prostitution as trafficking and all prostitutes as victims of trafficking. Between these two views there is little common ground, making it very difficult to adopt national legislation against trafficking without accepting one view and rejecting the other. Indeed there seems to be no clear agreement on exactly what problem it is that states should be addressing. Is it forced labour and labour exploitation; organised crime; prostitution; migration, or all of these?

Given the difficulty of defining the problem, it is no wonder that the matter of quantifying trafficking is fraught with inaccuracies.

Research methods and the problem of numbers

Global estimates (based on undisclosed methodology) put the turnover from trafficking for sexual exploitation at some $7–10 billion a year. Indeed, reflecting the general consensus in the anti-trafficking literature, Julie Cwinkel (2005) asserts that trafficking is 'seen as the best cost/risk-benefit ratio of all criminal activity' (306). She argues that not only is the trade in women for sexual exploitation growing, but that they are an invisible labour force, and therefore nearly impossible to access and research. Unfortunately we do not have a similar assessment of the amount of money that is provided to intergovernmental organisations and NGOs to counter trafficking, nor the amount spent by national governments to put in place policies to deal with trafficking.

The assumptions expressed by Cwinkel about trends in trafficking mentioned above are frequently repeated in the literature about human trafficking. Other commonly held assumptions are that there is a constant and growing demand amongst clients of the sex work industry[5] for new and exotic women, a demand which drives supply; and that trafficking claims extremely large numbers of victims and generates substantial profits – all while there is general consensus (even amongst anti-trafficking activists) that estimates of these are unreliable. Much of the literature about trafficking tends to include extensive accounts of the constraints to using acceptable and rigorous sampling techniques when researching trafficking, using this as an excuse for small samples from which generalised conclusions are reached.

Authors Frank Laczko and Marco Gramegna (2003), researchers for the IOM, grappled with the methodological challenges of doing research on human trafficking. They concurred that 'despite the growing literature on human trafficking, much of the information on the actual number of persons trafficked is unclear and relatively few studies are based on extensive research' (2003: 180). One of the problems of determining the prevalence of trafficking is that few governments collect data on trafficking, and in the cases where information is collected it is seldom systematically analysed. Laczo and Gramegna point out that 'many countries ... mingle data relating to trafficking, smuggling and irregular migration' (2003: 181). This can only result in a confusion, and probably inflation, of the numbers of trafficking victims.

Laczo and Gramegna critiqued the figures that are often quoted for the number of women and children believed to be trafficked on an annual basis, saying that they are, at best, estimates, usually given without any reference to how they are derived.

The Trafficking in Persons (TIP) Report produced by the US Department of State is one example of a report that provides estimates of the number of women and children trafficked without providing any justification or explanation of how the numbers were arrived at. Unfortunately, as an official document produced by the Department of State, the figures in these reports are frequently and uncritically repeated in NGOs reports and press reports to support claims about the extent of the global trafficking problem (Hughes 2001, Raymond *et al.* 2002). Yet few studies have sought to determine a more accurate assessment of the scale of the phenomenon – and we are thus left without any firm basis upon which to make effective policy and allocate resources.

Laczo and Gramegna (2003: 182) refer to a 1998 IOM study of 25 European countries that found that only 12 of the surveyed countries 'could produce data on trafficking in women and only seven countries on cases of trafficking in children'. It would appear that none of the countries collected data on trafficking in men and boys for purposes of labour exploitation or sexual exploitation. Indeed, there appears to be little consistency in the type of data that is collected in those countries that do so. Unfortunately Franz and Gramegna fall into the same trap as Cwinkel. While lamenting the lack of data, they claim that 'trafficking is an under reported crime for which the majority of cases remain undiscovered' (2003: 183). Indeed, while the authors argue that better data on migration would assist in detecting and countering trafficking, they provide no substantiation for this comment and its not clear quite how better migration data will do this. They posit that indirect indicators of trafficking should also be used to determine the numbers of trafficking victims. One such indicator, they argue, would be to count the number of *au pair* visas or visas for 'entertainers'. This assertion was based on a 1995 IOM study that had found an increase in the award of such visas to Russian women entering Switzerland, and that victims of trafficking had been found to enter countries with such visas. Yet, it would appear that using this kind of data again allows for a confusion of numbers that will inevitably result in an inflation of the numbers of suspected victims of trafficking. They do not provide substantiation for the claim that victims of trafficking make regular use of these kinds of visas to enter a country, nor do they suggest how it may be possible to separate out the number of 'genuine' visa applications from those awarded to victims of trafficking. Indeed, there may be any number of reasons for the increase, other than that the women were trafficked.

Yet several research initiatives have suggested that it is not impossible to obtain more accurate estimates of the numbers of trafficking victims; or have used methods that could be replicated to arrive at more accurate estimations of prevalence. A 2002 research report by Thomas Steinfatt *et al.* describes a methodology to determine the number of trafficked women in the sex work industry in Cambodia. These authors were critical of reports on human trafficking that provided unsubstantiated estimates of the number of women believed to be trafficked into sex work in Cambodia. Steinfatt's methods involved mapping the sex work industry in Phnom Penh, Cambodia through the use of taxi drivers who were knowledgeable of the industry because they ferried clients to brothels. Several drivers drove researchers around the city pointing out agencies that they knew. These included *inter alia* up-market establishments, large brothels, small brothels, brothels that catered to poorer clients, discos, nightclubs, and areas where women solicited outdoors. On this basis a list of locations was drawn up. Taxi drivers then visited each of the locations, made an initial observational estimate of the number of people working there, then asked the managers how many sex workers they employed, of which nationalities, and how many were working to pay off a debt (using the excuse that certain clients like these kinds of sex workers).

Through this method and statistical modelling the researchers were able to arrive at a point-in-time estimate for the number of sex workers in the city of Phnom Penh (n = 5,250) (Steinfatt 2002: 8). They were also able to determine how many indentured sex workers were working in the city – workers were counted as indentured if the managers said that they were currently working off a debt, or had worked off a debt in the past. The researchers were also able to determine how many were of foreign nationalities. While acknowledging that not all indentured sex workers would have been trafficked, Steinfatt *et al.* allowed for an overestimation of the number of trafficking victims by counting all indentured sex workers as trafficking victims.

To this the researchers added information about the number of sex workers along key routes, as had previously been mapped by the UNDP study that sought to map HIV vulnerability, and an estimate of the number of sex workers who would be found in the rural areas where the viability of commercial sex is significantly reduced by lower population density; and through statistical modelling the researchers derived an estimate for the number of trafficking victims in the sex work industry in Cambodia. Although, by their own admission, the figures were inflated by several factors (not least the conflation of trafficking victims with indentured sex workers), the researchers presented a rigorous model for deriving more reliable estimates than had been available up to that point – and found that the numbers of possibly trafficked women were significantly lower than had been presumed by NGOs and advocacy organisations working to counter trafficking.

The research conducted in Cape Town by SWEAT and the ISS was informed by studies like this and others, including a study conducted by the Poppy Project in London (Dickenson 2004) and a study by Rao *et al.* in Calcutta (Rao 2001). The South African study mapped the size of the sex work industry in Cape Town. Extensive interviews were conducted with brothel owners and sex workers, and a telephonic survey was conducted to establish a picture of working conditions, reasons for entry into the industry and the extent of human trafficking (Gould and Fick 2008).

There are a number of research initiatives that offer good ideas for how research in the sex work industry can be undertaken, and which could lead to more reliable data about the prevalence of trafficking, at least in the sex work industry. However, the utility of research to determine the prevalence of human trafficking is called into question by the very nature of the discourse itself. Some argue that the phenomenon defies attempts to determine prevalence because trafficking is a 'hidden' phenomenon; the corollary of which is that it is impossible to quantify because it is impossible to find. This creates a conceptual space in which the issue can be made to be as big as an analyst wishes it to be in order to meet their own agenda – which may be altruistic, or may be to ensure continued access to funding. Attempts to provide an assessment of the scale of the problem that suggest that the large numbers proffered in much of the anti-trafficking literature are overestimations are not welcomed by the anti-trafficking movement.

Consider the statement made by Hughes (2001: 9):

> Trafficking in women and girls for the purpose of sexual exploitation is a shadow market valued at US7 billion annually. Women are trafficked to, from and through every region in the world. This highly profitable trade poses relatively low risk as compared with trades in drugs or arms. They moneymakers are transnational networks of traffickers and pimps who prey on women seeking employment and opportunities. These illegal activities and related crimes not only harm the women involved; they also undermine the social, political, and economic fabric of the nations where they occur.

By making the statement that there is no country in the world unaffected by trafficking, while at the same time saying that every aspect of public life is undermined by the practice, Hughes feeds into the moral panic that characterises the discourse. Additionally, through presenting the issue as one that seeks to help the most vulnerable, who are apparently unable to assist themselves, the discourse is presented as morally unchallengeable.

Critiques of the trafficking discourse

The most outspoken critics of the anti-trafficking lobby are organisations representing sex workers who hold that the current moral panic about human trafficking is inherently linked to a moral aversion to sex work. But, increasingly, the trafficking discourse is also receiving criticism from researchers in the field of migration studies who analyse the discourse in terms of the way in which it divides migrants into criminals or victims on the basis of sex and gender (Chapkis 2005: 52).

Advocates for sex worker rights such as Jo Doezema (1988, 2000) and Alison Murray (1998), who participated in the meetings to draft the Palermo Protocol, have documented the political processes leading up to the adoption of the Protocol, noting that organisations that explicitly hold the view that prostitution is an expression of abuse against women and should be abolished (such as the Coalition Against the Trafficking of Women) played a significant role in determining the nature and scope of the definition of trafficking that was ultimately adopted. Similarly, Melissa Dittmore (2005) refers to the antagonistic schism that developed at the Protocol drafting meetings between pro-abolitionist feminists and those who advocate for the rights of sex workers to be recognised. Indeed, the avid involvement of these two factions in the development of the Protocol, and the success of the abolitionist movement in determining the focus of the Protocol on 'women and children', is evidence of how integrally related the issues of human trafficking and prostitution are.

According to Doezema, notions of trafficking (of women and children) were born out of the early social purity movement which developed the stereotype of 'white adolescent girls who were drugged and abducted by sinister immigrant procurers, waking up to find themselves captive in some infernal foreign brothel, where they were subject to the pornographic whims of sadistic, non-white pimps and brothel masters' (1998: 36). Doezema argues that research established that even at that stage many of the so-called trafficking victims were in fact sex workers who had migrated in search of better opportunities. It is the division of migrant women into victims, or if they are willing participants in the sex industry – criminals, that human rights activists and migration experts object to.

Agustín (2005) offers a slightly different analysis of the historical origins of the relationship between trafficking and prostitution. She analyses the discourses around women and work as they have developed over time, to discover how the agendas were formed of organisations that apparently seek to help and rescue female victims of abuse. She poses the following questions, which are relevant to the framing of the trafficking discourse:

> Why do so many feminists who want a different, better world propose solutions based on policing and punishment? Why do they appear to make no (personal) connection between a guilty class of men ('clients') and their own male friends and relations? Why do middle-class women assume they need to save working-class ones? Why are the diverse impulses that have led people to sell sex not taken into account? What would happen if we questioned the centricity of families and why many people wish to leave them? (Agustín 2005: 69)

She argues that the creation of a discourse that places family as the central organisational unit of society, which emerged before and during the Industrial Revolution, had as its flip-side the effect of seeing those who did not find themselves in families as deviant. In the late nineteenth century, women who worked were regarded as deviant and as presenting a threat to the proper order of things (a similar discourse exists in South Africa amongst traditionalists). While women of independent financial means were able to eschew the roles society demanded them to play – this was not the case for working-class women.

Agustín describes the growth of an industry driven by middle-class women who found that while it was unacceptable for them to work in many occupations, involvement in 'social work' was acceptable as it fitted well with accepted notions of femininity. (Agustín 2005: 75). She shows that between 1850 and 1860 the number of charities in cities around Britain grew exponentially, many of which focused on saving wayward women and girls. In France a similar phenomenon took place with the mushrooming of charitable organisations such that by the start of the twentieth century there were over 1,300 'associations devoted to the protection and 'raising up' of girls' (Agustín 2005: 76). But as much as this occupation provided affluent women with relief from the boredom of domestic life and ultimately with much greater freedom, their efforts did little to emancipate the working-class women they sought to save, and for whom the only acceptable form of employment remained domestic service.

The result of the successful campaign of the social purity movement at the turn of the century was two international instruments: the International Agreement for the Suppression of the White Slave Trade, Paris (1904) and the International Convention for the Suppression of the White Slave Traffic (1910). This was followed by the adoption of two Conventions by the League of Nations: the International Convention to Combat the Traffic in Women and Children (1921) and the International Convention for the Suppression of the Traffic in Women of Full Age (1933). Sixteen years later the United Nations adopted the Convention for the Suppression of the Traffic in Persons and the Exploitation of the Prostitution of Others (which combined and replaced earlier agreements). Between 1949 and the late 1970s the issue dropped off the international agenda. There are different analyses offered as to the reason for the re-emergence of the issue on the international agenda in the 1980s (see Kempadoo 2005: xi and Doezema 1998). Whatever the stimulus for its re-emergence as an issue of international attention, the focus on trafficking has very real implications for women in the sex work industry.

In her critique of the current anti-trafficking discourse, Sanghera (2005) argues that the current anti-trafficking discourse is based upon a mythology about the nature of the activity of trafficking and the role of perpetrator and victim. The common assumptions about trafficking that make up this mythology are flawed, she argues. This results in interventions that fail to adequately address the needs of the victims, or fail to recognise their own motivations and agency and thus perpetuate inequalities and abuse rather than ameliorating them.

The securitisation[6] of the problem of trafficking

Why human trafficking has emerged as an issue of international concern at particular historical moments has been the subject of a number of articles and papers, many of which offer an analysis of the emergence in the late 1800s of concern about human trafficking. These sources also reflect on the disappearance of the issue from the international agenda after the adoption of international law in 1949 until the issue re-emerged in the 1970s. Many of these are texts authored by feminists who believe that women should have the right to choose the work they do, even if in the sex work industry. Many of these writers argue that by 'prioritising crime, punishment and immigration control' (Kempadoo 2005: xvi) the current anti-trafficking movement fails to acknowledge or address social injustice and is more likely to result in the violation than protection of the rights of migrant women and prostitutes. These sources challenge the arguments of abolitionist feminists such as Kathleen Barry of the Coalition Against Trafficking of Women (CATW) (see Doezema 1988, Doezema 2000, Doezema 2002, Agustín 2005, Kempadoo 2005), who argue that in all cases, prostitution is abuse against women and as such should not be tolerated by states.

In the writings of Kempadoo, Doezema and others, the argument is made that the international focus on human trafficking (particularly for purposes of sexual exploitation) emerged in both eras in response to increased migration of poor working-class women. They argue that the most recent attention paid to the issue is a consequence of the emergence of a shared agenda between religious organisations, those who are anti-immigration, and those who advocate for the abolition of sex work. However, it is also instructive to consider the analysis of the emergence of international concern about trafficking from a political science perspective, such as that offered by Jackson (2006).

Jackson (2006) notes how human trafficking became an urgent security issue in post-Soviet Central Asia. She questions why international organisations have attempted to securitise trafficking, how the process unfolded and whether it has yielded successful strategies. An issue becomes securitised (in other words expressed as a threat) through the language used to refer to it by states, NGOs and international organisations. This language or discourse may not reflect reality, or be underpinned by an examination of the reality of the perceived threat. In her article, Jackson considers the role of the UNODC, the IOM, the Organisation for Security Co-operation in Europe (OSCE) and the European Union (EU) in the securitisation of trafficking. She identifies these organisations as having a vested interest in the securitisation of the issue for several reasons: they shared an understanding of 'evolving geopolitics and the emergence of "new threats" in the region', had a similar reaction to terrorist events and were motivated by possible post-9/11 funding (Jackson 2006: 305).

The 'new' threats, she argues, were as much a manifestation of the realities of political and territorial changes in Central

Asia as they were about the new role that organisations such as the OSCE had to carve out for themselves after the end of the Cold War. An alliance between newly formed states in Central Asia and international organisations was mutually beneficial, as 'many of the countries' leaders understood that they could not secure their borders on their own and needed external funds and expertise' (Jackson 2006: 306). These factors, combined with the 'War on Terror' and the 2001/2002 focus of the United States and its allies on Afghanistan, led to international organisations making this region a focus of attention. That was both because the organisations shared the same threat perception as the US and its allies, and because for these organisations anti-crime and anti-terror activities in the region were a source of revenue. The pairing of the issues of narcotics trafficking and terrorism in the early 1990s provided a rationale for the involvement of international organisations in the region and an added imperative for states in the region to work with them. However, Jackson (2006) argues that at this early stage there was no impetus to include human trafficking in the threat analysis.

While illegal immigration was a concern for states in the region, it was not regarded as a security threat by those states, nor by the West. Indeed, she argues that before the re-emergence of the discourse, trafficking was regarded as having some positive benefit, both by individuals and states as the activity of trafficking 'allow[ed] people to work (abroad or domestically) and survive in a poor home economy when the state cannot help them. At the same time, they can also be a source of revenue for the states themselves' (Jackson 2006: 309). This, she argued, was one of the many factors that ultimately and unsurprisingly undermined efforts to counter trafficking in the region. Despite this, however, over time the pairing of issues in the language of the international organisations such that narcotics, human trafficking, terrorism and organised crime became a single package of threats, 'encouraged the adoption of similar traditional security strategies to counter these largely distinct areas' (Jackson 2006: 310).

Administrative changes within the UNODC further cemented the process of securitisation when the organisation adopted an integrated approach to drugs, crime and terrorism. The location of international anti-trafficking legislation as a protocol to the United Nations Convention on Transnational Organised Crime is evidence of the success of the process of securitisation which has been institutionalised through the allocation of resources to counter trafficking in this context. However, on the final question of whether the securitisation of human trafficking has led to successful strategies, Jackson's conclusion is less than positive: in the case of trafficking in persons, these strategies are not only severely limited, they are often harmful to individuals (Jackson 2006: 315).

Jackson's paper shows that the application of a political science analysis to the emergence and response to trafficking in this region leads to much the same conclusion as that reached by those who argue, from a human rights and social justice perspective, that the current 'law enforcement' response to trafficking is unlikely to lead to a reduction in the prevalence of trafficking. Indeed, as several authors point out, making it more difficult for economic migrants, particularly women, to cross borders is more likely to lead to them relying on unscrupulous third parties for assistance.

Conclusion

This chapter attempts to show that in many ways the discourse around human trafficking is informed and inspired not by the actual lived experience of victims of human trafficking, but by the imperatives of organisations, states and movements who benefit in one way or another from human trafficking being the focus of international concern. In summary, challenges to the anti-trafficking discourse include that (a) the impetus behind the anti-trafficking movement appears to come from an intention to abolish prostitution, rather than from a genuine attempt to address human rights abuses in the process of migration; (b) research on trafficking is frequently methodologically weak and resorts to the reiteration of commonly agreed myths about the nature and quantification of the activity; (c) the anti-trafficking discourse is sexist and fails to recognise that law-enforcement responses to the migration of women will not improve their circumstances; and (d) the conflation of women and children in the discourse infantilises women and fails to deliver solutions that are appropriate to either.

This is *not* to deny that there are individuals who experience extreme abuse and exploitation by labour brokers and employers in a range of industries, nor that there might be a significant number of men, women and children whose vulnerabilities as migrants are exploited by others. However, there is limited evidence available to back up the claims that organised international syndicates are behind the large-scale trafficking of humans, and little empirical evidence to support the claims that huge profits are made from the exploitation of the victims. Indeed, the discourse does not seem to require empirical support for these claims to sustain the moral panic about trafficking. While support to victims of labour exploitation and abuse and the prosecution of those responsible wherever it occurs should be welcomed and encouraged, it is not clear that the kind of support offered by anti-trafficking movements or by states is indeed in the best interests of those exploited. In addition, the allocation of resources to counter trafficking necessarily means that those resources will not be available for other activities. If only for this reason, there is a need to insist that more empirical research into the extent of the problem be conducted.

Notes

1 This chapter is based upon the book *Selling Sex in Cape Town: Sex Work and Human Trafficking in a South African City*, Institute for Security Studies (2008).

2 This study involved qualitative interviews with sex workers, brothel owners and pimps; focus group discussions with sex workers from the brothel- and street-based sectors; and a survey of sex workers based on a random sampling method.

3 The 118 were made up of both sex workers who work indoors and street-based sex workers. 8,7 per cent of the indoor population were surveyed and 14 per cent of the outdoor population. Population estimates were point-in-time estimates based on a mapping process that is described in full in Gould and Fick 2008.

4 It goes on to refer to child trafficking in the following way: '(c) The recruitment, transportation, transfer, harbouring or receipt of a child for the purpose of exploitation shall be considered "trafficking in persons" even if this does not involve any of the means set forth in subparagraph (a) of this article; (d) "Child" shall mean any person under eighteen years of age.'

5 This was one of the assumptions tested by the ISS/SWEAT research. Sex workers and brothel owners were asked whether

clients ask for foreign women or young girls, and whether the frequency of such requests had increased. We found, almost without exception, that there was neither a particular market demand for exotic women or young girls, nor had requests for foreign women and young girls increased.

6　The concept of securitisation grew out of the notion that the security agenda should be broadened to include threats 'beyond state and military security ... to include individual, social and global concerns' (Jackson 2006: 300). In this context, securitisation is 'understood as "the move that takes politics beyond the established rules of the game and frames the issue either as a special kind of politics or above politics"' (in Jackson 2006: 301).

CHAPTER 4

Sex, choice and exploitation: reflections on anti-trafficking discourse

Ingrid Palmary

Introduction

This chapter reflects on the ways in which trafficking has become a central preoccupation when working with migrant women and children in the Southern African region. I will argue that there are multiple investments in the issue of trafficking that reflect long histories of preoccupation with the sale of sex, the shaping of the colonies and associated racial profiling that mean that victims of trafficking and their experiences of being rescued are hard to find within these debates. In particular, I want to pay attention to how discourses surrounding the agency of women and children function to curtail the kinds of interventions deemed feasible to victims of trafficking. This infantalisation of women (Burman 1997) is not a new phenomenon and many authors have critiqued the conflation of 'womenandchildren' (Enloe 1990, Yuval-Davis 1997). In a context of immigration control this conflation creates both familiar and new exclusions. Similarly, trafficking and its assumed links to sex work, whilst posited as a new and rising phenomenon, on closer inspection raises familiar discourses of power, agency and morality that have been a longstanding preoccupation in feminist and women's studies. This chapter thus reflects on continuities in the discourses on sexual exploitation and agency and the ways they have been mobilised in the most recent proliferation of anti-trafficking campaigns.

I want to consider three problems with the ways that trafficking has been taken up and responded to in the southern African context and its gendered manifestations. The first is the way that the agency of women and children is represented to create a partial and subtle conflation of the needs of women with the needs of children. This is accomplished through an immigration rhetoric that locates the natural place of both as 'home' and fetishises home (Ahmed 1999) by identifying being away from home as the source of women's vulnerability. Home is a fraught notion that has seldom been adequately interrogated in studies of migrations for its assumptions and exclusions. These notions of home and choice are at the heart of the debate on trafficking, the creation of the Palermo Protocol, its resulting local legislation in many Southern African countries, and indeed the eventual deportation of trafficking victims. But these are notions that function in ambiguous ways that reproduce a number of racialised sexualities familiar to the colonial project (see Arnfred 2005 for a more general discussion). Whilst there has been a feminist critique of these, it has failed to adequately interrogate the notion of agency with its implications of age and gender that is at work.

Second, the current discourse on trafficking relies heavily on racial stereotyping in the detection of traffickers, the representation of victims and the responses we envisage. This racial stereotyping manifests in the crucial ways that current immigration practices imagine and insist on national difference.

Finally, this means that many of the perpetrators of trafficking are the families of the victims in this context and the way trafficking of women and children has been debated and prioritised means that old-style intimate colonialism (see Summers 1991) continues to function through this kind of immigration policy.

The problem of trafficking

Anti-trafficking campaigns have attracted a great deal of funding and are arguably one of the most widely supported areas of work in migration responses. In the area of child labour, they are the most common interventions in the southern African region according to a database of services held by the Forced Migration Studies

Programme. The International Organization for Migration (IOM), one of the primary organisations driving trafficking interventions globally, has spent over a billion US dollars on its African programme since 2005 to cover three areas of work – one of which is trafficking (International Organization for Migration 2009). In South Africa, this concern with trafficking began at the moment (in 2007) where South Africa was placed on the tier-two watch list in the Trafficking in Persons report issued by the US government; that is, a country requiring special scrutiny either because there are thought to be particularly large numbers of trafficking victims or there has been a failure by the country to provide adequate evidence that it is taking steps to combat trafficking (United States Department of State 2009). Since this time, the South African Law Reform Commission has begun the process of developing a discussion paper and drafting a proposed Bill on trafficking (South African Law Reform Commission 2006). Its progress through parliament has been astonishingly fast given that, for example, the Children's Act, written in 2005, still has substantial parts that have not been operationalised, nor have any of the 2007 amendments. Similarly, Zambia, Lesotho and a range of other African countries have been no less swift in their development and passing of anti-trafficking legislation. However, questions have been raised about how widespread trafficking really is (see Consortium for Refugees and Migrants in South Africa 2009, Gould and Fick 2008) and how much of a concern it should be for African governments. Claims have been made about billions of dollars of easy money being made by traffickers each year and estimates of 700,000 people trafficked into the sex work industry alone have made newspaper headlines. The Trafficking in Persons report has been heavily criticised for providing no adequate sources for its claims about the extent of the problem. Similarly, there has been a major shift of donor funding, into anti-trafficking initiatives, which has necessarily taken place at the expense of funding to address other forms of exploitation. Perhaps even more intriguing is the fact that the sex work industry has been cited as the major industry that receives trafficking victims (International Organization for Migration 2009). There has been far less attention to other sectors that may well rely on trafficked labour such as farm work or domestic work and may equally be associated with widespread exploitation. This chapter begins with an analysis of just one small part of this seemingly sudden alarm over trafficking into sex work

– the concept of choice and agency that is at work – and argues for how this approach is rooted in colonial histories that have re-emerged in the new context of immigration control.

Reflecting on choice and agency

The Palermo Protocol adopted by the United Nations in 2000 and ratified by South Africa in February 2004 outlines the conditions that constitute trafficking. It defines trafficking as:

> the recruitment, transportation, transfer, harboring or receipt of persons by means of the *use of threat or use of force or other forms of coercion, of abduction, of fraud, of deception, of the abuse of power or a position of vulnerability or of the giving or receiving of payments or benefits to achieve the consent of a person having control over another person*, for the purpose of exploitation. [My emphasis]

Thus there are three central conditions that need to be met for trafficking to have occurred. The person must have been (1) moved, harboured, transferred or received, (2) using some form of coercion or deception (3) for the purpose of exploitation. In this section, I want to reflect on how the notion of coercion has been conceptualised in anti-trafficking materials and how this is embedded in notions of infantalised femininity (see Burman 1997 for more) and a pathologising concern over the sexuality of women. More than this, it is a concern over women who move – with all the associated implications of leaving home and children – where home is considered the most appropriate place for women and for expressions of female sexuality.

As in much law, age is significant in determining the degree of consent that one can give in situations of trafficking. Therefore, children (defined as everyone under 18) cannot consent to being moved or recruited into exploitative labour. This is a telling move, typical of most child protection law, which is rooted in assumptions about children's innocence, their need for the protection of adults, and their immature decision making that are frequently contradicted in practice. This has been well documented in the general literature on child labour (Bourdillon 2006). However, what I want to consider is the conditions that are considered to make up *women's* deception, coercion or agency and how this compares with children's. Just the fact that the protocol emphasises the trafficking of women and children is telling and fairly typical of the conflation of 'womenandchildren' (Enloe 1990, Burman 2008). This has been extensively critiqued in the feminist literature and I do not want to rehearse these critiques here. Rather, I want to examine the notion of agency that this conflation of women and children rests on. An extract from an awareness campaign run by the IOM indicates the reasons why women and children might be similar:

> Potential victims are often so desperate for a better life or for access to some form of income that they become oblivious to traffickers. They are naïve and are unaware of the dangers that they might face from trusting strangers or acquaintances who make them false promises of a better life somewhere else. Women and children are particularly vulnerable in situations where poverty is rife. Women, often the breadwinners of the home in such areas, would usually look for work opportunities outside their immediate environment. This makes them vulnerable to traffickers. (Sihlwayi 2009)

The assumption that women who are poor are open to having their labour exploited is not one that I would disagree with. However, this curiously becomes conflated with a woman being naive and overly trusting of strangers. For women, deception takes place at the moment that their behaviour is considered to be more culturally childlike; where they lack the (implicitly) masculine, adult qualities of rationality, risk aversion and reasoned decision making. The strangeness of 'another place' functions to emphasise women's domestic rootedness (a topic I will return to) and childlike innocence of the dangers of those places away from home. This occludes the ways that poor women's labour in the region has been heavily reliant on migration, from domestic workers under apartheid who were required to live with their employers whilst their families were not permitted into the city, to seasonal work on farms in rural areas. What is evident in this kind of argumentation is the hierarchies of abuse and exploitation that exist around the movement of people. Indeed, the asylum system, which offers protection to those fleeing political persecution but not those fleeing famine, is equally an example of hierarchies of violence that shape the responses deemed necessary.

This conflation of childlike women with a lack of agency is not uncommon and indeed is a trap that feminists too have fallen into. For example, Weekes (2006) has presented a well-argued critique of how the proposed South African anti-trafficking legislation might result in the restriction of women's freedoms and deny their agency. She argues that 'treating adults, and particularly women, as equal to children within legislation relegates adults to a position of vulnerable victims who have no agency and therefore need the relevant authorities to act on their behalf' (2). This of course sets up women and children in an equally artificial dichotomy as the argument that conflates them. Children too have agency and more of it in some settings than others. Furthermore, it fails to capture how notions of childhood and agency have equally changed over time and in different contexts. This is an argument well presented by Smart (1999) in her article reflecting on the history of child sexual abuse and its (re)construction at different moments through a combination of medical and legal approaches that changed the nature of the notion of consent and of what constitutes childhood more generally. For example, British law (which has heavily influenced South African law since the British took control of the Cape colony in 1806) has seen the age of consent for sex raised from 10 (in 1861) to 13 (in 1875) and then to 16 (in 1885) (see Smart 1999 for more). This has reflected an ongoing reconstitution of what childhood is and what the nature of children's sexuality ought to be.

And yet, in spite of a general acceptance of these arguments, there is no doubt that agency has been a vexing topic for feminism. As Ahearn argues:

> Feminists have sought to establish the seriousness of their struggle by demonstrating the pervasiveness and systemacity of male dominance. This has led to the development of theories that emphasize the constraining power of gender structures and norms, while downplaying the resisting capacities of individuals and groups. On the other hand, feminists have also sought to inspire women's activism by rediscovering lost or socially invisible traditions of resistance in the past and present. (Ahearn 2001: 115)

Therefore, there has been a tension between an overstated homogeneous approach to power that allows no space for agency and an overly romanticised understanding of resistance that both sees it everywhere and celebrates its effects too easily. In particular, this is a notion of agency that conflates it with free will, unfettered by relationships to others, and that equally draws on the much-critiqued notion of the rational, self-contained individual of enlightenment thinking (see Henriques *et al.* 1984 for early critiques). Thus, as Abu-Lughod (1990) argues, 'we could continue to look for and consider nontrivial all sorts of resistance, but instead of taking these as signs of human freedom we will use them strategically to tell us more about forms of power and how people are caught up in them' (42). Returning to the above example, what is most compelling about relegating women to the category children is the power of the globalised assumptions about child need and innocence that functions to render women's vulnerability taken for granted.

Nevertheless, whilst coercion is a requirement to meet the conditions of trafficking, its ambivalent treatment is stark in the awareness campaigns against trafficking. This is particularly true when we are considering women trafficked into the sex work industry. This concern over whether women can choose sex work has been a longstanding debate and it takes on a particular salience in the context of trafficking because of the requirement that coercion be proved. Sex work is where choice becomes most impossible for many groups to believe. For example, The New Life Centre in Johannesburg, which 'rehabilitates women and children who are commercially sexually exploited and trafficked', has refused any distinction between sex work and trafficking. Arguing against the decriminalisation of sex work in South Africa, they called a meeting to 'stop the decriminalisation and legalisation of prostitution because (1) it is not work but exploitation, (2) it is not a service but slavery, [and] (3) it contributes to human trafficking' (unpublished pamphlet, 2009). In their discussion paper on trafficking, the SALC noted that many of the commentators recommended special cases of trafficking to be where women are trafficked into sex work and some commentators argued that the requirement of force should not be in place for establishing trafficking into sex work.

These themes have a long tradition in anti-trafficking campaigns. For example, writing on the work of the social purity reformers in England in the 1800s, Gorham (1978) notes how, contrary to the claims of the social purity movement, there did not appear to be much evidence that the young prostitutes they sought to rescue were being held in sex work against their will. Nor did they show much enthusiasm for being rescued. She claims that:

> The national vigilance association, which in public portrayed itself as dedicated to the rescue of innocent maidens from the jaws of procurers, discovered that there was little work of this nature to be done after its foundation in 1885. One of the activities that the organisation became involved with instead was the management of a small 'preventive' home. The minutes show that the inmates often ran away. (375)

This is equally evidenced in the IOM focus on 'community stabilisation'. These are interventions that provide income-generating activities to prevent the re-trafficking of victims – a common problem after victims have been 'repatriated'. That this is a problem suggests that there may be a need to deal not with individual evil traffickers but rather with economic inequalities – a point equally made by Gorham (1978) in her analysis of Victorian England. She argues that:

> In much of the reform rhetoric, the young prostitutes are portrayed as sexually innocent, passive victims of individual evil men. This imagery of individual sin, with its corresponding possibility of individual redemption, may have been comforting to these late-Victorian middle class reformers because it did not threaten the images of womanhood, childhood, and family life that formed an essential part of their world view. (Gorham 1978: 355)

Indeed a fascinating parallel has been at work in the South African discussions about trafficking, which have questioned the value of the term 'abuse of power or position of vulnerability' in the definition of trafficking. At a recent workshop on methodologies for studying trafficking a magistrate raised the concern that this could arguably include any poor person as a victim of trafficking. Whilst it clearly is not the intention of the legislation to include all poor people as trafficking victims, programmes for all those working under exploitative conditions may well be more meaningful. The continued focus on sex work over other forms of exploitative work that middle-class families directly benefit from, such as domestic work, shows up the class inequalities in the framing of the trafficking agenda. The concern with the possibilities of alternative constructions of women's agency as threatening to the family is at least part of the explanation for why then, as now, the preoccupation is primarily with women and children trafficked into the sex work industry rather than with other forms of coerced and exploitative labour.

However, the fact that trafficking victims often are either re-trafficked or are unwilling to be rescued has been explained in a number of ways – most of which draw on popularised psychological ideas about women's passivity (and indeed masochism). For example, the IOM in their 2009 'eye on trafficking' newsletter draw on the notion of Stockholm syndrome to claim that:

> After a long period of servitude to the trafficker, some victims become emotionally attached to the trafficker and chose [sic] to remain with him/her, even if it means working under exploitative conditions. Furthermore, because of the fear of being deported, a victim may develop loyalty towards his/ her trafficker or even try to protect him/her from the police. (Lifongo 2009)

Thus, in spite of the requirement that women be forced or deceived into a trafficking situation, through the use of popular psychological notions, this lack of agency may not be apparent to the woman herself. Although no detail is given as to how one might know when a woman is being forced into a situation when she claims she hasn't been, behind this 'syndrome' one can glimpse a psychological expert who would be called in to assess her 'true' intentions. Furthermore, describing the control mechanisms traffickers may use, brainwashing is mentioned as something that can cause 'some victims, especially women, (to) blame themselves for their involvement in trafficking and prostitution' (Lifongo 2009: 4). Here again, the slide between trafficking and sex work is evident, as is the assumed individualised guilt associated with both.

Re-imagining home

A second criterion for establishing whether trafficking has taken place is that the person must have been moved. Whilst it is often assumed that this means movement across an international border, it has recently been claimed that it can equally apply to movement within a country (usually from a rural to urban area). Either way, there are a host of meanings attached to women's movement. For the most part, in studies of migration, women's movement has been treated as a problem, or at least indicative of a crisis, at 'home'. Implicit in much of this literature are the notions of home that are evoked. Home in the migration literature is an ambiguous term associated at the same time with violence, safety, stability and mobility. Its association with the well-being of the family makes women's migration a particular source of anxiety. Nevertheless, different conceptions of home are shot through with notions of race, class and gender, giving different kinds of homes very different meanings (see Webster 2003). In the previous quote by Sihlwayi (2009) it is the description of homes where women are the breadwinners that is cited as an anomaly that can cause women to leave the home. This notion of home stands in contrast to middle-class notions of home as a place of leisure or consumption (see Webster 1998) and it is only in comparison to this middle-class – and normalised – notion of home that we can lament migrant women's loss of home. Drawing on these notions, home is evoked as the natural place for a woman and mother and one she would only leave under extreme duress. The particular salience of the African mother that has been (re)constructed through the colonial project (Summers 1991) has reproduced these notions of the African woman as only ever domestic and shaped by her duties and responsibilities to family. Once again this is a mythical notion that stands against the ways that domestic work, as an example, has often required African women to leave their families in order to care for the children and homes of other women – a contradiction that is glossed over in the assumed natural link between women and home. This stands in stark contrast to the approach to agency discussed above which locates agency in the individual and assumes that individuals are the only possible site of agency. It also begins to explain why some groups (including poor, black women) can never, within the current framing of the problem, be attributed the agency that others have/are. However, the commonality of re-trafficking shows that home is an ambivalent space for poor women and children. The assumption that to move away from home necessarily involves a loss of some kind (Malkki 1992) is a highly gendered one that has been used to limit women's employment opportunities and justify differential migration laws for men and women (as in, for example the inheritance of citizenship only through patrilineal lines).

Thus, it is precisely the strength of such evocations of home as the natural place of women that legitimates the ignoring of notions of coercion in some instances of trafficking. This is most evident where we consider the programmes the IOM implement to reunify women and children. In the proposed South African Bill as well as in many of the current activities of the IOM and other organisations intervening with trafficking victims, the recommended solution (after the prosecution of the trafficker) is voluntary repatriation. However, this simply means repatriation paid for by the IOM rather than the 'less dignified' (International Organization for Migration, 2009) version of deportation by the government. It is not automatically the choice of the victim whether they will return to their country of origin. Rather a return home becomes governed by immigration law and its control ethos rather than the needs of the trafficked person.

Colonial legacies

I have already hinted at the way that trafficking targets poor women in ways that, rather than addressing their poverty, implicates individual traffickers and pathological families with absent or mobile mothers and children. This eclipses a number of factors that, again, are predictable ones for how they shape the interventions deemed possible and desirable. At a recent conference co-hosted by the Forced Migration Studies Programme and Save the Children, UK on child migrants, discussions in one small group centred on how community awareness programmes on trafficking faltered because in many instances the traffickers would in fact be the child's parents (Save the Children, UK and Forced Migration Studies Programme 2009). This is particularly the case where parents required their children to cross the border to South Africa to find work. This is a common occurrence for children from neighbouring countries when they become too old to qualify for free education (which, for example, is age 12 in Mozambique). This work often includes work on farms, domestic labour or begging, all of which are arenas of work with high levels of exploitation (Palmary 2008a). The solution proposed at the conference was to get trafficking messages to be taken up by respected community members to avoid the impression that they were being imposed by outsiders. However, the way that trafficking is conceptualised results in the focus being on the child's parents rather than the conditions of their work or on wealth disparities. Similarly, the most recent training manual designed by the IOM for DHA officials in South Africa proposed that bride inheritance[1] is a form of trafficking (International Organization for Migration 2009). The assumption inherent to this is that bride inheritance must inevitably involve coercion and cannot conceivably constitute a legitimate marriage. It thus draws on a normative discourse of marriage and sex that holds idealised and mythical notions of 'marriage as love' as the basis for establishing coercion in other kinds of marriage relationships. In this way, longstanding practices that previously have not been associated with moral indignation become criminalised and pathologised acts.

As in previous outbreaks of concern around trafficking, this has been seen largely as a problem of the poor (but not of poverty), who are set in contrast to educated, self-aware and less naive wealthy women. Because of this construction, the solutions concentrate on the individuals and families, also thereby creating an extensive system of surveillance of migrants. For example the discussion document of the South African Law Commission recommends a database of victims be kept, that border control be tightened and that the police have greater powers of search and arrest. These policing-focused responses are remarkably centred on the surveillance and control of the victim of trafficking given how much emphasis there is on rescuing victims within the trafficking discourse. In addition, none of these measures are likely to make the movement of women (or children) safer nor are they likely to improve the conditions of their work.

Nationality (and with it assumed race) equally figures in the way that research on trafficking has emphasised the need to create 'profiles of victims and perpetrators'. For example, the International Organization for Migration in their magazine 'eye on trafficking' (2003) claims:

Malawi is characterized by three different trafficking patterns. *Firstly*, Malawian businesswomen recruit young women to pursue employment or educational opportunities in Europe. Sometimes payment is made to the victim's parents. Upon arrival in the Netherlands, the victim is sold to a Nigerian madam for US$10 000, and told that she must work as a sex worker to pay off a debt of US$40 000. The Nigerian madam will ask her for underwear, hair, and nail clippings in a ritual that threatens death by magic if the victim does not cooperate. The victim is then sold to another Nigerian agent from Belgium, Germany, or Italy, or rented to local brothels. One brothel in the Netherlands brands with an identifying mark the sex slaves who work there. If the victim does not perform sexually to the satisfaction of the brothel owner, she is beaten, and given sex lessons, or resold. (Martins *et al.* 2003)

These claims have been heavily critiqued, as in many instances they were based on only one or two interviews with trafficking victims or officials. However, leaving aside their overgeneralised claims, the way in which victim and perpetrator profiles are established is largely by their national identity and related (but unspecified) cultural practices. Presented as a neutral and rational fact, this kind of statement is equally evident in other reports on trafficking. Sources of information are extremely difficult to trace and in many instances involve simply asking border officials how many people they think come across the border and who they think the perpetrators are (see, for example, Martins *et al.* 2003). Through methodologies like these, stereotypes are recast as facts in a research language that contributes to disguising their discriminatory underpinnings. As a result, the image created is of a well-organised syndicate with consistent methods that use extremes of force and deception. The parents are mentioned only in passing as someone who might receive payment. Nevertheless, the above discussion shows how, in many instances that can be defined as trafficking, this is not how it takes place. Rather, practices that might well involve exploitation but are commonplace, such as child labour across borders or bride inheritance, are recast as trafficking in ways that undermine the decision making of poor families.

Conclusion

Whilst we should have systems for dealing with the kinds of exploitation many migrant women and children face, this cannot be done through drawing on sexist and racist stereotypes of poor women and children. To do so risks losing the priorities and concerns of these groups and potentially making their movement increasingly dangerous – either by further criminalising it and therefore making migrants even less able to receive services or by ignoring the priorities and concerns of those affected by trafficking. This chapter has attempted to reflect on the notions of trafficking that are evoked in trafficking responses, and the racist and sexist notions that underpin some of them. Indeed, agency is so thoroughly conflated with race, gender and class that it is impossible for some groups to ever achieve agency, and the implicit assumption is that those who are marked as being without race, gender or class will make choices on their behalf. This risks continuing a long history of colonial intervention into the bodies and practices of African women in the name of their own protection in paternalistic and potentially violent ways.

Note

1   Bride inheritance is when a woman whose husband has died is taken in by her husband's brother and she becomes his wife. Whilst this typically involves a broad relationship of responsibility, the focus of much writing on bride inheritance has been on the sexual relationship.

PART 2

Asylum

In this Part the critiques of *how* women have been rendered visible continues with chapters offering different analyses of aspects of the representation of women's claims to asylum. Each of the chapters in this Part show how, in spite of generalised rhetoric about women's vulnerability in times of violence, their asylum claims are rendered implausible precisely because of the gendered nature of conflict and violence. Underlying this ambivalence towards women's assumed vulnerability is a notion of gender that maps it onto male and female bodies in uncontested ways such that the diversity and complexity of experiences of forced migration is foreclosed. Thus, a focus on women's asylum claims is inevitably also a focus on the way that the asylum system is set up to respond to mythical divisions between political and domestic, state and family violence. This theme is taken up in Julie Middleton's chapter which is based on gender-related persecution cases in South Africa and in Khatidja Chantler's chapter which analyses women seeking asylum in the UK. Although operating in different geo-political spaces, both chapters explore the ways in which gender and culture are essentialised and serve to cast gender-based violence as personal, cultural or both. The chapters highlight the mobility of concepts of gender, culture and conflict and interrogate the public/private dichotomy. Sajida Ismail's chapter addresses the fallibility of the concept of 'internal flight' which is posited by governments as a solution to limiting asylum claims without proper attention to the viability of such a solution.

In this Part of the book, therefore, we see most clearly how the discursive practices by which gender and migration has been rendered visible as a topic of analysis and intervention – with gender as an uncontested identity – shape the credibility of some migrants. The asylum system insists on separating out different reasons for migration and in so doing sets up models for credible claims that recreate gender, nation and race as natural identities that can be used to identify difference, and indeed need. Hence the ways that bureaucratic systems shape credibility through selective attention to the gendered nature of migration are most clear in Erica Burman's chapter, which utilises a discourse analytic approach to illustrate how the banality of official responses masks the complexity and complacency of government agencies in relation to gender and asylum. This Part of the book highlights the demand within these systems for a particular performance of gendered vulnerability that is, at the same time, denied by official claims to objectivity.

CHAPTER 5

Barriers to protection: gender-related persecution and asylum in South Africa

Julie Middleton

Over the last two decades, recognition of gender-related persecution in asylum law has grown, with many countries[1] issuing directives on the adjudication of claims by refugee women.[2] While such moves have increased awareness, they have also been criticised as largely symbolic, stopping short of fundamentally changing the approach of asylum systems towards gender and therefore limiting any real redress for refugee women (Valji 2001, Ceneda and Palmer 2006, Oxford 2005, Macklin 2004).

Based on research into gender-related persecution cases in South Africa,[3] this chapter assesses the manner in which asylum decisions are made. It looks at how the asylum system defines legitimate refugees, and the interplay of fluid interpretations of gender, culture, conflict and the political. Asylum determination is discussed from a social science and feminist perspective, as opposed to a legal studies angle, evaluating the ways in which understandings of the law are formed, and how they affect claims of gender-related persecution. In doing so, the chapter attempts to balance the need to position its analysis within the boundaries of asylum law, while also challenging the essentialist assumptions which that law legitimises and is based upon.

Two main themes were seen during interviews with South African asylum officials and refugee claimants, as well as in the analysis of individual asylum decisions. Both themes demonstrate a reliance on patriarchal and essentialist notions of the political and personal, as well as of the nature of conflict and culture. First, there is an emphasis on overtly political or officially sanctioned human rights abuses as grounds for asylum, as well as a dismissal of gendered claims as personal and common and therefore less serious or even irrelevant. Second, gendered harm is frequently only seen as persecution when it occurs during the time of an officially recognised conflict, or where it can be associated with a foreign culture, or cultural backwardness.

Finally, it is argued that the transformation of the asylum system towards considering gender-related persecution claims requires more than a change in law (i.e. the inclusion of gender as a ground). Rather, a dramatic adjustment is needed – one which interrogates and alters the narrow lens through which asylum seekers are viewed and the law is interpreted and applied.

The South African asylum system

While amendments to South Africa's refugee law were being debated in parliament last year, one change seemed to pass relatively unnoticed.[4] The 2008 Refugees Amendment Act brought 'gender', a term previously incorporated in the Refugees Act of 1998 under 'particular social group', to new prominence as the seventh ground for asylum, along with race, tribe, religion, nationality, political opinion or membership in a particular social group. Although passed without fuss, this small change distinguishes South Africa as the only country in the world to explicitly include gender as a binding ground for asylum. Other countries that recognise gender-related persecution, including Canada, Australia, the USA, New Zealand, the UK and other European states have chosen not to amend their legislation, but have instead created non-binding guidelines of how gender can be included within the definition of a particular social group. South African officials have said they hope this change will reduce ambiguity and raise the status of gender within the Act, generating greater recognition of gender-related persecution cases.[5] Whether it will have this affect, however, is a question that goes beyond just a change of law.

The South African 1998 Refugees Act incorporates the 1951 UN Refugee Convention and its 1967 Protocol, and the Organisation for African Union 1969 Refugee Convention (OAU, 1969) in its definition of a refugee. While new amendments to the Refugees Act will alter the definition of a refugee, at the time of the research a refugee was recognised as someone who:

(a) [having] a well-founded fear of being persecuted by reason of his or her race, tribe, religion, nationality, political opinion or membership of a particular social group is outside the country of his or her nationality and is unable or unwilling to avail himself or herself of the protection of that country, or, not having a nationality and being outside the country of his or her former habitual residence is unable or, owing to such fear, unwilling to return to it;[6]

(b) owing to external aggression, occupation, foreign domination or events seriously disturbing or disrupting public order in either a part or the whole of his or her country of origin or nationality, is compelled to leave his or her place of habitual residence in order to seek refuge elsewhere. (Refugees Act 1998: Articles 3a, b)

A social group is defined as including, 'among others, a group of persons of particular gender, sexual orientation, disability, class or caste' (Refugees Act 1998: Article 1xxi). How gender should be understood within the Refugees Act, however, is less clear. The Act and its regulations (Refugee Regulations 2000) do not define the meaning of gender, nor what types of harm could qualify. The United Nations High Commissioner for Refugees (UNHCR), however, published guidelines in 2002 (UNHCR 2002), meant to inform and guide adjudication around gender-related persecution. Although not binding, they are the most widely recognised and distributed, and hence, are referred to in this chapter.

As set out in the Refugees Act, No. 130 of 1998, Refugee Status Determination Officers (RSDOs) hold the responsibility for deciding on the validity and credibility of all asylum applications in South Africa. They interview applicants and determine whether their claims can qualify for asylum under the definition of a refugee as set out in Section 3 of the Refugees Act. At the time of the study, they had three options: they could either accept the claim, decide it is unfounded, or declare it manifestly unfounded. If it is unfounded, the claimant then has the right to appeal to the Refugee Appeal Board. If it is manifestly unfounded, meaning that it falls outside the definition of a refugee, the case is sent to the Standing Committee on Refugee Affairs. The Standing Committee reviews the case and decides whether it falls within the definition. If it does not, the application is rejected; if it does, it is sent back to the RSDO to either accept or reject the case.[7] Although asylum seekers who are initially rejected at the RSDO level are able to appeal their case, only few actually do so. RSDOs are thus the most crucial actors in the system. Their understanding of gender-related persecution determines how such cases are evaluated, and eventually whether they are accepted as valid.

The adjudication of gender-related persecution must be considered within the context of the South African asylum system more generally. South Africa is in the unique position of being the only country in Sub-Saharan Africa that has a formal policy of integration for refugees, unlike its neighbours which often rely on policies of containment in camps and settlements. Because of the nature of its policy, South Africa encounters many of the same issues faced in the northern developed states; however, it remains within the socio-economic climate of a developing country in southern Africa. Asylum seekers in South Africa come up against numerous procedural hurdles – lack of adequate official interpretation, backlog of asylum cases and fast tracking of claims, overburdening of asylum officials, and inadequate technology. Such problems inevitably affect the way claims are assessed and decisions made.

Xenophobia and high levels of violence against women in South Africa also influence how cases are viewed by asylum officials, and the personal security asylum seekers can enjoy. There is a certain irony that South Africa, a country with one of the highest levels of gender-related violence in the world, seeks to offer asylum to those fleeing similar harm (Human Rights Watch 2009, Hirschowitz *et al.* 2000, Jewkes and Abrahams 2002). As in most circumstances, however, granting asylum provides merely contingent protection at best (Macklin 1995). Although South Africa can offer its borders as protection from a perpetrator in another country, it cannot guard against gendered violence absolutely. It cannot guarantee adequate protection, or even an appropriate response by the police or legal system, should she become a victim of gender-related violence in South Africa.

The asylum system and the legal rules which govern it are the product of a historical process that is 'constantly evolving as a reflection of social and political values' (Shuman and Bohmer 2004: 396). Likewise, interpretations of gender, as well as what is considered political and cultural, are also dynamic, and continually shifting. The actors involved in the asylum system are inevitably affected by such fluid notions, and are informed by societal perceptions and experiences of gender, culture and politics, and levels of tolerance of interpersonal violence (Bhabha 1994, Palmary 2003, Shuman and Bohmer 2004, Razack 1995, Oxford 2005).

Common crime vs. persecution (personal vs. political)

According to the UNHCR handbook, asylum cannot be granted solely on the basis of personal injury (UNHCR 1992), creating a hierarchy of harm where only overtly political violence committed by the state is undisputedly accepted as a basis for asylum. Referring to the 'privatisation' of violence in the Dutch asylum context, Spijkerboer (2000: 98) observes that domestic and sexual violence are often viewed as private by adjudicators because they are seen as taking place in the family context, or because of the personal motives of the perpetrator. Such crimes are dismissed as common and arbitrary acts by which women around the world are affected. As a result, adjudicators often fail to recognise that domestic violence and rape and the lack of protection from abusers are systematic, societal and political in nature. This emphasis on public (political) forms of violence as persecution and the dismissal of gendered harm as private (personal) or common inevitably influences the way decisions are made by officials. It shapes the way questions are asked, what parts of the applicant's story get noticed and ultimately the decision that is made (Palmary 2003).

Additionally, most modern feminist writers, such as Greatbatch (1989) argue that assumptions of a public/private dichotomy ignore the diverse contextual realities of women's experiences. While something appears to occur in the private sphere, it may be extremely political. African feminist writers have also critiqued the public/private dichotomy as inapplicable in Africa, in that women have traditionally inhabited both spheres simultaneously, determining social organisation and hierarchy through other social constructions, such as seniority (Bakare-Yusuf 2003). Despite arguments against such a dichotomy, a reliance on it continues to exist throughout the South African asylum system, relegating gendered harm into the untouchable realm of the personal and private.

During the interaction between an official and an asylum seeker, the asylum seeker may emphasise certain parts of her story, and neglect other aspects, while the official may only pick up on outwardly political connotations. Asylum seekers often interpret their experiences of gendered harm as personal, rather than political, and as a result fail to present their experiences in political terms. Rape victims, for example, may see their rape as a personal attack rather than an example of gender violence (Shuman and Bohmer 2004). As Shuman and Bohmer (2004: 396) note in their study of the US asylum system, to meet criteria for political asylum 'applicants need to reframe what they often understand as a personal trauma into an act of political aggression'. Although it is impossible to absolutely separate the personal from the political, the asylum system frequently neglects to interrogate the political in seemingly personal accounts. As a result, many asylum seekers slip through and are rejected by the system without ever recounting the most important part of their stories.

The experience of a Ugandan asylum seeker illustrates this. Her application was rejected because she failed to fully tell the RSDO about her experiences. Her first husband, a former member of the Lord's Resistance Army (LRA), was killed when he refused to rejoin and, at the same time, she was also beaten and raped. Her brother in-law inherited her as his wife, but he was later also killed by the LRA along with her son. During the RSDO interview, she:

> Decided not to tell anyone because it is a shame and it is hurting, and I thought maybe it is not necessary to mention. The only question was why I left my country so I just said the things that I was comfortable with. And I didn't know where those information was going.

Her story is certainly political, but she was unaware of the need to share something she interpreted as so very personal. Like her, asylum seekers who fail to frame their experiences in political terms are similarly rejected, without officials ever attempting to dig deeper into seemingly personal experiences. This artificial distinction between personal/political serves to undermine and delegitimise the experiences of asylum seekers, as well as discriminates against those who are unaware of the necessity of portraying their experiences through politicised lens.

While South African asylum officials acknowledge that persecution can be committed by either a state or non-state actor, in practice the emphasis is clearly on cases where the state is the perpetrator. Where the state is involved the case is usually seen as undoubtedly political, requiring external protection. Where harm, particularly gendered harm, is committed by a private citizen, officials seem to see it as the domestic concern of the state and the community, even when there are no obvious mechanisms or willingness to prevent or prosecute it. As a result, during interviews, asylum officials at various levels showed inconsistencies in their approaches, often dismissing cases involving domestic violence, forced marriage and sexual orientation as too personal or common to qualify for asylum.

In discussing domestic violence, the Chairperson of the Standing Committee said that although they have seen a number of such cases, they are not seen as fitting under the definition of a refugee, and so are rejected.

> We have a number of domestic violence cases, but domestic violence is not easily covered by the definitions. So we would get a case where the woman claims her husband beats her up or the husband's family doesn't like her or something like that, but seeing her as a particular social group and suffering domestic violence is difficult to currently bring into the Refugee Act. Those that we have seen have been decided as manifestly unfounded.[8]

Here the Chairperson of the Standing Committee diminishes the harmful impact of domestic violence. He compares 'her husband beats her up' to 'the husband's family doesn't like her or something like that', trivialising the significance of a claim based on domestic violence. Such claims are rejected, not based on the merits of the cases, but because violence in the home or family is perceived as private and accepted as too commonplace to be persecution.

In contrast, demonstrating the variety of interpretations at play, the Refugee Appeal Board reported they would consider cases of domestic violence under particular social group (gender) grounds. 'It's the same as what you get with female genital mutilation, we would classify that as social group and we would allow those appeals,' said a member of the Board.

Within the South African Refugees Act, the ground of social group is defined to include, along with gender, sexual orientation. While it is explicitly mentioned in the Refugees Act as separate from gender, sexual orientation is clearly related to gender. Under the UNHCR Guidelines (2002), persecution based on sexual orientation is seen as relating to a claimant's refusal to adhere to socially or culturally defined gender roles. Most of the officials interviewed recognised that a claim based on persecution for sexual orientation could be accepted under South Africa's asylum law. As discussed earlier, however, prejudice within the asylum system inevitably influences decisions. For example, a Tanzanian man was interviewed who claimed persecution on the basis of sexual orientation. In his rejection letter from the RSDO, it states: 'You said you left your country because of your family problems. You said that your family chased you out because you are a gay. You also said that ... your religion (Islam) does not accept gays, even your tribe (Sukuma) doesn't.' When handing him his rejection letter, the RSDO reportedly told him, 'you don't look like a gay', with little other explanation. The rejection letter not only does not address the substance of his claim; it also trivialises it, describing it in purely domestic (i.e. personal) terms as 'family problems,' rather than questioning whether such harm is actually symptomatic of broader societal or legal discrimination. In addition, the RSDO's assertion 'you don't look like a gay' demonstrates how stereotyped perceptions, in this case of gay men, negatively affect the reasoning in asylum decisions.

Turning to forced marriage claims, 6 of 28 RSDOs interviewed said they had heard forced marriage cases, and almost all of them had rejected the claims. Only one said she had approved the claim. In a July 2007 decision, however, the Refugee Appeal Board approved a claim based on forced marriage. The appeal concerned a Cameroonian woman whose uncle sold her into marriage with an older man at the age of 14 after her parents passed away. Her husband and his other wives abused her for several years, prompting her to flee to South Africa. She had approached the Cameroonian police on several occasions, but they had refused to intervene. In this presumably landmark decision,[9] the Legal Resources Centre in Cape Town, which acted on behalf of the woman, argued that she was a member of a particular social group, in particular, according to the heads of argument:

Women forced to marry in exchange for bride price and who are subjected to severe and prolonged physical abuse at the hands of their husbands and who are unable to seek protection from the State because they are customarily considered the property of their husbands.

The decision is a breakthrough for gender-related asylum in South Africa as, specifically utilising information from a United States State Department country report looking at the position of women in Cameroon, it accepts that this woman is a member of a particular social group. In his decision, Mr Damstra, Acting Chairperson of the Refugee Appeal Board, states: 'It is accepted that the appellant falls within this category, i.e. she is a woman and as a group they are unprotected by the state in Cameroon.'

While the above decision presents hope for other women in similar situations, the emphasis placed on the appellant's decision to approach the Cameroonian police for help is worrying. It is questionable whether the Refugee Appeal Board would grant such a decision if the woman involved had not reported the situation to the police. In fact, asylum officials appear to require that claimants report the matter to the authorities, even when it is well known that they will do little to help. Also, the decision to present 'Cameroonian women', generally, as a vulnerable social group, while successful, also creates a possibly unreachable standard for other gender-related persecution cases (Bhabha 2006). In order to prove persecution, the lawyer and adjudicators were forced to essentialise all women in the country as vulnerable to persecution. While common practice internationally, such expectations may make future successful gender-related persecution claims all the more unlikely.

In domestic violence cases, as with forced marriage, RSDOs emphasised the need for claimants to prove local authorities could not provide such protection. One RSDO said, referring to domestic violence:

> You mean she has run away from the country because her husband is beating her? That claim is not credible because ... I don't know the constitutions of all countries, but anywhere where someone can be dealt with, they can deal with that ... What did you do before coming to South Africa? Did your parents know? Did his family know? Before even you

can go to the police. That's really where you need clear information – about what she did.

This response seemed to imply that domestic violence would not be a legitimate reason for women to flee their country, underestimating and trivialising its possible impact. The RSDO also falsely assumed that women could acquire assistance for such a common crime: 'anywhere someone can be dealt with'.

However, despite the assertions of asylum officials that asylum seekers who experience gendered harm should approach local authorities, few of the people interviewed for this study went to their local police for help before leaving their countries. When asked why they had not, all said they knew the police would refuse to intervene to help them. As a result, both the local police and the asylum officials participate in a process of undermining gendered violence as a rights violation. The asylum seekers who experience such harm are left caught between two systems – the local that refuses to protect because of unwillingness or discriminatory laws, and the international that, ironically, refuses to offer refuge because of its belief in the former's ability to protect.

Safe/unsafe, peace/war?

'Violence against women happens in peacetime, is intensified during wartime, and continues unabated in the aftermath' (Pillay 2001: 36)

The all-encompassing nature of modern conflict means that the continuum of violence transcends the simple diplomatic dichotomy of war and peace, and resists any division between the private and public realms (Giles and Hyndman 2004). Neatly drawn diplomatic concepts of peace as simply the absence of armed conflict view peace solely in the public realm, the space of typically male-dominated armies, political negotiations and peace deals, and ignores the less obvious violence that takes place in homes and communities and may continue long after the official end of a war. In fact, heightened sexual violence often outlives the period of armed conflict itself (Valji 2001, Bhabha 2007).

South African asylum officials have shown a willingness to grant asylum to women who have fled rape or other gendered violence, often by soldiers or rebels, during war. Once a conflict is deemed to be over from a diplomatic point of view – and therefore no longer designated as a '3b' country under the Refugees Act – such claims are rejected *en masse*. Section 3b of the Refugees Act refers to a situation of generalised violence in the country 'seriously disturbing the public order', most often war. Asylum officials make blanket assumptions that 'peace' automatically means a country can provide effective protection against gender violence, without conducting adequate investigation into the capabilities of local authorities. There is a failure to assess the country situation and whether, realistically, authorities are able and willing to provide any substantial protection. As a result, women who flee to South Africa after being raped by soldiers and rebels during wartime are not given refugee status if their asylum claims come up for evaluation only after peace – no matter how tenuous – has been declared.

According to an RSDO:

> You must look at the causes of the rape. You find that she was raped because of section 3b because of foreign domination, aggression, violence ... Because those rape cases are due to uncontrollable situations in his or her country ... Because of foreign aggression, rebels, maybe there was an attack on the village and raped women, I believe that such a person, I would give that person status. The claim is not based solely on the rape, but you've checked on 3b and it falls within the 3b, so that person deserves status. But based on 3b.

Another RSDO said:

> Most ladies from the Sudan will claim that they have been involved by the soldiers when they were trying to run away, when there was violence. And some are having kids from the rape. Others they are suffering with HIV because of those rapes ... [but] no, it's not just the rape ... they are fearing the events when there was violence.

In these comments, RSDOs use the assumed dichotomy between war and peace to draw a corresponding division between rape as persecution and rape as a normal part of life. During war, rape is seen as atrocious, a random act of violence associated with political upheaval. When there's peace, rape is accepted as commonplace, a normal form of interpersonal violence. As shown in the quotes above, according to asylum officials, asylum cannot be 'based solely on the rape' but on the existence of conflict. By relying on such distinctions, the asylum system creates and perpetuates the myth – a 'rape myth' – that persecutory rape can only happen during war, and as a result, denies and trivialises the majority of rape cases (Lonsway and Fitzgerald 1994).

Outside the asylum system, studies on the tolerance of violence have noted that respondents (police, judges, general public) often dismiss sexual assaults that do not conform to the stereotypical rape scenario (i.e. an armed stranger leaping out from a dark alley) (Du Mont and Parnis 1999). Such societal acceptance has serious consequences, especially when it influences the views of law-enforcement and legal professionals, prejudicing the treatment of victims of rape within judicial systems (Du Mont and Parnis 1999). Among asylum officials in South Africa, rape myths – 'the mechanism people use to justify dismissing an incident of sexual assault from the category of 'real' rape' (Burt 1998: 27) – appear to similarly influence who is deemed to be a refugee. In the above comments, RSDOs clearly articulate that asylum is never dependent on the fact of the rape alone, but on the circumstances of war in which it has occurred. No matter how heinous the individual experience of violence may be, the overriding factor is the existence of conflict. Rape itself, outside war, is seen as a normal or even 'personal' part of life, and thus is dismissed as an invalid basis for asylum.

Many of the women interviewed, as well as case files reviewed, by this study were from the Democratic Republic of the Congo (DRC), a country where a fragile peace has been negotiated but conflict is omnipresent (International Crisis Group 2008, International Alert 2005). Between the five women from the DRC who were interviewed, one was given refugee status (although she did not convey her story of rape), and four were rejected even though they shared their stories of rape or fear of rape. In a further seven rejection letters obtained by this study, sent between April and November 2007, RSDOs systematically rejected refugee claims of rape and forced marriage to rebels. As is demonstrated below, RSDOs seemed to merely 'cut and paste' one rationale for each of the decisions: that negotiations in the DRC are underway between the government and the rebels, so therefore the country is safe, ignoring the possibility of ongoing violence against women in the country.

In a rejection letter from August 2006, an RSDO states that country reports from the Department of Home Affairs claim the DRC is able to offer protection and assistance to all its nationals. In addition to suggesting the claimant – who arrived in 2004 – could approach the authorities for assistance, or move to a more peaceful part of the country, the RSDO wrote:

> The applicant claims that the rebels were raping girls in your area. There can be no well founded fear of persecution that be established from the fact that the rebels were raping girls. Rape is a crime that appears to be rampant all over the world. There appears to be no indication that the applicant experienced or witnessed the incidents that she claims was taking place ... The circumstances that compelled the applicant to flee from the DRC are not justifiable considerations that would lead a reasonable person in the circumstances of the applicant to flee from her country of origin.

One woman fled the DRC after she was raped and forced to become the 'wife' of one of the rebel soldiers. Solely based on the political negotiations between the ruling party and rebel groups, the RSDO who interviewed her wrote, 'The government protection is easily accessible to people who avail themselves for state protection. The government of the DRC will protect you against any ill treatment.'

What is most disturbing about these decisions is the assertion that rape on the scale that has been seen in post-war DRC (Gettleman 2007, International Alert 2005) is not accepted as a form of widespread persecution, and the insinuation that it is something normal. The RSDOs clearly disregarded the experiences of the applicants, rejecting the possibility that rape, a crime 'rampant all over the world', could be the basis of a legitimate asylum claim. They blatantly failed to consider that rape, when the government is not able or willing to prevent it or apprehend its perpetrators, can be considered a form of gender-related persecution. The assumption that rape is persecution only during wartime prejudices the judgement of the asylum officials; rather than interrogating the state that allows such acts to continue, they accept as normal and apolitical those rapes that occur during 'peace'.

Culture as political

The reality for those who claim asylum based on gender-related persecution is that the practice of asylum law relies on and expects simplified and stereotyped views of society, politics, conflict and culture to establish a basis for intervention. To prove persecution in cases where the perpetrator is a non-state actor, it must be shown that there is serious harm in conjunction with inattention or inaction by the state to provide adequate protection. Visweswaran (2004) argues that when a state's failure to make or enact appropriate laws begs the question of 'why', rather than attributing it to poor policy or lack of political will it is often blamed on the force of culture. Hence culture becomes equated with the political, and acts previously seen as personal are recognised as political. In South Africa, female genital mutilation (FGM) appears to fall into this category – a 'personal' form of harm deemed political by its basis in a foreign culture.

FGM, also known as female circumcision or female genital cutting, has received tremendous attention around the world and in South Africa.[10] Although FGM is not practised in South Africa (UNICEF 2005), it is seen in at least 28 countries stretching across the centre of Africa north of the equator (Althaus 1997). In contrast to other forms of gendered harm discussed, South African asylum officials seem more willing to accept FGM as a form of persecution. Revealingly, they also associate FGM with culture, in particular, a non-South African culture. As has been also noted in other asylum systems, South African officials seem to fall into the trap of cultural essentialism and ethnocentrism when assessing the legitimacy of gender-related persecution claims (Oxford 2005, Sinha 2001). FGM is practised by Other Africans and so more easily judged as barbaric and clearly unacceptable. In contrast, domestic violence, rape and forced marriage, which occur at an equal or even greater prevalence inside South Africa, even if assumed to be cultural, are less likely to be seen as persecution and a basis for asylum (Vetten 2005, Van Schalkwyk and Mhlanac 2007, Mathews *et al.* 2004).

An explanation by the Chairperson of the Standing Committee provides an illustrative example. When questioned on the distinction between FGM and domestic violence claims, he explained that FGM is a cultural practice and therefore requires a greater degree of state protection:

We see a difference; domestic violence would very seldom
cause you to leave your country, whereas genital mutilation
can quite easily cause you to leave your country. Domestic
violence, you don't usually have to depend on any state
assistance to avoid it, whereas mutilation you would
almost definitely need state assistance to avoid it, active and
successful state intervention. It's two very separate things.
FGM is more of a cultural thing.

While in this case culture is used to justify asylum, it is a dynamic
concept that can also be used interchangeably to undermine claims.
In other asylum systems, domestic violence is often dismissed exactly
because it is considered cultural. Cultural practices are thought to
be common and personal and therefore affecting everyone equally
(Spijkerboer 2000). In fact, even in the above statement by the
Chairperson of the Standing Committee, domestic violence is seen
as so common it does not even require state assistance. As Homi
Bhabha (2004) argues in *The Location of Culture*, concepts of
culture can never been assumed to be static or uncontested, as they
are constantly being renegotiated and reasserted. Similarly, the use
of culture as an explanation within the asylum system is also fluid,
being redefined by asylum officials according to the situation.

The borderline engagements of cultural difference may as
often be consensual as conflictual; they may confound our
definitions of tradition and modernity; realign the customary
boundaries between the private and the public, high and
low; and challenge normative expectations of development
and progress. (Bhabha 2004: 3)

While in other circumstances culture may be used to justify the
exclusion of asylum seekers, here it is used to argue for their
inclusion. Rather than a fact of life and commonality, culture
is demonised and on a par with the political as justification for
asylum.

In human rights reporting and feminist literature, culture has
frequently been portrayed as a non-Western phenomenon (Kapur
2002, Visweswaran 2004, Mohanty 1994, Spivak 1994). Chandra
Mohanty (1994) and Gayatri Spivak (1994) critique 'Western',
particularly feminist, writers for a tendency to portray third world
women as monolithic cultural others. Rather than unpacking their

unique experiences, differences and individual agency, they argue that such writing appeals to its readers' neo-colonial sensibilities to save third world women from their uncivilised cultures (Spivak 1994). In contrast, however, when Western women – usually cast as liberated, empowered and on a par with men – experience gendered violence, culture is not as easily used as an explanation. 'Culture is frequently invoked to explain the kind of violence experienced by women in the third world, though it is not invoked in a similar way when discussing violence against women in various Western contexts' (Kapur 2002: 14). In other words, culture is often portrayed as something 'others' have and are oppressed by.

More than a decade after the introduction of the gender guidelines in the USA, researchers have also found a differentiation based on culture arising between the types of gender-related persecution that are more likely to be recognised by asylum officers and judges, and to some extent even legal services providers. Certain types of harm, such as female genital mutilation and honour killings, that are seen as only occurring outside the country of asylum, are more readily accepted as grounds for asylum, while domestic violence and rape, that also occur in the country of asylum, are less likely to be seen as gender-related persecution or considered a legitimate basis for asylum (Oxford 2005, Sinha 2001). According to Oxford (2005), the American asylum system demonstrates insecurity with ethnocentric harm and fear of exotic harm. 'Female circumcision, unlike domestic violence, signifies cultural backwardness – a cultural practice exclusive to migrant women' (Oxford 2005: 24).

In her analysis of gender-related persecution cases, Jacqueline Bhabha (2006), states that the US legal system requires lawyers to simplify and use stereotypes, to depict countries as backward and undeniably oppressive of women. She asks, addressing fellow lawyers, 'How many of us have not pressed "our" country experts to simplify their affidavits, to present as clear a black and white picture as possible of a culture, a situation, a danger, in an effort to persuade a court?' The implicit danger in using stereotypes and ignoring the complex understandings of culture within any one country is that it sets too high a benchmark for access to asylum. An asylum case will not succeed unless it is able to establish that within the applicant's country all cultural views on gender are homogeneously oppressive. Such a requirement jeopardises the basis of future asylum cases, as background depictions become more and more exaggerated and removed from reality (Bhabha 2006).

Despite criticism, the demonisation of FGM as a cultural practice has clearly allowed women who flee FGM to be granted asylum in a number of countries, including South Africa. Reliance on cultural explanations, however, has serious repercussions for those women whose claims involve persecution that cannot be blamed on culture, or a cultural practice. As Kapur (2002) warns, such portrayals of culture distract from the real issue: the failure of the state to provide real protection for human rights. When women are seen as victims of their own cultures, the state is excused. Rather than focusing on culture itself, Visweswaran (2004) asserts it would be much more effective to place the emphasis on political systems' denial of rights and the intrinsic interface between culture and politics, putting the responsibility to protect against gender violence back on 'the shoulders of the state'.

Conclusion

Much of this chapter critiques the essentialism found in the South African asylum system. It also recognises, however, that essentialised portrayals of refugees are central to its operation, and that of the international refugee regime. To be successful, applicants inevitably have to play into a system that demands stereotypes (for example, 'Cameroonian women' at risk), bases defences on the demonisation of culture, and understands harm in only clear political terms. Aside from setting the standard unreasonably high, such a system also fails to hold the state accountable for prevention of and protection against gender violence, and instead places the blame on personal failures of the applicant and her 'culture'.

Although efforts to ensure the visibility of gender within the Refugees Act should be applauded, without an improvement in both knowledge and procedures any enhancement in the legal protection of women in South Africa's refugee law may sadly go unnoticed by those responsible for its implementation. Instead, the application of asylum law must be reframed towards a political understanding of gender-related violence and a clear recognition of the responsibility of states to protect. At the same time, improved training on the adjudication of gender-related claims for officials in all levels of decision making and the development of clear guidelines will go far in enhancing understanding and improving decision making. Only with greater emphasis on understanding and implementation, in addition to legal assurances, will those who flee to South Africa be able to realise the protection that the Refugees Act promises.

Notes

1   Among others, Canada, Australia, the USA, New Zealand, the UK and most European states all recognise gender-related persecution as a ground for asylum.

2   Due to the disproportionate effect of gender-related persecution on women, as well as the particular challenges women face in the asylum process, this chapter will primarily focus on women. It does, however, acknowledge that men can also be victims of gender-related persecution, and a number of these cases were examined by the research.

3   The research for this chapter was carried out as part of a larger project examining gender and asylum through the Forced Migration Studies Programme (FMSP) at the University of the Witwatersrand. The methodology employed key informant and participant interviews and documentary case study analysis. South African asylum officials were interviewed, including Refugee Status Determination Officers (RSDOs), members of the Refugee Appeal Board, and the Chairperson of the Standing Committee for Refugee Affairs. Twenty-two asylum seekers (three men and nineteen women) whose gender-related applications were originally rejected were also interviewed.

4   The amendment moving gender from under a particular social group to a seventh ground was not mentioned in any of the public hearing summaries available online; http://www.pmg.org.za/report/20080326-refugees-amendment-bill-b-11%E2%80%932008-public-hearings. Only the United Nations Human Rights Commission (UNCHR) noted the change, applauding South Africa for further acknowledging gender-related persecution as a basis for asylum.

5   The Chairperson of the Standing Committee on Refugee Affairs recalled a consultation regarding the amendments: '... [Participants] said rather put it in there; take out all the ambiguity, stop all the arguments that might take place in the future because not everyone sees gender as a particular social group.'

6   The Refugees Amendment Act changes 3a to read 'owing to a well-founded fear of being persecuted by reason of his or her race, gender, tribe, religion, nationality, political opinion or membership of a particular social group'.

7   The 2008 Refugees Amendment Act dissolves the existing Standing Committee for Refugee Affairs and the Refugee Appeal Board and establishes the Refugee Appeals Authority. It also removes 'manifestly unfounded' as a possible category for decision.

8   'Manifestly unfounded' according to the Refugees Act, Article 1, means 'an application for asylum made on grounds other than those on which such an application may be made under this act'. The UNHCR (1983) states that these cases are those 'which are considered to be so obviously without foundation as not to merit full examination at every level of the procedure'.

9   The Refugee Appeal Board could recall no other cases of forced marriage being granted.

10 Female genital mutilation/cutting (FGM/C) involves the cutting or alteration of the female genitalia for social reasons. Generally, there are three recognised types of FGM/C: clitoridectomy, excision and infibulation. Clitoridectomy is the removal of the prepuce with or without excision of all or part of the clitoris. Excision is the removal of the prepuce and clitoris along with all or part of the labia minora. Infibulation is the most severe form and consists of removal of all or part of the external genitalia, followed by joining together of the two sides of the labia minora using threads, thorns or other materials to narrow the vaginal opening.

CHAPTER 6

Safe to return? A case study of domestic violence, Pakistani women and the UK asylum system

Sajida Ismail

Introduction

This chapter draws from findings in a transnational study[1] which examined the ambivalent position of Pakistani women who seek protection from domestic violence within the framework of the 1951 Refugee Convention.[2] The chapter draws particular attention to the increasing use of an international legal device by UK decision makers for rejecting asylum claims. This is commonly referred to as the 'internal flight alternative' or 'internal relocation' and, in practical terms, often results in the involuntary removal of women back to their country of origin. In the UK, the study was principally concerned with examining ways in which the Border and Immigration Agency,[3] the immigration judiciary and other relevant services addressed the legal and support needs of Pakistani women asylum seekers. In Pakistan, the study examined the nature and extent of domestic violence, of service provision across all sectors, and documented women's experiences of attempts to gain safety, with particular reference to the viability of the 'internal flight/relocation' concept.[4]

The chapter explores the forced nature of Pakistani women's migration, which places them in positions of legal, practical and psychological vulnerability. It frames the discussion on gender and migration within feminist and other discourse on notions of culture, 'new-age' Islamism and domestic violence. It draws attention to how women's experiences are minimised within nationalised and Islamised framings of gender and culture and the ways in which the Pakistani and UK states manipulate these concepts in advancement of their political ambitions to sustain systems of political and migration control. The chapter concludes by considering whether 'internal relocation' realistically offers a Pakistani woman an appropriate safe haven from violence.

Background

South Asian women appear to be visible largely as victims of static patriarchal cultures. This awareness underpins much of the international interventions aimed at enhancing Pakistani women's status, for example international economic development initiatives and women's health programmes, designed to promote greater agency. Such interventions are reliant on significant development funds, such as those provided by the UK government. Yet, Western nations have historically paid little heed to any such discourse on oppressive practices, whether feminist or otherwise, during the process of assessing and determining South Asian women's *asylum* cases. An awareness and understanding by Western governments of the intersection between culture and political systems in South Asia is required to enable a more effective consideration of gender-based asylum claims emanating from South Asian countries (Visweswaran 2004). This is particularly so in South Asian women's asylum cases that allege domestic violence (Chantler 2007). But what are the additional concerns that identify *Pakistani* women as a 'special case'?

The specificity of Pakistani women's domestic violence claims lies in the conflation of notions of morality, sexuality, nation and religion with laws in Pakistan (Khan 2003). This conflation creates the structural conditions in which domestic violence takes place and is socially accepted. Khan's emphasis on the need to move away from traditional 'culturalist' explanations for domestic violence and instead to stress the role this conflation plays in subjugating Pakistani women had particular relevance for the study, and is amplified by her examination of how the Zina Ordinances in

Pakistan came into being. Khan's thesis that General Zia's military regime promulgated the Ordinances as a component of the new moral order in Pakistan in 1979, essentially to bolster its own political base through alliances with right-wing religious parties (Khan 2003: 89), is a compelling demonstration of the state's role in regulating women's morality. Ultimately, such state-endorsed regulation severely curtailed Pakistani women's ability to access redress against any form of gender-related harm.

Khan's analysis has particular significance for Pakistani women. Their status, attributable to cultural, societal and state-level discrimination and abuse within Pakistan, has been endorsed in the UK's landmark case of 'Shah and Islam'.[5] The case enhanced the definition of 'Membership of a Particular Social Group' in accordance with the spirit of the Refugee Convention and, specifically, its applicability to Pakistani women. The significance and specificity of 'Shah and Islam' itself justifiably warranted further examination of the situation for women in Pakistan in the period since this ruling.

Furthermore, analysis of South Manchester Law Centre's legal casework involving Pakistani women drew attention to the specific nature of the discrimination Pakistani women experience and of the Pakistani state's continuing role in maintaining legislative and other structures by which Pakistani women remain subjugated, demanding more in-depth enquiry.

Other studies (Batsleer *et al.* 2002, Burman and Chantler 2005) have examined the process by which, in the UK, government policy, structural violence and familial abuse coincide, with particular reference to women from minority groups, illustrating the particular vulnerability of Pakistani women caught in the system of asylum and immigration controls. However, increasing public and political scrutiny of Pakistan and Pakistanis also suggests that specific hurdles exist, which impact exclusively on Pakistani women.

In order to cast a comprehensive lens, the research consisted of 8 case studies across the two nations. We also interviewed 46 service providers in Pakistan such as crisis centres, and the police; 28 similar organisations in the UK; 25 women in Pakistani shelters who had experienced domestic violence; 8 women in the UK who had claimed asylum on the basis of domestic violence, and 8 group interviews/discussions across both nations. We obtained one written response from the UK Border Agency.

Overall, the study consisted of Pakistan-based research in the geographical regions of Punjab, Sindh and the North West Frontier Province and UK-based research in England and Wales. This presented the research team with numerous challenges, notably the need to pay attention to the risks of over-homogenisation, of over-culturalisation, and to the various uses and meanings of the terminology associated with the themes reflected in the final report. A range of research approaches, tools and analytical frameworks were used in response to the different national contexts. It was important that the research paid attention to difference, as well as commonality, in participants' responses. As a means of avoiding stereotyping, the selection of dispersed geographical regions emphasised the cultural and regional diversity of Pakistan. This diversity underpinned the research design and provided a constant check on over-homogenisation. Paradoxically, attending to differences also drew attention to cultural and regional commonalities, in particular, in relation to the socio-economic position and status of Pakistani women across the four regions and the dominance of men in all decision-making sectors of society. The study aimed to generate more indicative information to amplify available knowledge bases, including for UK asylum decision makers.

The study was not focused on children. However, the researchers identified a range of circumstances in which women were regarded as not fully adult, mothers were themselves treated like children, and where children were deemed to be women by virtue of the domestic, sexual and state violence they had encountered. Children did not directly participate in the research in the sense of being interviewed *separately* or having their specific perspectives taken as the topic of study, with one exception.[6]

A transnational focus on gender, culture, racism and domestic violence

The need to deconstruct our understanding of domestic violence in order to build a strong conceptual framework which recognises the complexity of women's experiences emerged as a critical issue. Thus, the study engaged with a wider arena of debate, drawing on current international discourses in academia, in the media and amongst practitioners on gender, 'culture', Islamism and racism. It enabled the researchers to highlight manifestations of violence which were perceived to significantly affect particular women (for example, honour killings and their prevalence within South Asian, specifically Pakistani families). Additionally, this approach highlighted the need to shift from 'culturalist' framings of violence, in order to examine the interplay between gender and race, and to understand both why and how violence against Pakistani women takes place. The research material demonstrated the ways in which cultural, racial and political frameworks in Pakistan and the UK intersected to create conditions in which women could be subjected to violence, a form of 'state-sanctioned' harm. In this respect, fundamental inadequacies and injustices within the UK government's immigration and asylum system emerged at a central juncture in these intersections. Within Pakistan, the research highlighted the way in which religious and cultural norms are bolstered by a corrupt political system. These norms are central to the way in which institutions, systems and states conceptualise domestic violence. Meanwhile, raging debates about the destabilisation of Pakistan as an Islamic nation-state (Pakistan's history, since its emergence as a new nation-state, has largely demonstrated only volatility and instability), its perceived 'Talibanisation', Islamophobia, racism and the 'War on Terror' have all intensified community concerns in the UK regarding a new wave of racism and distrust in the state. Furthermore, in the UK, regressive change has taken place particularly in the field of immigration and asylum. This is apparent in recent legislation to 'secure' UK borders, in which the issue of immigration and asylum was inextricably, and lamentably, linked with fears of terrorism (the UK Borders Act 2007). These fears seemed to have contributed to a decrease in the reporting of incidents of domestic violence amongst Muslim women, indicating an urgent need for both Muslim community groups, and service providers, to refocus on the issue of domestic violence.

How does this context connect to contemporary representations of Pakistani women? The prevailing simplistic perception in the UK asylum system is that the 'typical' asylum-seeking woman, such as 'the Pakistani woman' is more likely to be an 'economic immigrant', irrespective of the conceptual difficulties of disentangling economic reasons from political reasons for migration. For this study it was important to develop an understanding of what lay beneath this, particularly as this perception fixes Pakistani women's identities within a singular framework of opportunistic migration.

Within the West a woman who seeks asylum is often perceived through negative discourses that construct her as an 'immigrant woman'. These constructions are usually defined by her connection to practices such as arranged marriage and gender subordination, which are perceived as somehow 'backward' (Gedalof 2007). Gedalof demonstrates how this discourse is a continuum of the gendered and ethnicised coding which keeps 'immigrant women' firmly sited as homogenised symbols of unchanging cultural traditions. Through this classification and stereotyping, the specificity of male and familial violence is lost. Gedalof's analysis was pertinent to the study as within this construction it appears that any claim a woman might make to a *particular* or additional experience of victimisation remains obscured, and yet, clearly, as a result of such powerful symbolisation, Pakistani women never cease to be victims.

The focus of enquiry for a decision maker concerning a Pakistani woman's claims can only encompass the more believable explanation that the desire or need for economic gain is her real motive. Gedalof's analysis also highlights a specific experience of domestic violence that is structured by a 'minoritised' woman's minority status as an immigrant or asylum seeker. In highlighting this difference she exposes the fact that in domestic violence discourse there has been a tendency to privilege 'gendered' experiences of domestic violence over 'race' or cultural identification.

Within Pakistan, much of the material drew attention to societal perceptions of the customary role of women (principally as wives, mothers, carers, dependants), which hindered women's capacity for agency. Significantly, within the UK's asylum system similar conceptualisations of Pakistani women (further bolstering Gedalof's analysis) exposed flawed approaches to decision making on their claims. One example concerns 'lone' Pakistani women. Whilst some women attempted, and sometimes managed, to live as 'lone' women in Pakistan, they did so at the risk of experiencing 'legitimised' harassment and serious consequences for their 'reputation' and their family members. An awareness and understanding of this gendered analysis was simply beyond the conceptual radar of many UK decision makers, resulting in expressions of disbelief that women who lived alone experienced any hardship.

There exist 'other' women about whom decision makers are equally sceptical, if not ignorant, among them being 'abandoned women' and non-Muslim Pakistani women (such as Christian women) and Ahmadiye women.[7] Abandoned women – for example, Pakistani nationals who arrived in the UK with spouse visas and were subsequently 'returned' by sponsors – often find themselves in 'limbo' in Pakistan. Throughout the study it became clear that most of these women have experienced spousal and/or familial violence and were subjected to accusations of committing acts of 'dishonour'. The difference lies in their inability to register an asylum claim should they wish to, as it remains unclear how, if at all, a woman could lodge an application at a British High Commission in Pakistan. These women do not fit into existing models of asylum and do not fit into prevailing conceptualisations around gender, violence and national responsibilities for service provision.

Post 9/11 and 7/7 (the London terrorist bombings in 2005 which killed 56 people), Pakistani women, as migrants, have encompassed and attempted to negotiate any one or combination of ambivalent identity markers; for example, their status as Pakistani nationals, their faith as Muslims, their experiences as immigrants and as asylum seekers, each of which is intrinsically bound to their experiences as women. Furthermore, the adoption of Islamic headdress and other external trappings of religious adherence, which appears to be on the increase, reflect this attempt to negotiate these complex identity characteristics but have also enhanced curiosity about their motives. It raises questions about whether women are independently aligning themselves to a 'movement' (this may include 'Islamic feminism' or 'political Islam') by manifesting outward physical signs of affiliation, asserting a modern self-constructed identity, or whether they are acquiescing to coercive religious ideologues in assuming prescribed roles within a specific Islamic revivalist agenda (Jamal 2009 and Zia 2009 offer insightful critiques on such developments currently being played out in Pakistan). Jamal goes so far as to question whether these are entirely 'post-terror' developments (31). Nonetheless, they require continual examination to provide an understanding of the context and meaning behind changing (self-) perceptions of Pakistani women.

Pakistan: specific issues

From an early stage in the study, it became clear that there remain serious and specific difficulties with the regime within Pakistan when addressing domestic violence and the harm it generates.

The Constitution of Pakistan (which at the time of publication of the report in January 2008 had been suspended following the declaration of emergency rule by President Musharraf) and the various instruments signed by the government of Pakistan demonstrate a theoretical commitment to equality and protection for all Pakistani citizens. However, government rhetoric on women's rights can be contrasted with its failure to implement domestic violence legislation and appropriately punish perpetrators.

By putting in place a credible political and judicial framework, foundations could be laid for a significant change in Pakistani society's perception of women. This foundation should include the introduction of appropriate punishments, the creation and implementation of legislation to protect women rights, prevention strategies, and the repeal of legislation that discriminates against or persecutes women. It is noteworthy that the Domestic Violence Bill, pending since 2003, was only passed by the Pakistani National Assembly in August 2009. It has yet to be approved by the Senate.

Furthermore, there is a need for the government to demonstrate a commitment to improving service provision. Whilst there have been some developments, notably in the creation of additional crisis centres, our study indicated that these will not meet the considerable demand from both the rural and urban areas. The existing poor provision by state-run Dar ul Amans prompts the need for a thorough review of both systems and resourcing.

Meanwhile, the Hudood Ordinances continue to present considerable risks to women and to Pakistani society, engendering further abuse by enabling perpetrators to commit crimes without fear of reprisal or punishment. The parallel judicial system, whereby certain forums for dispute resolution function alongside, but to the exclusion of, the ordinary courts, with accompanying dual religious and state laws, creates both confusion, scandal and injustice within Pakistani society, often on issues relating to allegations of gender-related violence. These different parallel systems have deeply entrenched historical and religious roots and require urgent review.

Pakistan and the UK: commonalities

The need to maintain a critical transnational perspective throughout the study was reinforced by the fact that certain themes referred to above, which appeared to be Pakistani-specific (for example, corruption and neglect on the part of Pakistani state agencies and service providers), emerged as themes that were also relevant to a critique of the UK.

Laws, political structures, cultural norms and socio-economic barriers that maintained women's subjugation were apparent in both contexts. Criticism of Pakistan can appear to reflect or feed into a homogenised common view of the country as 'corrupted by its practices'. Yet much of the material within the context of Pakistan presented a more complex picture, demonstrating both corruption and a lack of access to justice, whilst also revealing resistance and campaigning on the part of organisations and individuals and an overarching oppressive regime that clearly impacted harmfully on women's lives. At the same time, within the UK context, women increasingly experienced poor-quality representation and support from services, and when cases failed as a result, they often 'disappeared' into an informal and exploitative socio-economic sector.

The lack of a welfare system in Pakistan has exposed women to destitution. Within the UK, a specific rule of immigration control – the 'no recourse to public funds' (NRPF) rule[8] – is a stark example of how lack of access to public funds prevents many women from leaving violent relationships. For women with insecure immigration status, who seek support against domestic violence, the 'NRPF' rule now represents a serious barrier to accessing both services and justice within the immigration system. Furthermore, the system of accommodation and financial support for asylum seekers administered by the UK Border Agency is removed once an asylum claim has failed. These risks associated with destitution, disappearance and detention pending removal for women abound.

The lack of effective regulation of the NGO sector in Pakistan has contributed to the chaotic, under-resourced services which struggle to meet demand. Zia specifically notes the 'complete failure of the non-governmental sector to propel a progressive politics' (Zia 2009: 40). In the UK, regulations, bureaucracy and the audit culture have hampered many service providers from responding effectively to women's needs. In Pakistan the nature of the relationships between state agents, some community-based agencies, men and their families are so disempowering for women that such inter-connectedness is unchallengeable and has effectively coerced many women to remain in violent circumstances; in the UK, a similar process of 'collusion' in the abuse of women is being played out in the immigration rules relating to domestic violence. This applies largely in cases where a woman in the UK on a spouse visa alleges that her marriage to her sponsor has broken down due to domestic violence. There appears to be a marked increase in the use of 'denunciatory letters' by sponsors, whereby the sponsor informs the UKBA of the marriage breakdown, for reasons other than his violence, and requests the authorities to activate curtailment of leave against the woman.

Service provision in the UK: service 'breakdown'

In the UK, services offering support following domestic violence are largely rooted in the charitable or voluntary sectors, with some statutory provision. Throughout the study, such services were consistently perceived to be poorly resourced, thin on the ground, oversubscribed, at times unsympathetic, culturally unaware or culturally inappropriate. They were also described as being at their most inadequate at 'crisis point'. The disjointed working relationships between women-specific and non-specific voluntary organisations, social services and health professionals has led to 'service breakdown' when women's needs have been at their most critical. Participants commonly perceived that such diverse providers were often unwilling to intervene. Whether that was due to complacency or to avoid being culturally insensitive, service providers unwittingly reinforced negative cultural perceptions of Pakistani women by simply failing to respond to their needs; for example, by accepting the wider family's request that allegations of domestic violence be treated as private family matters, thus 'closing their files'. However the prevailing perception was that the system of asylum and immigration control determines and 'regulates' service provision to women asylum seekers and women with insecure immigration status, heightening women's vulnerability to harm.

Previous studies (Batsleer *et al.* 2002 and Chantler *et al.* 2001) described the ways in which 'minoritised' women who are subjected to domestic violence were similarly treated inappropriately, or not at all, by service providers in the UK. These studies explored such issues in the context of informing policy and practice in domestic violence services. Their findings regarding racism were also reflected in the material for this present study; in particular, participants were consistent in their allegations of racism permeating the UK's asylum decision-making processes. For a woman who might be considering protection from a violent family situation, her fear of racism from service providers *and* the immigration and asylum system is more likely to limit her disclosure of violence, and consequently, to perpetuate it.

Furthermore, legal services were specifically highlighted as increasingly under pressure as a result of continual reductions in the level of legal aid (public funding for people on low or no income). Additionally, the immigration and asylum system and the regulation of the sector as a whole came under criticism for a general lack of knowledge, understanding and expertise in domestic violence cases. Inconsistent police practice across the UK was also described as a critical barrier to women's access to support and safety. Some perceived this to be indicative of the police's inability to create uniform practices to tackling violence. References to Pakistani women's negative experiences of police involvement in Pakistan parallels some police practice in the UK, leading many women to decide not to approach the UK police. The provision and quality of interpretation services also came under scrutiny. Participants described fundamental flaws in the nature, quality and delivery of this vital service, which they argued, contributed to the ill-treatment that women experience. These included inaccurate interpretations during asylum interviews, concerns about protection of confidentiality, and inappropriate discussions with applicants. Reliance on children as interpreters raised ethical difficulties, which competed with practical and often urgent demands. The need to attend to training and awareness issues within legal services, the police and, critically, interpretation services remained a pressing issue.

The UKBA practice of dispersing asylum seekers throughout the UK presented further legal and support issues. The dispersal system was regarded with suspicion and frustration by practitioners not only because it interrupted necessary care and support, but also because it created inconsistency and a lack of quality within legal representation in women's asylum cases. Furthermore, the UKBA has provided contradictory responses to women's refuges about whether they will provide resources to enable women asylum seekers to move to safer spaces (following domestic violence from partners whilst in the UK or whilst in the asylum system).

This has led to much confusion about its stated policy, a problem compounded by further inconsistencies in practice across different regions.

Service provision in Pakistan

The lack of access to appropriate provision in the UK can be compared in some respects to the inadequacy of provision in Pakistan. However, the severe lack of provision in Pakistan creates extreme difficulties for women who are fleeing domestic violence. This inadequacy of service provision can be seen at all levels, from a lack of legislative protection, to oversubscribed women's shelters which are limited in number and resources, and to the lack of rehabilitation or aftercare for women who have recently been housed but reach the end of their tenure. There is no system of re-housing women who have left their family homes; this fact alone plays a major role in the decisions many women make to return to violent relationships. This is exacerbated for many women by their weak socio-economic position, lack of education and employment opportunities. In addition, the attitude towards 'lone' women that pervades society in Pakistan often results in their isolation and ostracisation, exposing them to further harm.

The study found that the majority of shelters in Pakistan are under-resourced and offer little or no childcare provision let alone counselling or educational support for children. Policies within shelters that exclude boys over the age of five create severe and traumatic dilemmas for women, and provide disincentives to access them. Shelters are usually overcrowded, provide substandard facilities, rarely operate a 'one-to-one key worker' system, and offer poor working conditions, no casework supervision, and no training or worker accountability. The workers also often appear to run shelters with very little input from the board of trustees, which has overall management and accountability functions. Leaving a shelter often results in a woman returning to a violent situation, remarriage or returning to her family *if* they are willing or able to allow her back. Indeed, some of the shelters researched ran informal marriage-broker services, while others had links with the sex trade. In the absence of any of these 'options', women are often open to sexual exploitation to support their children and overcome the risk of destitution. Two crucial issues prevent women from living independently: the need for re-housing and for financial assistance. Unlike the UK, in Pakistan there is no such provision after leaving a shelter apart from the *Bait-ul-Mal* (a *zakat* fund)[9] collected by the government and distributed at its discretion, if at all. No woman interviewed for this study had been provided with funds from this source. Once a woman leaves a shelter there is no mechanism for protecting her within the framework for women's services. There is also little tracking of what happens to women after they leave the shelter, and workers often rely on newspapers to discover reports of honour killings of women previously in their 'care'.

Women's service providers in Pakistan often attempted to provide 'holistic' services, such as legal advice, counselling, arranging remarriages, identifying employment and facilitating reconciliations. Despite this willingness however, poor working conditions, a lack of management, monitoring and accountability structures, low wages, and under-resourcing, impact on their ability to adequately provide any of these. Often, shelters were not able to provide the specialist skilled workers required to address the particular needs of some women seeking help; for example, women with burns or who had been subjected to gang rape. Furthermore, the absence of specific provision for young women and girls again reinforced the ambivalent representation of 'adult women', particularly when viewed through a Western lens.

Using men as trustees of some shelters, and as employees, appears to be a common and acceptable practice. The support of male counterparts to engage in culturally sensitive and religiously contentious issues is a key element in raising awareness of domestic violence both within political discourse and within wider communities. Male presence as a protector and educator is, seemingly, a necessary intervention in the refuge services. However, it is also highly indicative of the nature and extent of risk to women, including women workers, in Pakistani society, and presents a fundamental ideological and political difference in practice between women's service providers in the UK and Pakistan, most notably that UK practice in the field of women's refuge provision has removed men entirely from this space, enabling women to determine and achieve agency. The role of international NGOs is critical, given their access to resources, and their responsibilities to facilitate development within services and to distribute resources. This presents considerable opportunities for partnerships which, in turn, can effect change in women's lives.

The 1951 Refugee Convention: protection 'home' and 'away'?

It is noteworthy that the analysis provided above appears to be largely absent in the discourse that has led to the development of the meaning of 'membership of a particular social group' (MPSG), a key strand of refugee law that has special significance for women seeking protection against domestic violence, and one of five grounds for which refugee protection is recognised by the 1951 Refugee Convention.

Legal discourse on this ambiguous Refugee Convention ground has gained momentum since the landmark case of Shah and Islam (see note 5). This House of Lords case widened the definition of MPSG to include Pakistani women. Further developments have since taken place in relation to the inclusion of girls and women from other nations who experience many other forms of gender-specific violence such as female genital mutilation. Nonetheless, recent decision making in Pakistani women's asylum cases has also been dominated by attempts to narrow its application, partly attributable to cultural ambivalence and misplaced perceptions. Furthermore, in the context of Pakistani women's claims, MPSG cannot now be considered separately from, and indeed appears to be inextricably linked to, the key concept of internal relocation.

This concept has a seemingly rational foundation. Asylum seekers are generally not entitled to refugee protection in a signatory state if they can safely flee to another part of their home country. They would need to demonstrate that it would be 'unduly harsh' to relocate in order to secure such protection. There is now a growing corpus of refugee case-law concerning this controversial concept (summarised in Bennett 2008), and yet the controversy surrounding internal relocation stems from a perceived lack of uniform and principled application of this by decision makers and the judiciary.

Evidence in asylum case-law

The research highlighted some fundamental problems in the treatment and interpretation of evidence in Pakistani women's asylum cases. There appears to be considerable resistance among decision makers to accept testimonies, even when evidence of the danger of internal flight is compelling. The research findings indicate that decision makers are unwilling to engage with the specific nature of 'undue hardship' presented by internal relocation within Pakistan. Significantly, whilst decision makers appear willing to attach some importance to the impact of internal flight on children, there is insufficient consideration of potential harm to women. This shift in emphasis towards protection for children is ultimately dangerous in its compromise of Pakistani women's separate entitlement to protection.

Such evidential issues affect asylum seekers from many diverse backgrounds; the difficulties associated with determining 'credibility' and the problematic ways in which the asylum system tackles concepts of 'objectivity' and 'subjectivity' impact on all those who seek asylum in the UK. For example, generic country reports generated by the UKBA for the purposes of assessing asylum claims are routinely accepted as independent and objective material by the judiciary. The reports of individual country experts (often distinguished academics) commonly produced by asylum seekers in support of their claims are frequently dismissed by the same body of people for lacking objectivity. Yet there remain specific concerns for this study regarding evidence in Pakistani women's cases. The formulation in refugee law that led to the recognition of Pakistani women as 'members of a particular social group' is undermined by misplaced and inaccurate perceptions of the nature of protection in Pakistan and the viability of internal flight within its borders. The depth of detail that emerged from interviews conducted in the UK and Pakistan is indicative of the oversimplification of protection issues. Furthermore, it is indicative of the structural and 'cultural' influences on decision makers that have prevented detailed scrutiny of these concepts in the context of Pakistan.

From the UKBA's viewpoint, the 'objective' country information for determination purposes is located in its Country of Origin Information Service country reports (COIS).[10] Yet criticism of the reports, notably that they lacked detail and 'objectivity', is supported not only by previous studies, but also by the UKBA's subsequent creation of the Advisory Panel on Country Information (APCI).[11] The APCI attempted to raise the standard of the reports. However, it had a relatively narrow remit, and the study's analysis of its assessment of the 2006 Pakistan country report demonstrates a flawed approach to its own scrutiny. For example, the APCI failed to address the lack of depth, detail and use of reliable sources in the 2006 COIS report concerning Pakistani women's particular position in society, the socio-economic structures within Pakistan that lead to women's ill-treatment and the considerable lack of attention to the complexities of internal flight.

It appears that other processes are in operation that influence decision making. When Pakistani women's accounts were found to be credible, the views of many participants suggested that their credibility is effectively immaterial to the outcome of their cases. Misplaced judgements about women's class, religion and other circumstances, misunderstandings about the nature of internal flight, and doubts about the 'credibility' of expert evidence all seemed to influence decision makers. Conclusions were often drawn on the basis of these misconceptions that Pakistani women, as asylum seekers, were rarely 'genuine' in the sense of needing protection outside of Pakistan. This response supported the widely held view that a 'culture of disbelief' permeates decision making in the UK asylum system.

Conclusion: safe to return?

This chapter argues that the option of internal relocation, which has been gaining ground in UK asylum decision making in relation to Pakistani women who have experienced domestic or sexual violence, is problematic. Whilst our research provides an indicative picture of domestic violence services in Pakistan, there is an urgent need for a thorough review and evaluation of existing services, including needs assessment for both rural and urban areas. This is essential so that internal relocation decisions are based on evidence of support available within Pakistan, so that, in turn, a realistic assessment can be made about the viability of such an option. The research team was also very mindful that the study did not focus on the specific needs of children, and this also represents a gap in current research and literature.

In Pakistan, women are required to travel vast geographical distances and to overcome considerable practical, cultural and psychological barriers to try to seek safety. Conversely, the vast geographical possibilities within the country are frequently cited in UK asylum contexts as an indicator of the 'safety' of relocation. The tensions presented by these opposing positions suggest a need to explicate what 'safety' in the context of the study means. Notions and concepts of safety, commonly associated with the provision of and access to physical, material, structural, social and psychological support, are heavily circumscribed in Pakistan. The study demonstrated the limited and temporary circumstances in which women reach a 'place' that can be deemed 'safe'.

Similarly, tensions abound when considering 'to where' in Pakistan a woman should 'return', since the study demonstrated that this does not, and cannot, refer to the place, house, family or situation from which many Pakistani women have fled. Whilst a woman's 'return' might take her to a new 'place' within Pakistan, her safety is not assured since, for example, she is likely to lack support networks, be isolated, and be unable to retain anonymity. In a UK context, return is more commonly associated with an involuntary process of removal to a 'safe' airport in the country of origin, beyond which the UK state absolves itself from any further responsibility. For the purposes of this study, this is indicative of further structural parallels between the UK and Pakistan, and, again, of misconceptions concerning the nature of 'safe return' and future dangers to women.[12]

Notes

1   South Manchester Law Centre conducted the study in partnership with Manchester Metropolitan University over two and a half years, concluding with the publication of a report in January 2008.
2   The United Nations Convention relating to the Status of Refugees and the 1967 Protocol.
3   Now called the UK Border Agency.
4   See C. Bennett, 'Relocation, relocation – the impact of internal relocation on women asylum seekers', *Asylum Aid*, November 2008.
5   Islam v SSHD and R v IAT ex parte Shah [1999] 2 AC 629 HL. This case concerned two Pakistani women seeking refugee protection against the threat of domestic violence in Pakistan.
6   We interviewed one female child living in a refuge in Pakistan. She was a victim of a forced marriage.
7   Whilst the Ahmadiye are a minoritised group, their beliefs are consistent with Islam, supporting the view that their 'otherness'

is in fact mired in historical and communal conflict within Pakistan.

8 Immigration Rules HC395 (as amended), paragraph 6. For a summary of this rule in the context of cases involving domestic violence, see 'Guidelines on Domestic Violence and the No Recourse to Public Funds Rule', South Manchester Law Centre, March 2009.

9 *Zakat* refers to the Islamic duty of almsgiving.

10 COIS reports are produced by the UK Border Agency's internal research team on each of the asylum-producing countries and address a broad range of issues, including the 'status of women'. The reports underpin the asylum-determining process.

11 The APCI was responsible for reviewing the country reports and making recommendations on their improvement. This is now the responsibility of the Chief Inspector, appointed by the UKBA.

12 It may appear to some that the position of women in relation to domestic violence pales into insignificance in relation to current events in Pakistan; that changes in leadership and senior administrators could render the analyses generated in this study less relevant, or even obsolete. This study suggests that the complexity of the relationships between domestic violence and cultural and political structures in Pakistan, including the parallel legal and administrative systems, means that much more than a cosmetic change of personnel, or even legal reform, is needed to alter this situation. Rather, changes that will make a significant impact on domestic violence rates, and service provision, will need to be structural and systemic. Specifically, changes will need to confront the 'men, money, mullahs and the military' and emerging Islamised national identities (Zia 2009: 30). It is anticipated that the analyses presented in the study will remain of substantial relevance until such time as these shortfalls in both the UK and Pakistan are addressed.

CHAPTER 7

Women seeking asylum in the UK: contesting conventions

Khatidja Chantler

Gender and migration covers a multitude of issues, practices and discourses. As Zavos (this volume) points out, much of the literature on migration tends to treat migrants as a homogeneous category and, by default, as male. Further, where women are depicted it is usually as a dependant of a man. To provide an alternative perspective, I focus in this chapter on (a) asylum, which can be understood as a form of forced migration and (b) adult women who make asylum claims in the UK as primary claimants rather than as a spouse or other dependant. This focus on women asylum seekers serves to highlight some of the specific issues facing them as well as placing these issues within wider debates around asylum.

This chapter has three main interconnected themes. First, it begins with a brief overview of some key statistics of those claiming refugee status worldwide and in the UK. These statistics help us to better understand the contribution made by the UK in comparison with other countries. They also help to contextualise the debate about the economic cost of hosting refugees. Second, the problem of gender in the United Nations High Commission for Refugees (UNHCR) definition of a refugee is discussed and the 'gender neutrality' of the definition is explored. In particular, the chapter debates the types of gender persecution experienced by women and the difficulties that have been encountered in fitting these within the framework of the Geneva Convention 1951 (Art. 1A (2)). This section of the chapter also comments on the attempts that have been made to develop gender-sensitive policies both by the UNHCR and by the UK government and courts in relation to women and asylum. Third, post-9/11 the UK alongside other Western states has become increasingly preoccupied with security, and I provide a brief discussion of the recent UK government strategy entitled 'Securing the UK Border' (2007) to highlight the dawning of a relatively new method of surveillance: biometrics. These three themes highlight significant concerns in relation to women seeking asylum in the UK.

Current statistical overview

The Office of the UNHCR provides detailed statistics of countries of origin of asylum applicants, as well as statistics and information about industrialised countries that asylum seekers lodge claims in, on an annual basis. In 2008 (the latest figures available at the time of writing), the UNHCR compiled figures from 44 industrialised countries to which asylum claims were made. It should be noted, however, that the majority of those in conflict areas are either internally displaced or flee to neighbouring countries. In the UNHCR's 2008 Annual Trends report, 42 million people are reported to be on the move, with 16 million people refugees or asylum seekers and 26 million people internally displaced (UNHCR 2009).

Within the report (UNHCR 2009), a distinction is made between refugees and those making (new) individual claims for refugee status in 2008. Given the current geopolitical context, it is unsurprising that the two countries which produce the highest number of refugees are Afghanistan and Iraq. A quarter of refugees (worldwide) are from Afghanistan, the majority of whom take refuge in Pakistan. The top five industrialised countries to which claims are made are: the USA, Canada, France, Italy and the UK. However, in 2008, South Africa received the largest number of individual asylum claims in the world, with Zimbabweans totalling just over half of total applications to South Africa. This expansion is a trend noticeable since 2002 and has resulted in South Africa being the foremost recipient of asylum claims. The UNHCR data on age and sex characteristics is less comprehensive, as not all countries have provided this information, so the picture is more partial and thus has not been included here.

Another measure which the UNHCR produces relates to the relative capacity of the industrialised nations to accept refugees. Here, the total number of claimants is compared to (a) the total population of the country and (b) to the Gross Domestic Product (GDP) of the industrialised countries. These measures offer a different perspective and illustrate for example that although the USA receives the largest number of claimants, in proportion to its population, it emerges as 27th out of 44 industrialised countries, while Cyprus and Malta appear in the top two. In relation to asylum claims and GDP measures in industrialised countries, France comes top, followed by the USA and then the UK. However, this needs to be seen in the context of developing countries continuing to bear the brunt of the costs. At the launch of the 2008 Annual Trends Report in Washington, the UN High Commissioner for Refugees, António Guterres, said that 'the overwhelming burden of displacement is borne by developing countries', and 'eighty percent of refugees are in the developing world. Generosity and wealth are not proportional to each other' (http://www.unhcr. org/4a37c9076.html). The country hosting the largest number of refugees is Pakistan, both in terms of absolute numbers and in relation to its economic capacity. It is worth noting that the first industrialised country that features in terms of economic capacity at number 26 is Germany. These statistics are useful given current preoccupations regarding the economic cost of protecting refugees (particularly in times of economic recession) and the perception that industrialised countries are being 'swamped' with asylum seekers.

Within the UK, the number of applications lodged has been steadily declining since the mid-1990s despite continuing political upheavals and military conflict in a range of countries. At the time of writing, the latest statistics available for the UK are as follows. The five nationalities accounting for the highest numbers of asylum applicants in the UK in 2007 were Afghan, Iranian, Chinese, Iraqi and Eritrean. Compared with 2006, applications increased from nationals of Afghanistan (by 4 per cent), China (by 8 per cent) and Iraq (by 93 per cent). Including dependants, there were 28,300 applications in 2007. The number of applications excluding dependants was 23,430. According to the UK Border Agency, 16 out of 100 were given refugee status; 10 out of 100 were given humanitarian protection in 2007. By the end of 2007, 6,800 applicants had not received an initial decision. Twenty-three per cent of appeals were allowed by Immigration Judges in 2007. The Home Office estimates that 16,800 people (including dependants) became 'failed' asylum seekers in the UK in 2007, in which year 13,705 asylum seekers (including dependants) were removed (voluntarily or otherwise). This is 25 per cent less than in 2006. Eighty per cent were under 35 and 70 per cent of principal applicants were men, 30 per cent women (source: http://www. homeoffice.gov.uk/rds/pdfs08/hosb1108.pdf).

The UK figures compared to global figures (discussed above) illustrate the fact that only a very small percentage of the world's asylum seekers end up living in the UK. Yet their presence looms large in the national psyche. In an attempt to distinguish 'economic migrants' from genuine refugees and *also* to keep the overall numbers of refugees low, punitive policies and practices have developed to discourage asylum seekers seeing the UK as a 'soft touch'. The category 'economic migrant' is somewhat spurious as, in practice, not only are issues of economics closely related to conflicts over scarce resources, but it can also be argued that abject poverty is a form of persecution and is often politically motivated. In the UK, however, the category prevails and interventions to deter 'economic migrants' have focused on increasingly draconian policies. These include: restricting access to the welfare state, restrictions on the freedom of movement, compulsory detention, dispersal within the UK on a no-choice basis, 70 per cent of basic benefits, refusal of permission to work, and the revision of refugee status from permanent to temporary refugee status for five years. People who have lost their claim and exhausted the appeal system have two choices: (a) to be deported or (b) to become invisible to the authorities. This has created a class of destitute people, particularly those with 'failed' asylum claims. Women in this category (of 'failed' asylum seekers) are particularly vulnerable to sexual exploitation and the sex trade. This stringent regime applies to all asylum seekers whether an 'economic migrant' or a 'genuine' asylum seeker. Similarly, this system applies to both men and women, but the position of women asylum seekers is of particular concern as many of the forms of violence perpetrated against women often remain invisible, e.g. rape, forced marriage and other forms of domestic violence. Further, providing evidence of this nature which is credible to the UK Border Agency of the Home Office is very difficult, thus placing women claiming asylum in an extremely vulnerable situation. These themes will be taken up later in this chapter, while for now it is relevant to consider the position of the UNHCR.

The UNHCR is clear that fluctuations in the number of people requesting asylum depends on two factors: the political situation in countries of origin, and the introduction of harsher regimes of asylum policy and practice in receiving countries (UNCHR 2009). This chapter focuses on the latter in the UK context, with particular reference to women asylum seekers. Central to the process of seeking asylum is the definition of who constitutes a refugee as defined in the 1951 UN Convention, and it is to this that I turn next to discuss the implications for women within the given definition.

1951 UN Convention and gender

The Convention defines a refugee as a person who:

> … owing to a well-founded fear of being persecuted for reasons of race, religion, nationality, membership of a particular social group or political opinion, is outside the country of his nationality and unable or, owing to such fear, is unwilling to avail himself of the protection of that country; or who, not having a nationality and being outside the country of his former habitual residence … is unable or, owing to such fear, is unwilling to return to it. (Geneva Convention 1951 (Refugee Status), Art. 1A (2))

One of the key criticisms made of the 1951 Refugee Convention is that its assumed equal protection offered to both men and women is erroneous because it does not pay due regard to the differences in the experiences of persecution based on gender. Particularly since the 1990s, there has been widespread recognition (including from the UNHCR, e.g. UNHCR Guidelines 1991, revised guidelines 2002) that the persecution experienced by women is different to that experienced by men in substantial ways. The UNHCR as well as many radical practitioners and agencies working in the field have urged governments to develop a gender-sensitive approach to asylum. In the UK, this has amounted to guidance from the Home Office on gender issues in asylum (e.g. Immigration Appellate Authority 2000, Home Office 2006, see also Burman this volume).

Interestingly, the UK guidance was issued five years after the USA produced theirs and seven years after that of the Canadian government. However belatedly, the guidelines open up a space for gender-specific forms of torture, e.g. rape in conflict areas, to be considered as legitimate grounds for claiming refugee status. There is now a general consensus that this type of persecution fits within the grounds of the Convention.

However, a second type of gender persecution is much more contentious in terms of the Convention definition. These are acts that fall within the rubric of violence against women, e.g. domestic violence, forced marriage, or female genital mutilation (FGM), which have occurred in countries of origin. In these situations it is argued by governments that it is much less clear whether these practices fall within the grounds of the Convention. By and large, violence against women has been represented as a 'private' concern (perpetrated by non-state actors) in contrast to the more taken-for-granted 'public' concern (perpetrated by state actors) as imagined by the Convention definition. It is often claimed by governments that issues of 'ordinary' domestic or sexual violence do not constitute grounds for refugee status as these were not intended to be included in the conceptualisation of a refugee. However, as gender-based violence disproportionately impacts on women, it can be argued that the Convention definition has not taken sufficient note of women's persecutions. The interpretation of the definition by governments, and its delineation of public and private, limit the protection offered to women. Importantly, as Sajida Ismail discusses (this volume), there have been major challenges via the courts to this traditional way of thinking. Landmark cases – e.g. 'Shah and Islam' in 1999 (domestic violence) and the Fornah case in 2006 on FGM – have shifted legal thinking such that, depending on the socio-legal-cultural context of the country of origin, it may be possible for victims of domestic violence to be considered as refugees where countries of origin do not offer protection to such victims. In these instances, women may be considered as members of a particular social group (MPSG). The significance of this cannot be overstated, as these judgments interrogate the usual understandings of the Convention definition and bring the issue of violence against women into the public domain. This shift of violence against women from a private to public issue has of course also been a central concern of feminists worldwide. However, it should be noted that it is still very hard for women to be deemed members of a PSG on the basis of such issues. In relation to FGM, the Fornah case in 2006 was only the second case in the preceding six years that has been successful in claiming FGM as grounds for asylum.

Whilst these challenges have been crucial, they also pose some troubling questions in terms of the constructions of asylum-seeking women. There are two key questions to consider. The first is to do with the argument that refugee women represented under MPSG are inevitably portrayed as victims of oppressive patriarchal cultures in their countries of origin. The second is to do with the difficulty of states perceiving women as political beings. Each of these is explored in turn.

In relation to the first issue – that is, asylum-seeking women as victims of oppressive cultures – the problem is that this sediments the view that, compared to the West, countries of origin are backward in respect of gender relations. Herein lies the crux of the matter in that, currently, countries of origin need to be portrayed as 'backward' in order that women experiencing 'ordinary' violence can have a chance of successfully claiming refugee status in the West. One strategy for avoiding feeding into colonial and racist discourses about 'other' countries is to reflect on gender inequalities in the West. This tactic helps to ground evaluation and to seek out commonalities in experiences of 'ordinary' violence even where such violence has taken place in different cultural contexts. This may help to partially alleviate the colonial gaze, but it is still flawed unless these observations also take account of the political and economic contexts of countries of origin. Even so, perhaps the bigger question is whether gender-based violence should be read as persecution per se under the terms of the Convention definition. If this was the case, then the analysis would need to shift to seeing gender-based violence as integral to the politics of the country of origin rather than as a 'private' or cultural issue (see Kneebone 2005 for a fuller discussion on this). As Susan Kneebone (2005) also points out, private and cultural issues are nearly always also political ones and this is in line with the feminist slogan that 'the personal is the political'. Furthermore, in countries where women are forced to observe religious practices because the nation-state has a religious identity exercised through its politics and via state structures that discriminate against women, then surely this should count as persecution on grounds of religion? The key advantage of this position is that, despite the challenges presented in the Shah and Islam case and the Fornah case in the UK, these do not appear to have set a cast-iron precedent. The Convention definition, however, is still likely to be interpreted in a conservative manner and women will have to continue to fight to be recognised as a member of a PSG in other similar situations.

Second, and importantly, reliance on membership of a PSG works to cast women as only cultural beings operating in the private sphere or at the borders of private/public spaces. This means that designating women as political, i.e. as occupying the public domain in relation to their politics or religious beliefs (in the way that men are perceived to), is still problematic. If women are portrayed only as 'victims', and it is on this basis that their asylum claims are decided, then it is clearly difficult to see them simultaneously as independent political actors. Increasingly, there is agreement that women can be implicated in political activity via association, e.g. because one's husband, father or brother belongs to a political grouping, and that women in such situations can suffer persecution because of familial relationships. However, this still does not construct women as autonomous political beings (however risky or dangerous, and however restricted owing to the public space afforded to women) and makes invisible their contributions to political struggles. So whilst, on the one hand, the legal challenges in relation to women seeking asylum and MPSG have been highly significant in paving the way for women's experiences of violence to be considered as legitimate grounds for refugee status, the largely conservative readings of the Convention definition appear to exert a more powerful influence. There is, therefore, much work to be done to ensure that women's experiences are seen as part of the political context and thus perceived as fitting the Convention definition. However, in the current context this seems to be particularly difficult to imagine as the UK government (amongst others) is arguing for a narrower definition of refugee status. It is to this that I turn next, as it will help us to better understand the current preoccupations of the UK government in relation to refugees.

The continuing importance of the 1951 UN Convention

Quite apart from the gender issues raised above, which highlight some of the challenges made in relation to asylum-seeking women, there has also been a movement in the opposite direction in relation to refugees (men and women). The UNHCR is concerned that there have been increasing calls for the 1951 Convention to be modified, as some countries consider it no longer fit for purpose. This is also the position of the UK government, first put forward in 2000 and reiterated in 2009. Within the UK government context the Convention is perceived to be too liberal as it does not readily distinguish between 'economic migrants' and 'genuine refugees'. As highlighted above, the category 'economic migrant' is not as clear-cut as might be suggested by the UK government. Further, the UNCHR is unequivocal that the Convention is still as relevant today as it was in 1951 and argues that it will continue to be so while conflicts persist.

The key principle of the Convention is *non-refoulement*, which means that receiving countries should not deport or return people to countries where they would face persecution or violence. This is an important principle and needs to be maintained for the Convention to be implemented in a way that protects the interests and welfare of those seeking refuge. The increasingly harsh regimes in countries like the UK, and the relatively low numbers of those seeking asylum being granted refugee status, indicates that countries like the UK – which are adamant that refugee numbers should be reduced (regardless of the geopolitical context) – are in danger of breaching the principle of *refoulement*. Where people are deported, in practice it is very hard to prove whether or not *refoulement* subsequently occurs; though people may face persecution or violence on their return, information concerning this is clearly difficult to collect.

Another central issue in this debate has been the increasing call for securitisation, particularly since 9/11. Since then, the desire to protect borders has escalated; the key rationale for this is the prevention of terrorism. So the refugee debate can in many ways be read as and conflated with the war against terror (Ahmed 2002, Chantler 2007). Migrants, including asylum seekers, have long had negative stereotypes associated with them, and now there is one more: that of terrorist. More insidious perhaps is the possibility that the legitimate aim of security is being used as a cover to restrict successful immigration and asylum claims. Within human rights circles there is a growing concern that the principle of *non-refoulement* is being compromised in the light of heightened security measures. The 1951 Convention (Art.

33 (2)) does permit *refoulement* for people for 'whom there are reasonable grounds for regarding as a danger to the security of the country in which he is or who, having been convicted by a final judgment of a particularly serious crime, constitutes a danger to the community of that country'. Significantly, this is only permissible in *exceptional* circumstances where there is a direct link between a person being granted refugee status and the danger that they pose to that country (International Helsinki Federation for Human Rights 2003). Even so, preference must be given to prosecuting suspects in the UK, and the *refoulement* principle must remain intact where it is known that a person will be subject to the death penalty or torture on return. In relation to terrorism, Bruin and Wouters (2003) argue that in practice it is difficult to exclude people on the basis of 'terrorism', as there is no definition of 'terrorism' in international law. Neither should being a member of a 'terrorist' organisation automatically be used as grounds for refusing refugee status.

It is within this context that the Home Office (which is the government department dealing with asylum policy for the UK) issued a new strategy in March 2007 called 'Securing the UK Border'. In the foreword to this strategy, it says: 'A strong border is what the public demands and what we will deliver' (Liam Bryne, Minister for Nationality, Citizenship and Immigration and Lord Triesman, Parliamentary Under-Secretary of State, Foreign and Commonwealth Office). In the next section, I explore, first, the notion of the need for a strong border, second, 'what the public demands', and third, the 'delivery' aspect of the above sentence.

Borders, public mandates and technology

In the statement above, the need for a 'strong border' implies that 'we' have a weak border at the moment; a border that is permeable and easy to enter. It is this sentiment that is the driving force behind much post-1999 legislation. As discussed above, two of the primary categories that have provided the major impetus for a new regime of asylum have been those of 'economic migrant' and post-2001 'terrorist'. These categories reinforce and reiterate the already well-established and familiar imagery of us and them, of others as marauding outsiders, of a line that must not be crossed. William Walters uses the term 'domopolitics' to consider the 'politics of home' (Walters 2004). Within his conceptualisation 'home' is conjured as safe, comfortable and secure. This warm notion of home functions as the line whereby those considered not to be 'family' are unwelcome, and serves to position those outside home as dangerous and unsafe. 'Home' and 'family' as an analytic to consider the borders of the nation-state is of course feminised, as is the language associated with countries in the English-speaking world: mother-land, mother-tongue and so on (Chantler 2007). Here it is important to note the way notions of 'home' slip from being located in the private domain at one point to the public domain at others. Nira Yuval-Davis and Floya Anthias have long argued that mothers in particular are seen not just as biological reproducers for the nation, but as cultural and ideological producers as well (Yuval-Davis and Anthias 1989). Hence the notion of 'home' in its multiple readings functions to create a well-loved place that values homogeneity. In addition to this romanticised notion of home, campaigners (e.g. 'No Borders' Network) argue that borders are unnecessary and so campaign for an end to all migration control (http:/www.noborder.org). This illustrates that the need for a strong border is not universally acknowledged.

However, from the strategy's perspective, to legitimise the strong border 'the public demand' is invoked. Here the 'public' is homogenised and no dissenting voices are permitted to feature in the representation of 'the public'. In calling upon 'public demand', agency is constructed as slipping away from the politicians to the hungry demands of the public. So in this representation, politicians are shown to have 'their hands tied', submitting to the 'will of the people', so that no other possible option is available. What is also happening is that in this very submission, in the symbiosis between politicians and public, the power base of the politicians is reinforced and magnified, and agency to the politicians is returned with a mandate. Used in this way, what the 'will of the people' does is allow for the empowering of politicians whilst absolving them of key moral and political dilemmas and responsibilities. In this instance it is the public's will that has to be satiated and this is seen as the politicians' primary responsibility. If anything, this becomes the driving force, and any other moral or ethical concerns to do with outsiders – e.g. the process for determining asylum, or the very basis of the proclaimed necessity of the strong border – become silenced, and their disappearing off the radar is legitimated. Clearly, 'will of the people' is a central feature of liberal democracies through which legitimacy and accountability are enacted. Yet there are many other situations where the will of the people is ignored – for example in calls for the death penalty, or the public protests against the war in Iraq. This illustrates the way in which politicians consciously select which aspects of the people's will they choose to acknowledge and adhere to. Thus in this context, by invoking the public's demands, politicians allow themselves to play into and feed nationalistic sentiments. The discourse of the 'strong border' combined with the 'public's will' act to reinforce one another so that no other option is deemed viable.

Having established that there is really no other course of action, and bolstered by the comfort of the public's demands, the third aspect of the sentence in 'Securing the UK Border' focuses on delivering. If the previous two aspects were not of sufficient concern, this third aspect is very worrying. It implies that whatever needs to be done to maintain a strong border will indeed be done. Again, the priority is the strong border, not the myriad human rights issues or the moral and ethical complexities of asylum. Indeed, the foreword also includes a firm statement of intent concerning how the border is to be made strong. The technology of biometrics is to be used with the introduction in 2008 of biometric immigration documents, including finger printing for all visa applications. Asylum seekers already have biometric ID cards. Whilst the government has met with stiff opposition to the introduction of (biometric) ID cards for British nationals, the UK government has not seen fit to take into account comparable issues of civil liberties and privacy concerns in the field of immigration and asylum. The key rationale is to be sure that identification of people is accurate and this measure is seen as getting round the issue of forged documents and identities. The Securing Borders strategy talks of 'fixing identities' and there is no mention of the limitations or errors associated with this form of technology. As with any technology, there are inevitably going to be errors. Even manufacturers of biometric ID cards signal the problem of both false negatives and false positives. My concern is not only with the use of biometric systems per se, but also that there appears to be no engagement in the strategy with the potential difficulties of using a system which has error in what the strategy calls 'fixing identities'. It is clearly believed that the use of a scientific technology can iron out all potential difficulties, regardless of the conceptual and technical problems inherent within the technology. On this point, it is worth noting that biometric information on such a large scale as proposed for UK citizens has not been tested and is therefore argued to be unreliable (LSE 2005). Numerous other problems have been presented to the Home Affairs Select Committee on Science and Technology (LSE 2006). Examples of these include inaccurate iris recognition where people have had cataract operations or have severe diabetes which impacts on vision (LSE 2005). In addition to this there are also inevitably going to be technical problems with the software from time to time, e.g. systems crashing, data not being secure enough, and so on. At a philosophical level, the notion of 'fixing identity' to a code on a bit of plastic so that the card 'becomes' you and vice versa is difficult to contemplate. For women seeking asylum who are already more likely to have their identities fixed as hapless victims, this is a further measure which seeks to reduce their identities.

By June 2009, the UK government had abandoned its intention to roll out compulsory biometric ID cards for UK citizens. However the system remains for asylum seekers and foreign nationals, thus introducing yet again a lower threshold of consideration of issues of privacy, autonomy and sense of self for asylum seekers and foreign nationals compared to British nationals.

Conclusion

This chapter focuses on the current UK context for women attempting to seek asylum in the UK. It is crucial, however, to have some awareness of the global context in order to appreciate that the majority of refugees are hosted in poor, developing countries. So the UK government's attempt to distinguish between 'economic migrants' and genuine refugees in order to keep costs down needs to be understood within the global context of richer countries not doing enough in comparison to poorer countries. Moreover, the harsh asylum regime introduced by the UK affects all people claiming asylum within the country, thus failing to distinguish between 'real' and 'bogus' or economic migrants (even if such categories are assumed to exist). I have offered arguments which provide a critique of such discrete categorisations. This inevitably includes discussion of the wider policy and practice issues that impact on both men and women, but focuses on women because of the different types of persecution they experience compared to men. Central to this analysis is the discussion of public and private forms of violence and the ways in which women's persecution is often represented as occurring in the private domain and therefore not perceived as fitting within the Convention definition. Two types of gender-based persecution were discussed: sexual violence perpetrated during civil war and conflict, and 'ordinary' domestic or sexual violence or what has been termed 'harmful cultural practices', e.g. female genital mutilation. Whilst the former is now seen as fitting within the Convention definition even though it may be perpetrated by non-state actors, it is proving more difficult to see the latter as such. Key legal challenges in relation to the latter include the Shah and Islam case and the Fornah case. Such challenges have successfully argued for victims of domestic violence and female genital mutilation which have occurred in contexts where there is no effective redress for women in their countries of origin to be seen as constituting 'membership of a Particular Social Group'. These landmark cases have been highly significant in shifting what were originally considered to be private or cultural matters in to the public domain. However, it is also important to be mindful of not restricting our constructions of women seeking asylum as only victims and to appreciate the political struggles of women.

What is being urged is a more expansive interpretation of the Convention definition of a refugee in relation to women. This has resulted in gender guidelines being produced to address the 'problem of gender'. The extent to which they are used effectively is debatable. Moreover, at the same time the UK has a punitive asylum regime and is also arguing for the Convention definition to be made narrower. Post 9/11, the emphasis on security works to conflate issues of asylum with that of 'terrorist', resulting in a heightened anxiety to 'secure our borders'. This tactic feeds into and simultaneously constructs a nationalistic perspective, intolerant of outsiders. Measures that are considered unpalatable for British citizens, namely biometric identity cards, have already been introduced for those seeking asylum and for foreign nationals in a bid to 'fix their identities'. Biometrics such as finger printing are more commonly used for criminals, and this association has the potential of criminalising all asylum seekers and foreign nationals. Within this environment, it is difficult to see any further widening in the interpretation of the Convention definition taking place in the near future. Indeed, as Sajida Ismail discusses (this volume), the use of 'internal flight' is another mechanism which is increasingly used to refuse refugee status in the UK. Despite some positive movement in relation to women, the wider UK context illustrates what a long distance yet needs to be travelled for women in particular to have a fair hearing in relation to their asylum claims.

CHAPTER 8

Explicating the tactics of banal exclusion: a British example

Erica Burman

Introduction

This chapter draws on some recent UK research to explore state bureaucratic discourses around asylum practice. Its analysis focuses closely on a relatively small amount of text which, through detailed discourse analysis, may illuminate wider interpretive strategies and assumptions underlying policy formulation and practices. Focusing not only on what is said, but on how what is said achieves its effects (the specificities of formulations and selection – and omission – of particular terms), is relevant for the analysis of practices of power such as state immigration. The overarching aim of this analysis is to tease out the gaps/fissures in the accomplishment of this text's statements as indicative of a particularly powerful 'regime of truth'.

The WASP project (Women Asylum Seekers from Pakistan) was a transnational project carried out between 2005 and 2008 investigating Pakistani women's access both to domestic violence support services in Pakistan, and to asylum support services in the context of marital breakdown (and so immigration status problems) in the UK, due to domestic violence.[1] The wider aim of the study is to improve service provision and especially decision making in relation to claimants seeking asylum on the basis of domestic violence. It is specifically addressed to legal advisors and decision makers, and is concerned with addressing the 'internal flight alternative' which is used to return Pakistani women in the UK to Pakistan (see Siddiqui, Ismail and Allen 2008).[2] The text I will discuss was generated from the Home Office as a key respondent within the WASP research project. It took the form of an emailed response to an interview schedule sent to them. That is, unlike other respondents, no one was willing to be interviewed face to face or on the telephone, but instead the project team received a request for questions to be sent in writing, to which an email response was provided.

My rationale in selecting this text for analysis here can be simply summarised. First, it stands out from the rest of the corpus of material as dramatically different in its formulation of the (lack of a) problem/issue. Hence the analytical challenge was to tease out why and how it achieves this. Second, such a text merits close study for what it reveals of wider debates. Third, precisely because of its predictability and banality, as well as its status as the 'official' state response whose hegemony the action research project aimed to challenge, this text was not extensively discussed within the WASP report beyond merely noting its receipt as appropriate for an initial research report. Yet it leaves uninterrogated the wider question of how large organisations, in this case a major governmental agency, accounts for itself and frames or warrants its practice.

There are obvious methodological implications of analysing a written, emailed, response, rather than (say) recording a spontaneously generated discussion or interview (Parker and the Bolton Discourse Network 1999, Parker 2003, Burman and Parker 1993). Crucially, it remains unclear who the 'respondent' is – since although emailed from a specific address this text could have been formulated either by a singular delegate or by a committee or 'cut and pasted' from existing Home Office documents. Indeed, we cannot know even why such a response was sent. Yet if we assume that the text is performative and so constructing as well as reflecting its topic, then the content may be less relevant than the fact of the response (indicating perhaps: that they felt they had to respond? That this will 'put the record straight'? That they are reasonable and convinced by their own account/arguments?).

One can assume that, as a written, emailed response, its comments are deliberate, and presumably carefully crafted. Given the context of the study and what we know of the generation of this text, it is probably fair to assume that it was generated in a climate of suspicion, rather than enthusiastic participation, such that areas of contention were likely to be smoothed over, rendered less evident. The kind of analytical strategies called for in dealing with this complex and crafted material therefore included attending to absences as well as presences (with these absences generated in part through contrast with other texts). A second strategy took the form of noticing the moves between 'conversational' and declarative (informative) genres. Amid the proliferation of models of interpretive approaches applied within social research, I drew upon my background in discourse analysis (including discursive psychology, critical discourse analysis, narrative analysis and conversation analysis). This attention to textuality invites a particular set of questions that can inform socio-political analysis, including asking: what kind of text is this? Generated for which audience? With what kind of readership/circulation? Who is included/excluded? Although this context may seem far from the arena of the critical and literary theory from which it originated, nevertheless two central ideas are relevant here: first, 'the death of the author', which moves analysis away from mentalist, intentionalist claims, is important since the actions or policies of major governmental agencies cannot be reduced to the intentions of specific individuals; second, the claim that 'there is nothing outside the text' challenges all analysts and activists to consider how all texts (including our own) are situated within social/political/cultural/historical contexts (see Burman and Maclure 2005, Parker 2007). Rather, we necessarily draw upon our membership of these contexts to generate our interpretations, yet we are also complicit within them.

This 'turn to the text' relies upon a set of assumptions about the interpretive character of the social world, so that 'facts' become texts for analysis, rather than self-evident truths, the claims of which can be interrogated in terms of how they accomplish their 'factuality'. This helps us to denaturalise or expose how certain contestable assumptions are presented as if they were natural. In the case of the usual popular and bureaucratic tropes of asylum discourse, typically a binary is set up between 'refugee' and 'asylum seeker'; and between 'refugee' or 'asylum' vs. 'migration'. This in turn draws upon the more longstanding division between 'economic' and 'political' migration (as if these can be absolutely distinguished). In terms of the contemporary global context, such binaries also overlook how migration is necessary to the contemporary structure of capitalism (as flexible flows of labour), such that it has become a 'normal' rather than abnormal condition, with patterns of migration no longer 'A-B' (from one stable place of residence to another) but multiple ('A-B-A', and 'A,B,C...'). In the UK, as in other states, there are significant material consequences of having an asylum application rejected. The status of 'failed asylum seekers' (i.e. whose application to the Home Office have been refused) means that they have 'no recourse to public funds' (i.e. are not eligible to access any public – health and social – services). As such they are usually (what is formally called) 'destitute', and support is only allowable contingent on agreement to voluntary repatriation, while they may in any case be forcibly returned to their country of origin.

Home Office discourse as performative

While the Home Office is a key organ of the British state, a discursive or performative approach enables exploration of how its practice constitutes the state as much as reflecting it. Indeed this too is the view of many critics of immigration control, seeing this technology as central to the definition of contemporary nation-states (e.g. Cohen 2006). More specifically, as the Home Office, its account has to negotiate a central tension between asserting its commitment to promoting women's rights vs. a subscription to wider discourses that connect the regulation of women to questions of national identity and belonging (Yuval-Davis 1998). What we might expect the text to have to achieve is the management of a double standard that structured contemporary British New Labour policy, as a party that can justifiably claim to have been very active on initiatives to counter domestic violence (within the rubric of public order) but that has remained insensitive to the specificities of the barriers for black and minoritised women's access to services, quite apart from specific issues around migration and asylum issues (Burman *et al.* 2004, Chantler 2006). The British state is of course not alone in this, since arguably the idea of 'Europe' could be understood as founded on the notion of the superiority to which women's rights/freedoms is central – hence instituting an exclusionary understanding of women. As Lewis points out:

> The claim to European specificity is an idea that translated into a claim of socio-political advancement and superiority

that rests upon an image of women's freedom and a particular kind of gender order between women and men. It is a symbolism that positions Europe and the European as the standard of humanity and closes down questions as to whose identity, autonomy, family and privacy are to be respected, at whose cost and with what consequences for Europe's potential for an economy of gender equality. In so doing, it throws back the issue of visibility, not only to ask who and what is visible but who sees what. (Lewis 2006: 92–3)

Thus the methodological/theoretical question 'what is inside/outside the text?' can be seen as a question of showing how a specific text links with/exemplifies wider discourses and institutional practices: in Lewis' terms above, of what it makes visible or topicalises, and what it overlooks, occludes and marginalises. The intersection between domestic violence and immigration can correspondingly be seen as a prime exemplar of two conjoinings of bio and disciplinary power: the state regulation of (hetero)sexuality and intimacy via the focus on marriage and of the flow of bodies across national borders. Thus it is crucial to focus on their mutual determinations and the exclusions that this gives rise to, with the 'immigrant (woman)' as a current key site by which to elaborate these (Lewis 2006, Mojab 1998, Mahalingam and Lei 2005). Specifically, the previous model of the migrant/asylum seeker as a single male, with women seen as dependants/appendages (Palmary 2006), is now shifting with the figure of the 'immigrant woman' being seen today as constitutive of an elitist and exclusionary European identity (Lewis 2006, Gedalof 2007). This is alongside a further gendered racialised trope whereby immigrant women are seen as the route by which men may enter as 'sponsored spouses' and so their sexuality rendered subject to state scrutiny and evaluation.

Talking institutions

Discussion so far has treated the Home Office as a reified and unitary entity, yet it is a complex organisation with many functions. It is the British government agency responsible for immigration issues, specifically a part of it. As with other arenas, with the decentralisation of the nation-state under neoliberalism, many of its functions have been outsourced. Hence there are somewhat blurry boundaries between government and non-governmental agencies, which – as Duffield (2001) has noted – has particular reverberations worldwide. This distribution of power can be unwieldy and even embarrassing – as when it was discovered (in December 2007) that the office cleaners of the central Home Office buildings in Croydon were illegal immigrants.

As Ismail (this volume) discusses, the specific focus on Pakistani women in the WASP study was tactical, since a key legal judgment (Shah and Islam, 1999) accorded them particular social group (PSG) status.[3] This status invites wider reflection upon whether invoking a general category 'woman' undermines its usefulness (as a specific instance of the 'commonality of sisterhood'/'what is a woman?' debates of the 1990s, e.g. Riley 1988). Such problems coexist alongside equivalent difficulties surrounding appropriate description of the kinds of violence that women have experienced. Feminist debates around this continue so that, for example, characterising 'violence' as 'domestic' reinstates the public/private opposition so as to overlook and exonerate state involvement (Hanmer and Itzin 2000) whilst also ignoring its gendered characteristics (see Shepherd 2008 for a recent analysis in relation to the wider theme of gender and (inter)national security). Similarly, the term 'violence' is too often equated with physical abuse and so occludes emotional, financial and sexual forms.

These general definitional dilemmas around gender and violence acquire additional, and potently racialised, inflections when combined with cultural, national or religious issues. Some common discourses that circulate widely within popular British discourse (including our previous research on domestic violence and minoritised communities), and that are also evident within the text analysed here, include such assumptions as 'domestic violence is acceptable in Pakistani communities', 'Pakistani women don't know they have rights …', 'It's a matter of religion, culture etc. …' These claims work to support a strategy of limited service engagement with women from such communities (see Burman *et al.* 2004).

But such overarching concerns should not overshadow the specificity and materiality of the text under consideration. For this might lead the analyst to pre-judge how the issues will be framed and thereby miss vital textual and indicative anomalies and instabilities. So, to be specific about the text under consideration here, it comprised just over six typed pages. It was composed of answers to questions (included in the text) posed by the WASP researchers to the Home Office (in June 2006). The questions were common to all 'providers', but adapted slightly to be relevant to each audience (see Appendix for the schedule).

(Un)Structuring the analysis

In terms of the approach taken to developing the analysis, I deliberately chose to bypass the central preoccupation of the text with the question of 'credibility' (which takes up over one and a half of the six pages). This was because it seemed a rather overworked theme in which the asylum system was overwhelmingly presented as 'firm but fair' (my gloss) and as 'giving the benefit of the doubt' to the appellant (repeated four times). Such claims were directly contradicted by those of a prevailing 'culture of disbelief' known to pervade Home Office decision making. So, rather than attending to what was probably the most 'polished' part of the text, I focused the analysis on other parts to explore how other aspects might illuminate the viability of the claims put forward.

Emotion in the text?

Overall, in terms of initial thoughts on structure, and borrowing from narrative analysis (Andrews *et al.* 2000), it was relatively easy to identify that there were more complex formulations at the beginning, with shorter responses towards the end of the text. Possible interpretations for this could include that the respondent(s) were getting 'tired', or fed-up, or even less well 'defended' towards the end. This might be indicated by the response given relatively late on in the schedule at the end of the questions on 'Knowledge/ information needs' (section 3). For in answer to our question 'Is there any other training that you think workers should have access to?' the answer was merely 'Not appropriate for comment.' This was in contrast to a response early on where a question about 'challenges/difficulties' (question 1b) was reframed in the answer to 'Interesting areas of the work include ...', thus indicating an explicit refusal to accept the assumption in the question that such challenges or difficulties exist.

Further indications were present in the response to our penultimate question, 'Is there anything that you think would help a woman to disclose any difficult or sensitive issues?', where the somewhat surprising answer provided was: 'A less adversarial attitude on the part of her representative.' This clearly puts the onus of responsibility for the conditions for maximal disclosure back onto her advocate, rather than considering the setting or the contribution of HO workers. Moreover, the 'adversarial attitude' would appear to be being attributed to the interviewers/ researchers (who were known to be 'representatives') rather than to other advocates, and thus should perhaps be seen as a metacommunicative statement about how the questions were being interpreted. This impression is confirmed by the response to the final question 'Is there anything else you'd like to tell us about this issue?' which was a mere 'No'.

Given that these (rather routine) questions would have been expected to elicit rather predictable responses confirming the organisation's efforts to be receptive to new perspectives to improve their practice, it was surprising to see such obvious indications of closed, and indeed even apparently 'hostile', responses. Further, given the crafted nature of the text, the fact that such traces remain is interesting methodologically. Such features would appear to be the closest we are able to get to an affective response. Even if one disallows the interpretive move to make claims of seeing 'emotions' within texts, such formulations can at the very least be understood as revealing tensions within the account – something of the strain or effort to sustain its coherence and as such of relevance to the analysis of institutional practices.

Subjects and objects: who is the respondent/subject?

A key way to generate a discursive analysis is to explore the forms of subjects and objects identified in the text. These do not merely frame the representation of physical or material objects but indicate prevailing forms of institutional power relationships (contests over which are already evident above) (see Parker 1992, 2003). Forms of subjectivity (and correspondingly objectivity) are lexically coded through temporal markers and 'voice' of verb tense forms used. Hence in this text, unsurprising for claims of authority, statements were made in the timeless (universal, omnipotent) present, with third person subject positions ('If caseworkers become aware of ...'), or else using the passive voice (thereby obscuring who exactly is the agent): ('Every effort is made

...'; 'Social group issues are covered in initial training courses', 'training is kept up to date ...'). Elsewhere a corporate plural 'we' was invoked ('As explained above, we can – indeed we must – give the benefit of any doubt to the claimant'; 'We have worked hard...'; 'It may sound trite for us to say that we are ... precisely what we do'; 'Our experience is ...'); 'However, as explained above we can – indeed we must – give the benefit of any doubt ...' Occasionally a speaking position of 'nation' was claimed ('The UK is one of two European countries to have published guidance ...'), while across the text the organisational hierarchy was invoked to clarify procedural accountability: 'screening officers are required to confirm ...'; 'decisions routinely sampled by senior officers ...'; '... caseworkers ... required to inform their Senior Caseworkers ... Country/Policy officers then collate/formulate ... to meet the needs of caseworkers'.

As already indicated, one of the challenges of this text was the inscrutability of the process of its formulation and embodiment of its author. Indeed, in some ways its authorial subject does appear as some kind of cipher, offering automata-like responses, as where our question 'is there any other training that you think workers should have access to?' merely elicited the answer 'Not appropriate for comment.' This invites an image of an interlocutor representing themselves as a de-personalised transindividual entity that is not 'programmed' for personal reflection or evaluation; or perhaps even that to answer otherwise would imply a singular, specified and reflective respondent (that perhaps was precisely not the case).

Forms of subject position function in relation to explicit and implicitly identified objects. The 'objects' in this text ranged from 'Applicants' (also qualified as 'Principal applicant and ... adult dependant ... any minor children ... spouses and partners', 'Applicant ... women'); as 'people', and as 'victim'. 'People' also became 'cases' ('Each case'), 'claims' ('Each asylum claim'), with frequent reformulations between personalised and bureaucratic designations (as in 'the person ... his asylum claim', 'the applicant to furnish details of her claim', 'claimants as witnesses in their own cause'). Children were rarely mentioned, and only when this was solicited via explicit questioning. Other 'objects' or parties identified included 'representatives' (classical legal-political discourse) – although this was only mentioned once ('A less adversarial attitude on the part of her representative'), while a more frequent formulation used was 'case owners' (reflecting perhaps a new business discourse that commodified asylum seekers further). There was a single mention of 'policy workers' and NGOs (specified as the Medical Foundation).

Initial impressions generated from this preliminary analysis indicated a picture of smooth and confident practice ('The UK is only one of two European countries to have published guidance specifically covering gender issues' – but this presupposed that 'guidance' translated into practice); of clear statements of 'commitment' ('We are committed to ensuring ...'); of sensitivity to gender inequalities ('The BIA's[4] published guidance on interviewing and on gender issues advises decision makers to avoid interviewing women in front of male relatives'); and to how the interviewing situation may be distressing ('We also have guidance on interviewing people who may be vulnerable and/or traumatised'). Corporate accountability was also invoked (as in 'Since the gender guidelines were introduced in 2004 ... decision makers are now bound to consider this aspect in all cases'). This corporate quality also appeared to function to limit or block further inquiry, as in 'operational guidance notes ... also access via senior caseworkers to policy and process specialists. It is not believed that more is needed', while (as already noted) there appeared to be some resistance to accept the possibilities of there being 'problems', as where 'Challenges/difficulties' in the question was reframed to 'Interesting areas of the work include ...'

A cursory attempt at identifying discourses

Discourses in this text can be divided between those present, or explicitly topicalised, and those that (to an attentive reader) are made conspicuous by their absence (remembering that every speech act silences others). Overall, the most obvious, present discourses were legal and managerial, and operational rather than strategic (i.e. it is not clear what happens in practice; e.g. 'It may sound trite for us to say that we are ... precisely what we do'; 'Our experience is ...'). This could be seen as indicative of the customer service model that presumes a 'caring' service provider (rather than, say, an anonymous/exclusionary bureaucrat). Such an interpretation would be consistent with the discourse of Home Office 'clients', rather than 'asylum seekers'. This managerial discourse functions alongside a discourse of openness/transparency, such as 'we feel we have made significant process with more to come', 'independent monitoring ... dialogue ... external input ... welcome more'.

What was absent from the account is any mention of human rights or entitlements, any mention of being 'Muslim', or of racism. While there is a description of the assessment process and claims of focus on the 'higher profile of gender', there is no mention of the impact of the recent change towards fast-tracking of claims (which prevents legal advocates from assembling adequate documentation to make persuasive cases, especially when detailed records are needed from countries of origin[5]). This, alongside recent cuts in legal aid funding, has made legal advocacy very difficult and many immigration sections within law firms have been forced to close. It is therefore worth reflecting that 'representatives' were noticeably absent or diminished in the text. Significantly, there was also no mention of how failed asylum seekers have 'no recourse to public funds'.

Subjugated or marginal discourses included that interpreters were only discussed when introduced by the question, and that issues for children were covered only minimally. As a consequence we might surmise that there was insufficient attention to the tensions in the relations between women and children, and how they figure within women's decisions to stay or leave violent relationships, and to how children figure within service policy and provision for women (see Burman *et al.* 2004, Burman and Chantler 2005). Reflecting the general policy polarisations between women and children (Burman 2008a,b), there was no acknowledgement of how girls can also be (treated as, and will grow up to be) women. This is despite the ways the issues of domestic violence and asylum also connect with those of child marriage and forced marriage – although interestingly here conflicts are discernible with recent UK government proposals on immigration in relation to preventing forced marriage, which (mistakenly) treat lesser age as a key criterion of vulnerability (Chantler *et al.* 2009, Gangoli and Chantler 2009).

Discursive motifs: structure vs. fluidity

After identifying and reflecting upon both prioritised and subjugated subjects/objects in the text, two overall discursive motifs emerged concerning structure and fluidity. These characterised the text's portrayal of both the functioning of the BIA and its treatment of gender. To summarise some of the arguments below, notwithstanding the paradoxes that emerge on closer scrutiny, the effect of presenting the work of the BIA in both structural and fluid terms sustained its claims to be 'transparent', while the discursive shifts from gender specificity to gender neutrality to 'social group issues' can be seen to sideline the particular issues facing Pakistani women asylum seekers.

The 'structural' features secured the reading of the BIA as a coherent, closed, rational, self-regulating system (but as also open to scrutiny – so 'transparent' and 'accountable'). On the other hand, portraying its procedures as 'fluid' and in process allowed for the 'procedures' and 'guidelines' not actually to affect the specific situations that prompted them, since the circumstances (and in some cases even the laws) might have shifted/changed by the time they come into effect. This fluidity also included covert changes within the immigration and asylum system that were not disclosed except, in each case, as a post hoc *fait accompli* (e.g. fast tracking of applications, raising of age for recognition of marriage for sponsoring a spouse from 16–21, with a double standard of marriage age being covertly introduced between citizens depending on whether they marry EU or non-EU citizens; Hester *et al.* 2008, Chantler *et al.* 2009).

The managerial speak – indicated by talk of reports, guidance, policies etc. – is currently so commonplace under everyday neoliberalism that is it hard to analyse. It seems self-evidently true; there is apparently little to dispute or find fault with. A banal de-problematisation of the issues is achieved. But what this covers over is how little acknowledgement there is of what these policies mean in practice. Shortcomings were addressed through outlining organisational responses, as in relation to a quality audit evaluation, as in: 'If caseworkers become aware of particular issues appearing frequently in claims for asylum then they are required to inform their Senior Caseworkers who are able to monitor the issue and escalate the need for further information.' Despite this account of monitoring and reporting, it was interesting to note how the reference to circumstances demanding further investigation was described as a need to 'escalate'. This depersonalises the process (since it does not specify who demands and finds this 'further information'), and also perhaps works to make it sound more efficient/certain/objective than it may be. The lack of clear specification of agency further failed to identify what the 'further information' was for, but also could work to ward off external scrutiny. In other words, despite the claims of transparency and accountability, the lines of responsibility were really not at all clear, disguising how, if caseworkers do not notice anything, nothing happens.

Mitigating this bureaucratic mode was a more 'personal', or subjective one. A recurring affective framing of aspiration marked the text's claims that could be summarised as 'We try'. Examples included: 'Every effort is made to comply with' (in relation to a request for same-sex interviewer or interpreter); 'Requests made ... as far as operationally possible'. The discursive effect achieved was that intention or effort can compensate for or even stand in for success, so that it is more difficult to identify blameworthy actual outcomes. I will now move to analyse a passage in more detail.

From gender-specificity to being treated as an individual

Interesting areas of the work include the difficulty of persuading people who are not used to speaking up for themselves to do precisely that. However hard we try to build a relationship of trust and openness, the public realm remains one in which some cultures tell women they have no place and this can be difficult to overcome. On the other hand, we need to avoid stereotypes. The current attention to gender issues in immigration is to be welcomed but it does carry with it the danger that women become stereotyped as 'gender cases', instead of being treated as individuals. We must also guard against any tendency to regard certain attitudes and certain forms of persecution as the exclusive preserve of women. Men can also be raped, for example, and may find it just as difficult to discuss during asylum interviews.

Many complex assumptions and arguments are compressed into this short but potent paragraph. It is worth highlighting the argumentative structure: 'However ... On the other hand ... The current ... to be welcomed but ... it does carry the danger

... must also guard against ... exclusive preserve of women ...
Men can also be ... and find it just as difficult ...' The passage
starts therefore with the acknowledgement that there is a (gender-/
culture-specific) problem. However a distinction is drawn between
'We' vs. 'the public realm' (i.e. the Home Office 'we' is not part
of/like the public realm in this claim about culture). This positions
the Home Office as not bearing any responsibility for what 'some
cultures tell women' and, beyond its recognition of the wider
'cultural' issues, for preventing women from being able to 'speak
up for themselves'. Here it is also worth looking at ambiguities
in the shifting referent of 'we' – from the Home Office 'we try' to
enlistment of us all, as in 'we need to avoid stereotypes', 'we must
also guard against'. The inclusive first person plural 'we' works to
enlist the reader into an assumed common set of assumptions.

After the claim about how others see women from some
cultural backgrounds (note religion is not mentioned), the claim
of gender-based persecution as a 'stereotype' is made. This would
seem to be an example of when assertion is denial. An opposition
is set up between a 'gender case' and 'being treated as individuals',
as if these were mutually exclusive. Moreover, in this context, for
a woman to be treated 'as an individual' appears to mean that her
gender-specific position then does not figure. Perhaps lurking in
the background here is the question of MPSG designation: At any
rate it appears that, in practice, 'stereotyping' of women as 'gender
cases' means that gendered violence against women is normalised
so that she has to be subjected to even more exceptional and
horrendous abuse for this to be considered 'persecution' (Cohen
2006). The third move in the argumentation of this passage is to
portray gender as a zero-sum relation: that is, by highlighting that
it is not only women who are gendered, this appears to work to
discredit the claims for gender-specific need or consideration.

Hence in this text there is a shift from a (desirable) distancing
from 'stereotyping' to designating gender-specific consideration as
unfair or 'exclusionary', since certain forms of persecution are 'not
the exclusive preserve of women'. The Home Office is of course
not alone in this kind of reasoning. It reflects the wider critical
literature that notes how the move towards gender-neutrality in
law has worked to the detriment of women's rights (Smart and
Sevenhuijsen 1989, Smart 2004), while some accounts portray
difficulties in disclosing sexual violence as transcending gender (or
even worse for men).

There are indications elsewhere in the text of resistance to acknowledging specificity. A response to the question late on in the schedule about staff training, which offers very detailed priming in terms of how domestic violence is viewed in Pakistan (including customary practices; issues posed in considering applications of women from tribal/feudal areas; honour killings; forced marriage; economic situation of women), characterises this concern as a 'social group issue': 'Social group issues are covered in initial training courses ... training is kept up to date through general presentations.' This of course leaves unspecified which 'social group' is being addressed and which 'issue', while the blurring of initial with general training obscures how it is unclear whether such training will have been undertaken by any specific caseworker, and as such be available as a knowledge resource.

Conclusion

This analysis of a British Home Office text has illustrated how the semblance of a just and coherent system is achieved, through a range of discursive practices of what I have called here 'banal exclusion'. Yet close attention to this text, generated as part of the WASP research project, also reveals that such institutions are not, at least at the level of discourse, monolithic or homogeneous. Crucially, since no text can be read in isolation, the analysis identified some tensions and fissures in the account of how the Home Office works, which puts the claimed 'rationality' of the organisation in question and correspondingly the adequacy of the functioning of its policies, procedures and 'guidance'. The analysis presented here was both informed by and consistent with the project's other participants' accounts of the arbitrariness of HO asylum decision making.

This discursive analysis has drawn on lexical, grammatical, narrative, argumentative, dilemmatic approaches. All these approaches to the analysis of text offered resources to move from detailed features (in the face of so elaborated and apparently seamless a text) to inform analysis of wider disciplinary practices. While it is important not to overstate the significance of any particular text, given the institutional role of an organisation such as the British Home Office (in particular the Border and Immigration Agency), such close readings of these small texts may offer some implications for understanding the performative and even fragile status of the nation / state of the nation.

Some wider theoretical connections can be made from this analysis, in particular in showing how gender specificity becomes neutrality, which then erases racialised difference in the name of equality. Seshadri-Crooks (2000) draws on Arendt's (1973) critique of bureaucracy alongside Bhabha's (1994) analysis to draw attention 'to the contradiction within the order of race as the institution of difference and the desire for sameness' (81). This analysis helps to explain the covert racial violence of 'rational', egalitarian law/bureaucracies, such as the BIA. As she argues:

> ... bureaucracy must not be understood as a simple and correctable error of colonial discourse; rather, it must be understood as the 'symptom' of the inherently contradictory claims of the rhetoric of colonialism (the impossibility of the rule of law) engendered as it is by an impossible desire ... The unconscious aspect of Whiteness guarantees just such a non-knowledge, while its illegal desire, articulated in the symptom of lawless bureaucracy in the scene of colonialism, supported by the latent equation of Whiteness with humanness, remains repressed and unacknowledged ... (Seshadri-Crooks 2000: 81)

Hence rather than seeing these discourses of immigration control as merely reflecting the nation-state, we might see them as actively constituting the nation-state and as such a key site for interrogation and intervention. In particular, there is a wide body of both anecdotal and systematic evidence currently emerging, suggesting that the climate of disbelief and distrust of women asylum claimants inhibits and so impairs their access to justice, the process of pursuing their claims even punishing and retraumatising them further (Bögner *et al.* 2007). The 'truth' of a claimant's account is assumed on the basis of its coherence, and corroboration of its accuracy. As Žižek' (2008: 2–3) points out, traumatised women may not be able to provide either of these. Moreover, notwithstanding – or rather paradoxically precisely because of the Home Office's narrative around 'stereotyping' – new orthodoxies are being generated about how women who have experienced terrible interpersonal (including sexual) violence should react, in ways that ignore geopolitical conditions and presume culture- and context-free (as well as gender-neutral) normalised responses.

Thus, as we documented in the WASP study, if a Pakistani woman could in fact provide a coherent and factual account of her journey and the abuse that precipitated it, then she might not be deemed credible, precisely because she failed to exhibit the behaviour deemed appropriate for the level of trauma associated with the violence to which she claimed to have been subjected. She is thus caught in a double-bind wrought from the fateful intersection of dominant cultural representations of her homeland and the status she is accorded there as a woman, alongside – equally cultural but naturalised through their professional status – representations of knowledge about responses to abuse. This is the work of symbolic and systemic violence, together with structural violence. These intersections – that are simultaneously political, cultural and gendered – have clear implications for a range of decision makers and providers across the spectrum of advocacy and support services in both the UK and Pakistan.

As indicated at the beginning of this chapter (and in Ismail's account, chapter 6), the WASP study was prompted by the draconian measures increasingly deployed within UK immigration practices, here specifically Pakistani women, seeking asylum on the basis of domestic violence. The challenge of seeking justice for Pakistani women poses in acute form the key questions of North–South relations, the role of gender-based violence, and general understandings of gendered status within both state and transnational policy, alongside how discourses of rights, the law and culture often converge, clash and even combine to exonerate key agents. This close reading of a Home Office account offers some indications of how such exonerations work precisely by mobilising discourses of gender, culture and (implicitly) racialisation.

Appendix: interview schedule

1. Policy

> a. How would you describe current Home Office policy in dealing with cases of this type?
> b. Are they the same as other asylum cases?
> c. Is there specific policy on domestic violence and asylum?
> d. Any differences in managing cases of Pakistani women?

  e. Is there specific guidance for decision makers / Home Office case managers?

  f. What issues do you face in working in this area of policy – challenges and difficulties?

2. Assessing a case

  a. What criteria do you use in the assessment of cases?

  b. What guidance is given in assessing claims of this kind? (Is there a need for further guidance to assist in the assessment? If so, please provide examples.)

  c. How important is the issue of credibility in assessing asylum claims in grounds of domestic violence? (What factors are important to you in the assessment of credibility?) Since you have been involved in the process of assessing cases, what changes (if any) have there been?

3. Knowledge/information needs

  a. Do you use country reports in your work?

  b. If yes, how useful are they in assessing a case (particularly in cases from Pakistan)?

  c. Is there any additional information that would help you in assessing these cases?

  d. Do home office workers or assessors have access to training in any of the following areas?

  e. How is domestic violence viewed in Pakistan?

  f. In-country conditions in Pakistan (e.g. customary practices)?

  g. Considering applications of women from tribal/feudal areas. Honour killings, forced marriage, economic situation of women?

  h. Is there any other training that you think workers should have access to?

4. Women's experiences

  a. What issues do you think women face when going through the asylum process?

  b. Are there any parts of the process that you think are carried out particularly well?

  c. Are there any parts of the process that you feel could be improved?

    d. How often are women provided with interpreters in these cases?

    e. Are there any issues which women are reluctant to discuss?

    f. Is there anything that you think would help a woman to disclose any difficult or sensitive issues?

    g. Is there anything else you'd like to tell us about this issue?

Notes

1   Elsewhere I discuss how the project team addressed the ethical issues concerning representational dilemmas around the image of Pakistan (in which the significance of the colonial relationship between the UK and Pakistan is not merely coincidental), the current political situation in Pakistan (which threatens to occlude any specific concern about gendered violence), the problem of colluding with the imperialist, Western model of intervening in the name of supporting black and minority women's emancipation (cf. the rationale for the invasion of Afghanistan). See Burman 2010; Siddiqui, Ismail and Allen 2008, and especially Ismail, this volume.

2   The title of the project and the report itself performs a discursive intervention in questioning the notions of both safety and return, see Siddiqui, Ismail and Allen 2008 and Ismail, this volume.

3   While practically useful in the formulation of asylum applications and appeals, the problems with this designation reflects a wider (international) problem in refugee policy with gender as a PSG ('particular social group') on both conceptual and practical grounds. A key conceptual difficulty revolves around the conundrum that half a national population could be a PSG, and poses the wider political question of what this does to the image of those countries so designated. As well as the political question of whether it is overall strategically useful to claim PSG status for all women within one country, there are practical and conceptual issues around how such designations may be inflected by class, 'race'/ethnic, regional and religious differences between women.

4   To be specific about the timing of name changes, the IND (Immigration and Nationality Directorate) – the section of

the British Home Office dealing with immigration and asylum – became the BIA (Border and Immigration Agency) on the 3rd April 2007; and the BIA subsequently became the UKBA (United Kingdom Border Agency) on the 3rd April 2008; i.e. after the research reported here had been conducted. I am grateful to Sajida Ismail for this clarification. We might reflect on the significance of the name change: 'borders' perhaps privileges 'security' issues, sounds more distanced from the 'centre', and connotes a specific 'European' discourse (after all, Britain is an island, therefore has physical rather than political/ territory-defined borders). 'Immigration' is now placed second, suggesting perhaps that migration rather than immigration is the current focus as reflecting recent changes in neoliberal capital which require flexible, mobile labour. Such a name appears more in line with post-9/11 and 7/7 preoccupations with managing flow of populations. The shift from 'Directorate' to 'Agency' sounds less grandiose, perhaps suggesting diminution of authority, or thereby implying it is merely carrying out the policies determined elsewhere (rather than 'directing' them), while the subsequent suppression of the 'I' (Immigration) is suggestive of the wish to make this issue disappear – from public view at least. Finally, there seems to be a displacement of the centrality of matters of 'nationality' – indicative perhaps of how remote the possibilities are of gaining British nationality for asylum applicants.

5   In August 2010 such fast-tracking was in fact ruled illegal, though in the face of all the other structural measures preventing appellants from getting adequate support, we have yet to see what difference this will make.

PART 3

Depoliticising Migration

In this Part, the exploration of the intersection of visibility, vulnerability and credibility shifts to focus on the kinds of migrations, migrants and violence that are typically rendered non-political. These chapters delve deeper into migrant relationships with family back 'home', how state responses legitimate and exacerbate supposedly domestic violence, and how intimate relationships are shaped and constrained by the status of being a migrant. This Part of the book continues the concern about the visibility of migrants by considering how different kinds of migrants might choose to avoid being visible and negotiate the kinds of visibility available to them. This is evident in the chapter by Isabel Rodríguez Mora, who considers the visibility of poor women as mothers within a disaster relief intervention, as well as by Caroline Kihato, who looks into how migrants represent their migration experiences to family members in their 'home' countries. In this section therefore, different kinds of visibility are examined and the implications are drawn out for a range of sectors that include but are also beyond the state, including family relationships and the development of intimate relationships in the 'host' society. The impossibility of such intimate relationships is a central theme of the chapter by Stavros Psaroudakis, while Monica Kiwanuka shows how examining these seemingly domestic relationships further challenges their seemingly non-political nature, since their 'contractual' and sometimes abusive characteristics could only occur in the context of the wider economic and political positionings rendered salient by their migrant status.

CHAPTER 9

Now you see me, now you don't: methodologies and methods of the interstices

Caroline Wanjiku Kihato

Introduction

> [C]an photographs, the very cultural objects that support
> dominant ideologies, also be used to resist and contest those
> ideologies? And how, in these opaque and ultimately flat
> two-dimensional representations, can this resistance be
> read?
>
> (Hirsch 1999: xiv)

The use of visual methodologies in social-science research
is fast becoming accepted as a viable and credible means of
better understanding populations that are politically, socially
and economically marginalised. Visual methods are considered
empowering, as they allow research subjects control over how they
are represented. They also provide new ways of 'seeing' population
groups that are often hidden from view, or who are known only
through how 'outsiders' perceive and represent them. This chapter
reflects upon the narrated visual diaries of 11 migrant women from
the rest of the continent now living in Johannesburg. The research
process is a performative act which provides insight into not only
the relationship between the researcher and research informant,
but also the informants' relationship to broader society. I argue that

migrant women live liminal lives, as if suspended in society. And this method allows us to see the socio-political and economic issues that arise from living in society's interstices. Paradoxically, while migrant women use the camera as a performative tool – as a way of challenging hegemonic discourses and stereotypes of migrants – they do so in a context where they wish to remain hidden and outside the gaze of the state. Thus, the camera is a symbol of the dialectical character of living in the margins – an ongoing dialogue between wanting to be seen and yet hidden, of needing certain forms of visibility but also requiring a measure of invisibility. This research outlines the complexities of visual methods, bringing into focus critical issues about the politics of representation, and the ways in which these are implicated in the research process itself. Migrant women's performance in the research process impacts upon what they choose to reveal, and how they project themselves to the world. Invariably, their images and words are embedded in the political, social and economic contexts of the margins.

The limits of words

My decision to use a visual method as a data collection tool was prompted by an awareness, during my fieldwork, of the failings of language to convey migrant women's migration experiences. My first reaction was to blame language barriers – particularly where I could not converse directly with interviewees because we spoke different languages. As the research progressed, I became convinced that it was not just that there were language barriers, but that there are times when no words *in any oral language* can articulate women's feelings, memories and ideas. In other words, there are situations and contexts that cannot be expressed or articulated orally. Scarry writes this of pain, suggesting that 'physical pain ... is language-destroying' (Scarry 1985: 19). Other feminist authors also illustrate the failings of oral techniques in situations that relate to, or trigger, traumatic events (see Motsemme 2004, Gasa 2007, White 1998). White writes:

> When listening to survivors speak about their experiences during the war we are left with the sense that ultimately our language fails us. The words we have available to us are inadequate to the task of conveying the systematic

humiliation and degradation experienced by European
Jews during World War 2; they cannot express the complex,
anguished feelings and mental imagery of the survivor.
(1998: 174)

In these contexts other forms of non-verbal expression become the
means through which people articulate their feelings. In her article
'The mute always speak', Motsemme writes about the significance
of silence as a vehicle for communicating to the Truth and
Reconciliation Commission the pain experienced by communities
under apartheid (Motsemme 2004). Giles-Vernick points to the
importance of reading bodily and spatial practices, as these are
ways in which women communicate about their situations and
experiences (2001).

As an attempt to overcome some of the barriers of oral
languages, I added a visual component to my data collection
technique. This approach did not seek to replace oral evidence,
but to use snapshots produced by migrant women to complement
our verbal interactions. In this context, the images worked both
as mnemonics and as sources of evidence in their own right. My
initial objective was simply to use images as visual confirmation of
migrant women's material conditions – revealing spaces which are
often invisible to outsiders. As the research progressed, however,
I realised that the images women produced went beyond their
material dimension, constructing meanings that lie behind the
image, and constituted as part of a complex meaning-producing
system. In this system, both the 'viewer' and the 'viewed' co-
construct meaning – the meaning of the visual sign is therefore
always a product of the articulation between the image and its
audience (Evans and Hall 1999).

Migrant women's narrated visual diaries reveal new insights
into their everyday lives in ways that uncover the complexities of
their socio-political locations and, in turn, extend our theoretical
and empirical understanding of the condition of migration in
contemporary Johannesburg.

Research method

Using a snowball technique, I approached 11 participants from
Cameroon, Kenya, the DRC, Zimbabwe, Burundi, Rwanda and

Uganda to participate in bi-weekly workshops over a period of six months between November 2007 and April 2008. At the time, the women were living in inner-city Johannesburg, in the suburbs of Yeoville, Berea, Hillbrow, the Central Business District and Rosettenville. As authors elsewhere remark, snowball sampling has limited 'breadth' because of its bias of some migrant networks over others (Jacobsen and Landau 2003). However, the study was less about obtaining a representative sample than gaining in-depth information about women's everyday experiences of migration to Johannesburg.

I worked with Terry Kurgan, a professional artist who uses the medium of photography in her work. At our first group workshop we introduced the concept of the visual diary to the migrant women and explained how to use disposable cameras. We deliberately wanted the brief to be as open as possible and did not want to dominate the activity by imposing too many conditions on their diaries. To achieve this we asked participants to reflect upon only two questions when taking images of their everyday lives: What happens in a typical day in your life in Johannesburg? What are the markers that punctuate your day?

We used group discussions as the platforms where participants could discuss the images they had taken. These conversations were digitally recorded. The group meetings were held at the Yeoville community centre, which was a central meeting place for all the participants. Every fortnight, the women would talk about their

9.1 The research group at one of our meetings

pictures they had taken over the last two weeks, and conversations – sometimes linked to the images, and sometimes about other issues – would take place. At each meeting they would get a new camera to prepare for the next group discussion. This continued until our last meeting in April 2008.

Group discussions have the advantage of eliminating the power dynamics between the 'researcher/expert' and the research informant. If conducted amongst peers, they reduce the inhibitions and self-consciousness that is sometimes present in a formal interview. But as Slim and his colleagues warn, the opposite can also be true. 'Groups can bring out the best and the worst in people. Sometimes, by taking the focus off individuals, they make them less inhibited, but the opposite can occur just as easily' (Slim *et al.* 1998: 118).

As the women got to know each other better, some of the inhibitions we witnessed in early groups faded away and their conversations became more candid and spontaneous. In fact, in some of the workshops, the participants took over, directing the discussions as they debated common themes in their experiences. In these discussions, our roles shifted from interviewers to moderators, instigating initial questions but leaving the conversation to take its own identity and direction.

As a research technique, group discussions are important in generating robust conversations. The group provides a platform for uncovering issues that are significant to a particular community, triggering memories of other group members, verifying facts, and challenging different views (see Slim *et al.* 1998). Through robust group discussions, researchers gain access to the issues that are important to a community and the various positions or debates around the issue. This dynamic interaction is often difficult to achieve in a one-on-one interview.

But this method of data collection also has its limitations. Group dynamics can result in the domination of some members over others. Terry and I had to ensure that everyone in the group had a chance to share their experiences. In this, the photographs provided a good platform for all participants to speak about their own images and experiences. By giving everyone a chance to discuss the photographs they had taken, and using the photograph as the focus of everyone's attention, we unwittingly overcame the problem of dominating voices, which can silence some group members. In addition, women's images prompted conversations around an event in ways that eliminated some of the awkwardness sometimes experienced when narrating personal testimony. Using the photograph as the point of focus took attention away from the narrator, making her less self-conscious about talking in a group.

There were instances when we realised that we were out of our depth, particularly when women were discussing traumatic issues around their past or present circumstances. In a session about the past, two of the women shared with us their experience of the Rwandan genocide, another revealed to us that she had just found out she was HIV positive. Under these circumstances, we found ourselves without the necessary counselling skills, and frequently questioned whether we had made the appropriate responses. What surprised us was the group's capacity to offer support to the narrator during these times. How we collectively responded to issues of trauma by listening empathetically and being present with the narrator was something I found reassuring. Nevertheless, due to the intensity of some of the sessions, we linked women who needed it to a service which provides free professional counselling.

Women's social economic and legal contexts in Johannesburg

South Africa represents the possibility for migrant women to become economically independent and provide financial support to their families back home. From the sample it is clear that not all women can be considered 'refugees' in terms of international norms and conventions. Nevertheless, they all face varying degrees of displacement. Economic migrants, while not facing the same levels of threat to their lives as those fleeing war, express the lack of economic opportunities in their countries as an immediate threat to their own livelihood and that of their families. They have in some ways been forced to leave their countries by the poor economic conditions there, in order to survive. All the women in the sample group had valid documentation to be in South Africa. While a few had temporary resident permits, most had a Section 22 asylum seeker temporary permit which allows the holder to work and study in South Africa. Typically, women pay 'agents' with connections to the Department of Home Affairs (DHA) (the office responsible for determining and issuing status documentation in the country) to get asylum seeker permits which allow them to work and study while their refugee status is being determined. This process is meant to take six months, yet it often takes years before an asylum seeker's status is determined. In the meantime, the permit holder is required to renew their permit every one or two months at a DHA office. While there are differences in their personal circumstances and it is obvious that some meet international conventions for claiming refugee status, all women face the same barriers to work, study and other opportunities in South Africa and experienced similar levels of fear and vulnerability to arrest and deportation. Despite these women having *de jure* rights to work and study, few employers recognise asylum permits as valid forms of identity. Mary (DRC) highlights the frustrations of not having a South African identity document:

> I cannot participate in South African life the way I would like to. Here, if I try to get a job I cannot because I am not South African, and I do not have an ID [identity document]. This makes me feel an outsider and also angry because it is not because I cannot do work, but because I am not from here.

Similarly, asylum seekers are unable to open bank accounts, sign a lease, get free health care or walk the streets without the fear that they will be detained by police, either having to pay a bribe or be denied access to essential services (CORMSA 2008). These institutional 'barriers to entry' imply that migrant women literally live as if suspended in South African society. And, because status determination can take a long time, being in this legal limbo can last years. Even those with refugee permits, while legally entitled to all the rights of a South African (except the right to vote), are not immune from exploitative and corrupt policemen or service providers who do not recognise their status.

Interrogating power in the research process

Much has been written about the empowering nature of research techniques that give participants control to determine the content of their experiences, and the ways they choose to represent them. Using written diaries amongst a group of women in Durban,

Meth argues that the method provides an opportunity to a group of marginalised women to have a say, and identify the key issues that affect them in relation to crime and violence (Meth 2004). Recognising the significance of visual methods in empowering vulnerable populations has led to its frequent use amongst children – becoming an important channel for understanding social experiences through their eyes and 'in their own terms' (see Young and Barrett 2001: 144). Similarly, Goldstein suggests that visual methodologies give research subjects control over the medium of representation, allowing them the latitude for 'identity-building' – constructing the way in which they would like to be perceived by the researcher and society at large (Goldstein 2002: 485).

Although my research interests determined the parameters of the visual diaries project, the method provided migrant women some measure of authorial control. It gave them a chance to compose the content of the images and articulate the meanings they attached to them. This was important, as the research aimed to understand how women's everyday lives – their subjectivities and schemas[1] – contribute to our knowledge of contemporary migration processes in Johannesburg, and, more broadly, on the continent. Echoing feminist methodologies, the research aimed at moving migrant women's experiences from the margins to the centre (to borrow from bell hooks 1994). In other words, the women were not 'objects' to be observed and studied, but rather, co-participants in the research process, sharing their interpretations of their life-worlds. Epistemologically, approaching the research in this way implies acknowledging that migrant women are 'knowers'. Their marginality and socio-economic locations create certain subjectivities which are not necessarily subsumed in dominant knowledge and power regimes but which, in fact, produce ways of knowing that either counter or reinforce existing dominant discourses. This epistemological location draws on Collins' (2000) thesis that black women's social locations produce knowledges that are related to their contexts but are often invisible from other viewpoints.

Having authorial control and being 'co-participants' does not erase the fact that I had a particular relationship to the women and to the research process that cannot be equated to that of a peer. It was *my* research idea, I coordinated the group, bought the cameras, developed the images, organised the food and venue, and, together with Terry, moderated the workshop. Despite giving women the latitude to determine the content of their contribution, it was clear that Terry and I were 'outsiders'. And by virtue of our position we were perceived as offering the group a different set of skills and opportunities than other members. In effect we represented the world 'out there', and migrant women were aware that they could leverage their participation in the project to determine the kinds of narratives and images we eventually published. At the first meeting, one of the questions posed by the migrant women was what benefit this project had to them and their communities: Here is an excerpt of the conversation:

> Florence: What is the project going to pay after, when we finish, the result, that is what I would like to know ... When we are sharing our experiences, our life. What are we going to do with it? I don't know if you understand me?
>
> Mary: What she's saying, maybe, is what is she going to benefit or something like that ...?
>
> Terry (artist and co-moderator): Is that what you mean?
>
> Florence: I mean we are going to make it, I don't know a book or album of photos, what's it going to do [so that] other people can benefit on it, I would like to know that.
>
> Helen: Same ja, what benefits are [there] how does it help the community, and where do we go from here?
>
> Caroline: What would you want out of this process? You don't know me and yet you decided to come together with strangers to share your life ... What would you want to see come out of this process so we can direct this project where you want to see it going?
>
> Florence: ... we want [that] it must affect other people, we must just have maybe for example a ... conferences, to invite other people, discuss all our issues, so that they are helping us, something like this. And we help them to know other difficult things, we can just do it like this, you see. To have the different experiences of people.
>
> Mary: To change the mind of other people, I don't know. To bring them to work. To bring them to ... bring out the value inside them. To help other women maybe that doesn't have their rights, it can help them. It's what I'm thinking about, if it's like that.
>
> Florence: Also maybe to educate the South African peoples, to show them that we are people just like them. We are not

taking their jobs (laughter) ... Whose jobs are we taking? Which jobs are we taking from anyone, we are making our own jobs!

The research participants were, quite rightly, concerned about what value the project would have for them and their communities (family, church members, women's groups, foreign migrants more generally). When we asked what they wanted to get out of the project, women's responses showed the need to use the experience of the group to assist other women or community members to address some of the difficulties they faced in South Africa. It was clear that they had an agenda too – and their participation in the group was in part informed by the role they saw themselves playing as the 'voices' of their own communities. This undoubtedly framed the narratives and images that they took and ways in which they represented themselves to us, and, by extension, the broader society.

This dimension of the research is important theoretically in terms of how we understand power in the research process. Where much of the literature on qualitative methods focuses on the power of the researcher to define and structure the process, little attention is paid to the agency of research participants and their role in co-constructing the dynamics of the process. Goldstein makes this argument of the anthropologist:

> ... many of these people recognize that the anthropologist who has come to study them will ultimately produce a written report about them, one that represents them, their needs, and their desires to a larger and more powerful world beyond their immediate domain, and they will attempt to exert some kind of influence over that final product. (Goldstein 2002: 488)

In the context of the research process, it is therefore important to conceptualise power not simply as embodied in the researcher, but as circulating in the relationship between researcher and informant(s) – shifting from one actor to another at different points in the research process. Foucault's understanding of power is particularly illuminating in this context. For him, power is fluid – not localised in a single individual, but rather articulated through a variety of actors (Foucault 1980).

Viewing the research process as a uni-directional power relationship, where the researcher has the power and the research subject has none, not only simplifies and misreads a complex process but, importantly, prevents a more critical appreciation of the data that is obtained. Understanding how and why research informants narrate their stories and, as in this project, take particular images, provides greater insight into the underlying meanings and messages they wish to convey about themselves, and the highly political context within which research occurs. As will become evident in the next section, understanding 'research as performance' provides critical insight into the politics of representation – unveiling ways in which marginal groups counter the asymmetrical and unequal power relations implicated in dominant modes of representation.

Research as performance

Recognising migrant women as knowledge producers with some agency in the research process also meant that I had to confront the fact that their words and images were not merely reflective mirrors into their worlds, unmediated by their contexts. Rather, they were representations of what they wanted to reveal of their lives. It is not only that their gender, class and specific histories influence how they narrate their stories, or what images they took. It is also that their *intentions* shape the content of the discussions and pictures. Goldstein refers to this as the 'performative encounter' where research participants actively shape the way in which they are perceived and represented in the world (2002: 486). Thus in understanding the data, I needed to move beyond migrant women's words and images seeking to uncover the hidden codes and meanings contained within them. This position is linked to a broader point made by Hall that visual and oral languages are not simply mimetic, reflecting or imitating a materiality (Hall 1997: 24), but are rather located within a context of signifying systems. No matter how 'marginalized' or 'dispossessed', women display agency in their words and images, not only by selecting what to reveal and what to conceal, but also by determining how and when they choose to do so.

At the first workshop, I was struck by the repetition of the narrative of despair among the group. When I compared it with subsequent discussions where many of the narratives displayed a more positive and confident demeanour, I wondered why there were these differences. Months later in a conversation with Lucy[2] I asked why:

> **Caroline:** In the first meeting we had, I remember you telling us that things were difficult in Johannesburg – you were unable to get a job, didn't have papers and so on – while now you talk about these difficulties, you seem so much better able to cope. Why?
>
> **Lucy:** When we first met, we did not know what the project was or what we could get out of it. I thought that maybe you could help with getting us jobs or papers. So I was saying my situation was bad in case you guys offered us something ... It's not that it's not bad; what I said was true, you know it's true.
>
> **Caroline:** So what changed later?
>
> **Lucy:** Ha ha! After a while we just took you as friends, just people who we meet and laugh and share together with ... and you know I also wanted to show people I am not stupid, and that I can make my own life even with difficulties.

Perceiving that we may be in positions to offer her something, Lucy told us what she wanted us to hear at our first meeting. Her problems with getting a job or immigration documents were not untrue, but she admits to highlighting these to get our attention, in case we could help her. In subsequent workshops, she wanted to display her agency – her ability to overcome the structural barriers facing an asylum seeker in Johannesburg. If I were to solely rely on the first discussion we had with the group, I could easily have misread Lucy as lacking agency, and being marginalised and weak. Yet she was conscious that while pulling at our heartstrings could get her some form of assistance, she did not want us to think of her solely as a victim. She adopts a language that she thinks can manipulate her listeners into helping her. These performative acts – her ability to assess her audience and choose the narrative she perceives as most effective – reveal her agency, as much as her statement 'I am not stupid'.

As the research progressed, it was clear that Terry and I were not the only audience that the women were speaking to, and the narrated visual diaries were used as avenues for 'talking back' to broader society – the state, South Africans, and communities back home. Migrant women's words and images of their daily lives are not neutral, devoid of their values, politics or aspirations. Living in Johannesburg, they are marginalised, excluded from participating fully in the country's socio-economic and political landscape. Despite having asylum seeker permits, or other legal documentation allowing them temporary residence and access to work and study opportunities, many of the women find it difficult to access these and other basic services. This conversation with Rose from Rwanda discusses the barriers she experiences as an asylum seeker in Johannesburg:

> **Rose:** For me [getting work] is difficult because I'm still having this asylum seeker permit so I can't get a little job. I just sell my bananas. So I was trying to ask to the Home Affairs if they can give me a permit for more than one month. They say decision, decision, until now they give me one month ... So every month I have to go now to renew my permit.
>
> **Terry:** So you have a refugee permit?
>
> **Rose:** No, I have an asylum seeker permit. I've been trying to get refugee status for many years because you can get one for two years and work if you get a refugee status. This asylum seeker permit can't allow you to get a job; can't allow you to open an account. Asylum seeker permits can't allow you to even rent your own house because you have to have all these things ... addresses. They ask for a little paper to show that you pay rent [in order] to get your own flat. Even the flat which we are living in is on another person's name because they don't allow us to rent the house.

Although she does not have a full-time job, Rose's images and narrations of her everyday life show her making a living trying to conduct petty trade – selling bananas, finding market space to start a telephone business, and renting a room in her house to raise money. When describing what she would change about being in South Africa, Mary, from the Democratic Republic of Congo, echoed Rose's frustrations:

> **Caroline:** If there was something you could change about your life what would that be?

Mary: Something which I can change, maybe to work hard, to be more productive, to assist society and my family also.

Terry: What do you feel is the barrier in the way of that?

Mary: Many, many barrier is here in South Africa. First, I'm not a South African; second, I don't have a document like South Africans. That's what is ... is not allowing me to go far. Yes.

The conversations with both Rose and Mary reveal the sense of dislocation experienced in South Africa because they lack documentation that is recognised by the service providers they encounter at an everyday level. Being in this limbo state where migrants have *de jure* rights to work, yet face *de facto* discrimination by landlords, employers, banks, health practitioners and so on, means that they are unable to fully participate in socio-economic life in South Africa.

In both women's responses there is a clear message to their 'audience' that they cannot be defined solely by the difficulties they face. In other words, they are productive beings with the ability to make contributions to the society in which they live if the barriers that they experience are eliminated. Despite the women's marginalisation, their narrated visual diaries illustrate their resilience, and their ability to make a living in Johannesburg even with the discrimination they face as foreigners.

Identity building: migrant women's self-portraits

It is in women's own portraits, taken by a family member or friend, that we encounter the stark contrast between how refugees are often depicted in media and their own modes of self-representation. In the image below, Florence is wearing an evening dress getting ready to go out. She sits in front of a dressing table (the mirror is cracked). We expect that this is where she puts on her makeup and does her hair – although all that we see in the photo are nappy wipes, and a toddler's clothes. This is an image that evokes sophistication, glamour and beauty and contrasts with representations of refugee women as impoverished, ugly and humiliated.

9.2 Florence getting ready to go out

Mary's portrait conveys similar messages. Her hair is done up, she is wearing makeup, and her eyebrows have been trimmed. She explains that a friend took this picture at the Yeoville market (a hawkers market located in one of Johannesburg's inner-city suburbs). At the workshop, she introduces the image: 'Here is me, Mama Africa, the mother of the community!' In this image, Mary reminds us she is an important figure in her community – she is a pastor's wife and is often called upon to counsel members of her church.

9.3 'Here is me, Mama Africa'

The significance of these images moves beyond how Mary and Florence look in the pictures. It is also about how they look to their audience, about the messages that their images convey of beauty, glamour and sophistication. Group discussions about the photographs often revealed the importance of looking 'good' in front of the camera – a convention that cuts across class, race and ages. There are some images that I have not been given permission to reproduce in public because the woman thought it did not portray her in the way she would like to be seen.

Some of the images also possess qualities of material wealth that women aspire towards. These images are aimed particularly at the audience 'back home', and are important in showing family members how successful the migrant has become in Johannesburg. The image (opposite) of Jean taken in a shopping-mall garage standing next to a luxury car represents her aspirations in Johannesburg. She explains that she took the picture 'to remind me of the things I want when I am a successful business woman'. To her family in Cameroon, the car that she stands in front of is a symbol of her success. She may not explicitly claim that it is her vehicle, but she may not deny it either. This conscious 'staging' of the image for her family reveals the complex familial relationships between migrant women and their families back home. Women's narratives and images revealed the pressure, both real and perceived, exerted upon them by family members and communities back home to be economically successful in Johannesburg. Part of this pressure emanates from the need to provide material support to families facing economic difficulties, many of who made material sacrifices to send the émigré in search of economic opportunities in another country. But improving one's social status (and by extension the status of the family within the community) is also important. For the migrant woman, journeying to Johannesburg is often considered a rite of passage – the route to becoming a 'real woman'. If it is accompanied by economic success and material support to the family, it confers upon her a higher social status and level of authority that she previously did not possess within her family. Yet while familial and community pressure to succeed in Johannesburg can build a resilience and creativity, it can also make women vulnerable to exploitative practices, especially when their option of going back home is diminished by the pressure to succeed. As a Nigerian woman said to me:

Ochu: Going home is like being between Pharaoh's army and the Red Sea. You hope to God that there is a rescue ship. If God does not answer your prayers, you have only one choice – to negotiate with the army. Jumping in the Red Sea is sure death.
Caroline: What is the Red Sea, Johannesburg or Lagos?
Ochu: No, no. The Red Sea is going back home with nothing in your hands; that is social death.

9.4 Jean in front of a luxury car in a mall

Women's snapshots respond to dominant media depictions of 'dirty', 'immoral', 'poor', 'ugly' migrants and refugees, countering these images by constructing alternative identities of beauty and glamour. These are images of resistance, in which migrant women overtly project how they want us to see them – as respected members of the community with a self-consciousness about looking 'good' in front of the camera. Images of wealth and aspirations not only reveal migrant women's dreams for material wealth but the way in which mobility is tied to dignity, honour and status in their communities. Thus, the photograph in this context transcends its opaque two-dimensional form, revealing more than it makes visible. Its layered meanings expose the politics of representation and allow us to reflect upon the unequal power relations embedded in the production of images – not only those of refugee or migrant women, but of marginalised communities across the globe.

Dialectic between visibility and invisibility

Photographs furnish evidence. Something we hear about, but doubt seems proven when we're shown a photograph of it. In one version of its utility, the camera record incriminates ... Photographs became a useful tool of modern states in the surveillance and control of their increasingly mobile populations. (Sontag 1977: 5)

Previous sections have discussed the camera as an empowering tool in the research process, particularly where research subjects are given the opportunity to author, through images and narratives, their own life stories. Indeed, bell hooks argues that '[c]ameras gave to black folks, irrespective of class, a means by which we could participate fully in the production of images ... Access and mass appeal have historically made photography a powerful location for the construction of an oppositional aesthetic (hooks 1994: 46). Yet despite the empowering quality of the camera, I was acutely aware of its potential use as a disempowering tool. While conducting research, I was often confronted with the dilemma of making migrant women's lives visible, yet acutely aware that particular modes of visibility could increase their vulnerability. On the one hand I wanted to use their narratives and images to humanise and break down the stereotypical ways in which they are constructed in public discourse. On the other, I understood the dangers of visibility amongst a group that often wished to remain invisible, particularly with respect to the state. Although we received consent from the research participants to use the images, and involved them in the selection processes for publication, the tension between visibility and invisibility continued to be one that concerned me.

As Sontag succinctly argues in the quote above, one cannot dismiss the role of the camera as a technology of social control and surveillance. The invention of the camera brought with it an authenticity – a true image of the object that previous modes of representation (drawings and paintings) could only hope to approximate (Berger 1980). Because of its power to produce '*visual facts*' (Hamilton 1997: 81), the camera has become an important tool for making populations *legible* (Scott 1998). The proliferation of closed-circuit cameras on city streets, at border control points, in public and private buildings, as both a surveillance and bio-data collection tool, serve to both control individual behaviour and make populations 'visible' to the state. In this sense, the camera is a central tool in Foucault's 'society of panopticism' (1994). The use of surveillance cameras is justified by arguments that they reduce incidences of crime, identify perpetrators, and protect the freedom of law-abiding citizens. But it is in a negative sense that theorists of the state like Foucault understand state surveillance mechanisms. In *Panopticism*, Foucault argues 'the supervision of individuals is carried out not at the level of what one does but of what one is, not at the level of what one does but of what one might do' (Foucault 1994: 70–1). For Foucault, the gaze of the state is less about effecting justice as about regulating, through disciplinary power, individual behaviour.

I was aware of this conception of the camera, and its power to *incriminate* (to use Sontag's term) a population that is vulnerable. This was particularly so when many of the women expressed their fear of the South African state, and their need to sometimes remain invisible to it. In a community where being 'seen' by the state or its agents can result in deportation, exploitation, evoke fear, or involve considerable risk, invisibility becomes a survival strategy. As a Congolese woman said to me: 'Here I am nobody. I hide from the police, I hide from the South African government, I hide from my government at home. Sometimes I even hide from my own countrymen ... you see this is how I survive.' Talking about how she navigates the city, another Congolese woman remarked: 'I do not like going down that street, Joe Slovo … you know it? … because under the bridge there are always police there. If you have to go to Bertrams, I rather take another route through Yeoville. It is very long but it's better than meeting the police.' Lucy's encounter with police illustrates the fear and anxiety it evokes. While the camera's 'incriminating' power would, in this encounter, expose the state agent, Lucy is fearful about what would happen to her were she caught documenting an incident of bribery with the police. In this case what remains invisible is the illegality of police actions, which she wishes she could make visible but fears the consequences of getting caught with a camera.

> Many times when we are going home from the restaurant in the evening in a taxi, we find a lot of police roadblocks. We all know these police are just there to target Zimbabweans because they know we have just finished working and we have money from tips. I would really like to take a photograph of a policeman taking money from us, but I don't know what they will do if they catch me.

At an empirical level, the discussions of the 'invisible pictures' highlighted the way women's routes through the city are shaped by fear. In particular, the two quotations discussed here illustrate how women avoid state agents for fear of harassment or deportation. At a methodological level, I realised that I could not presume the empowering nature of the camera. First, the possession of a camera, even a cheap disposable one, could have made the women targets of criminals on Johannesburg's streets, or of state agents and others not wanting to be captured on camera. Moreover, the incriminating qualities of the camera meant that women had to continually negotiate between self-authoring their life stories in ways that countered negative hegemonic representations, and avoiding the exposure that could compromise their security and well-being in South Africa.

These experiences point to the complicated and contradictory workings of photography, particularly as a social science method for understanding marginalised populations. What women's experiences with photography in this project have shown is that modes of representation are inherently political. Allowing research subjects the space to build their own identities provides the opportunity for reflection on the power differentials present in the representation of displaced (and marginalised) populations. It brings to the fore the asymmetry present in the circulation of images, and how certain images tend to dominate the public realm more than others. These observations raise questions around the institutional dynamics surrounding the production of images. Who has access to what media? What is their agenda? Who controls image production and circulation?

So, just as migrant women take images that are located within specific socio-political contexts and personal agendas, so too are dominant media images of refugees or displaced populations which tend to depict women as disempowered and weak. At a research level, this project has sharpened our understanding of the power relationships within the research process. Research participants are not merely neutral informants devoid of any agency in shifting research outcomes, but are rather active agents within it, often using the process to project their own agendas to the researcher and the society at large. Yet while the use of the camera in this way can be empowering, it can also increase the vulnerability of research subjects. Do subjects want to be seen and known? In what ways do they wish to remain invisible? And in which ways do they choose to be visible? These questions are significant, not only because they highlight the struggle for more humane modes of representation, but also because, at an everyday level, they unveil the politics of living in the margins. In other words, we are able to see how a group of marginalised women in Johannesburg avoid certain aspects of the state's gaze, providing clues for understanding the nature of state relationships with certain urban populations.

Conclusion

This chapter reflects upon the use of narrated visual diaries as a vehicle for understanding the dynamics of gender and migration experienced by a group of migrant women living in South Africa. The use of photographs taken by the research participants has provided the opportunity for reflecting upon the research process, and rethinking power relations between the researcher and 'subjects'. The project shows how migrant women use the research process to articulate the barriers they encounter living in Johannesburg, in the hope that voicing these issues will raise awareness and lead to policy changes. Beyond their materiality, migrant women overtly seek to counter stereotypical characterisations of being foreign in Johannesburg by highlighting their resourcefulness, entrepreneurial skills and ability to survive in Johannesburg, despite their difficult circumstances.

Theoretically, the use of images raises questions about what can be captured by the camera, and the spaces that remain hidden and beyond its reach. Analysing the invisible spaces provides clues about how women live in Johannesburg, how their fear of state agents shapes their experiences of the city and everyday urban practices. Ultimately, the snapshot is not merely a mirror reflecting migrant women's lives; it is a signification of the political, social and economic realities they face in their everyday experiences. When interrogating visual methods, it is important to understand the complex locations within which they are produced. It is through this analysis that we can gain insight into the realities facing communities that live in the margins of society.

Notes

1 I define schemas as the ways in which migrant women organise, understand, interpret and infuse meanings in events in their everyday lives.
2 Not her real name. I have used pseudonyms for all research participants.

CHAPTER 10

For love or survival: migrant women's narratives of survival and intimate partner violence in Johannesburg

Monica Kiwanuka

Introduction

This chapter is concerned with some of the ways that immigration, legislation and the social context in South Africa heighten migrant women's vulnerability to intimate partner violence, and the influence these two factors have on the means of survival some migrant women later employ. In the analysis I discuss the impact of migrant women's cohabitation with South African local men as a survival strategy, and the implications of this in relation to migrant women's experiences of and responses to intimate partner violence. The discussion shows how the state and contextual factors in the host country indirectly contribute to intimate partner violence among migrant women and the choices of survival some make. The chapter is drawn from a qualitative study conducted in Johannesburg and Pretoria, which is based upon in-depth narrative interviews of 15 African migrant women[1] (Kiwanuka 2008). The study utilised the social constructionist approach and feminist theory emphasising women's knowledge as socially and contextually constructed, combining to produce multiple experiences and standpoints of their lived realities during migration (Stanley and Wise 1983, Burr 1995).

Background

The link between migration and women's vulnerability to intimate partner violence has been extensively discussed. A multifaceted interaction of culture, poverty, host country immigration laws and policies, and other contextual factors appear to exacerbate migrant women's vulnerability to gender-based violence in contexts of migration (Menjivar and Salcido 2002, Raj and Silverman 2002, Erez 2000, Bui and Morash 1999, Lefko-Everett 2007). With regard to intimate partner violence, migrant and non-migrant women's experiences, coping mechanisms and obstacles to leaving abusive relationships are similar. However, key distinguishing factors increasing migrant women's susceptibility to intimate partner violence are embedded in their immigrant status (Burman and Chantler 2005, Menjivar and Salcido 2002). These factors include, among others: exclusionary immigration policies that limit access to services and other support; being undocumented, which heightens dependency on the perpetrator and severely restrains some migrant women's options to respond to intimate partner violence; and the impact of social contexts of crime and xenophobia, which, further, produce different women's experiences and responses to intimate partner violence (Raj and Silverman 2002, Kiwanuka 2008).

The main aim of the study was to investigate how migrant women understand and explain the effect of migration on domestic violence. Purposive and snowball techniques were utilised to identify study participants, and data collected through semi-structured narrative interviews. The analysis of data employed a combination of content, and narrative analysis. This chapter, however, focuses on the views and experiences of only a half of participants from the above study. This group of women were undocumented and all had relationships and cohabited with South African local men. This, as they explained, was a conscious strategy they chose, mainly to obtain the South African Identity Book (ID) and other means of livelihoods to enable them to secure their stay in South Africa in order to undertake different economic activities and thus better their welfare.

The immigration context and migrant women's undocumented status in South Africa

Increasing levels of poverty and unemployment, combined with the rising demand for female migrant labour, especially in Southern Africa, have given rise to migration being undertaken increasingly by women as a livelihood strategy (Crush and Williams 2005). Although there are just as many male migrants, in South Africa and elsewhere women form a significant proportion of cross-border and internal migrants who continue to move independently in search of livelihoods, a better life and/or protection from political repression (Lefko-Everett 2007, Sigsworth *et al.* 2008). Female migrants are more likely to be found in urban areas where employment opportunities exist; and they are mainly engaged in less skilled and informal work (Dodson 1998). Literature presents conflicting outcomes related to their gains and challenges when they migrate. For example, GCIM (2005) and Lefko-Everett (2007) indicate that, among some women, such movements have yielded positive results such as financial independence, leading to the ability to salvage their families from poverty as well as overcoming repressive family relationships. On the other hand, Burman and Chantler (2005) and Raj and Silverman (2002) point to the impact of discriminatory immigration legislation in combination with gender inequality as continuously placing migrant women in even more vulnerable positions. The section below thus looks at the influence of host country immigration policies and specific contextual factors in influencing the choices migrant women make in their continued struggle to live in South Africa, and the resulting consequences of these.

The dearth of research on female migration in the region notwithstanding, many women (as supported by this study) move as independent actors in search of better livelihoods and other means of protection. A significant proportion enter and/or remain in South Africa as undocumented migrants given difficulties related to acquisition of visas and other related financial expenses (Black *et al.* 2004, Lefko-Everett 2007).[2] In many instances such undocumented persons have been at risk of arrest and deportation for violation of immigration laws (Sigsworth *et al.* 2008, Landau 2006). Although some women negotiate being arrested for their illegal status through bribes, studies also indicate that some undocumented migrant women without resources trade sex with security officers to avoid detention so as to continue living in the host country and find means of survival (Lefko-Everett 2007, Landau 2006, Sigsworth *et al.* 2008).

In this study, while some of the participants had found and lost temporary jobs, in general they reported a difficulty of finding gainful employment, as this requires one to have legal documentation to stay and work, and the country has a high level of unemployment, at almost 24.5 per cent.[3] The lack of employment is further exacerbated by difficulties related to approval of foreign qualifications among those who are skilled (Sigsworth *et al.* 2008). This limitation makes it likely that some poor migrant women will be left at a risk of having their basic needs unmet. In South Africa, undocumented migrants not only find it difficult to access the asylum system and lodge claims, given the existing numerous complications involved (see CORMSA 2009), but the need to present legal documentation for access to services (in terms of the Immigration Act of 2002) means that undocumented migrant women and other migrants with insufficient incomes and limited networks may find it difficult to approach and access health and other essential services provided by government. This may severely compromise the health of those without income or other means to seek health care at private clinics. Although South Africa's legislation guarantees access to emergency medical care (South African Bill of Rights 27(3)) and recently introduced anti-retroviral therapy (ART) to all in South Africa (Department of Health 2006); studies continue to reveal denial of access to some migrants on the basis of lack of legal documentation, which risks the health of such migrants (Vearey, Nunez and Palmary 2007, Sigsworth *et al.* 2008).

In their narratives, participants explained that this background generally affected them in two ways: first, through limiting their help-seeking initiatives for fear of deportation; and second, through increasing levels of helplessness, as participants felt they would not be able meet their health and other basic needs without support from South African local men with a South African identity document. Thus a combination of restrictive immigration policies and the resultant consequences above had a bearing on the choices of survival adapted in the host country.

Migrant women's inability to cope on their own could also be explained by the lack of, or weak, social networks, especially combined with contextual factors in the host country such as high levels of generalised and hate crime. Significantly, these, according to the participants, functioned to increase their fear of finding alternative livelihoods and/or means of protection apart from cohabitation.

Survival love and intimate partner violence

In their narratives, migrant women explained that they chose to cohabit with local South African men in the hope of marriage, which they hoped in the long term would result in acquisition of South African citizenship; in the meantime, they hoped to receive assistance in acquiring aslyum seeker permits.[4, 5] Interesting to note is that none of these participants mentioned the need of a refugee permit, which is at least more permanent than the aslyum seeker permit. Nevertheless, they felt that they would be able to settle peacefully and permanently in the host country if they acquired citizenship, as their narratives below indicate:

> … I was with him because I was not settled, even how we hooked up it is because I had no place to go, no food and most of all I had to attach myself to a South African to help me get papers [legal documentation] … Even from the way we hooked up, he knew he is the only person I trusted and depended on and counted on. He used to do this [abuse me] because he knew there is nowhere else I can go and that is why he used to do this. (Martha, 26 years, single)

> I had no alternative being in a foreign place, no job, no one to turn to, no money. So I had to accept this man even if I would not have done so if I were in my country, but I needed him to help me out in terms of survival … that was my only concern. Since he was born here, and had hinted on marrying me and changing my status, I thought he was the perfect person to help me get papers and more especially a South African identity document. I endured all the abuse in the hope that one day I will get the papers and live my life but, day by day, I only got beatings instead. Until I gave up and I just live with my problem. (Cindy, 29 years, single)

The participants' narratives show that the need for legal documentation and basic survival in the host country have the effect of emphasising the material function of marriage and/or relationships. This is not to say that all women in this category would respond similarly, given that poverty may not be the overriding factor for all women to engage in exchange-based relationships (Chatterji *et al.* 2004). To migrant women these cohabitation relationships with local South African men were a coping and survival strategy for basic needs, and, more importantly, a way of acquiring legal documentation in the absence of adequate protection by the host government. To these participants, and indeed to the rest of irregular migrant populations in South Africa, the importance of regularising one's status is paramount. This, to some degree, would mean less chance of deportation and other related exclusions. These migrants would also be able to work and support themselves since the policy allows asylum seeker permit holders to engage in work. Given that the asylum seeker permit does not hold the same benefits and permanency as the identity book and clearly classifies one as a foreigner (Landau and Monson 2008), some of the migrant women felt that they would not be able to acquire the benefits they sought entitlement to in the future, if they did not possess a South African identity book.

The rights and privileges associated with this identity book as a system of national identification in South Africa, and indeed with South African citizenship as compared to the asylum seeker permit, meant that some of the undocumented migrant women in this study viewed heterosexual relationships with South African men as a meaningful opportunity to acquire benefits they were excluded from. To the women, acquiring an ID book was not only a means to a livelihood and protection in South Africa, but would also entitle them to access other resources that would benefit those they left behind and remained responsible for.[6] They seemed to be negotiating rights and membership into a system they had been excluded from because of their citizenship status. Acquisition of the South African identity book was thus a long-term strategy pointing to women's agency, related not only to minimising dependency on their partners, which they felt exposed them to intimate partner violence, but to giving them the capacity to meet obligations towards their families and especially children left in their home countries.

The importance of an identity book, even for a local South African, as the basis for access to rights and essential services cannot be underestimated, as the minister of Home Affairs stated:

'When you write matric, register at university, open a bank account, start a business, want a driver's license, you need an ID and that comes from Home Affairs.'[7] Possession of an identity book not only implies inclusion and a sense of identity as a South African, but, as migrant women explained, it also means access to benefits such as citizenship and/or documentation, guaranteeing them – among other things – an escape from poverty. It is interesting to note that, to these participants, the acquisition of an identity book did not mean being identified as a South African among their own people or country, but served only to secure identification by South African authorities so that they could access resources and services in the country (Landau 2008).

One of the participants, Jackie, goes to great pains to emphasise the irrelevance of love for her partner in her relationship, which she entered primarily to secure an identity book and thus ensure her livelihood and permanency in South Africa. In such cases, migrant women's accounts suggested that local men were conduits for acquisition of identity books and other resources associated with citizenship and extensive networks.

Studies that focus on heterosexual relationships involving exchanges tend to centre on young women, adolescent girls and non-migrant populations as well as sex workers. Some highlight single women, widows and divorcees as those mostly involved in transaction or exchange-based relationships (Chatterji *et al.* 2004). There is less focus generally on migrant women who cohabit for survival. However, one study that investigated marriage as a survival strategy – focused on local Zimbabwean women – found that whereas single women allowed men as intimate partners to move into their homes and live with them, they were expected to contribute towards rent, food and household chores equally. In this way, women had more power in determining the nature of the relationship they had with such men (Muzvidziwa 2001).

Although financial rewards, survival and the need to enhance status, especially among the young girls, are documented as main motivators of transactional relationships (Hunter 2002, Luke 2003, Longfield *et al.* 2002, Chatterji *et al.* 2004), in the context of migration in South Africa the need for legal documentation and, specifically, acquisition of a South African ID book was indicated by some of the participants in this study as the main motive for their relationships with local South African men. To use Brennan's (2004) argument while describing sex workers in Sosua who targeted foreign men because of the benefits their citizenship brings,[8] these migrant women employed innovative strategies to attain survival and protection in South Africa as a rational choice. They were thus not entirely passive victims who are exploited, trafficked or forced into sex work or some such relationship (Brennan 2004, Hunter 2002). Unlike the Zimbabwean women who cohabited with men but on their own terms and to their own advantage because of the resources they had (Muzvidziwa 2001), migrant women's agency was, however, limited to identification of this survival strategy and some of the benefits they got out of it. They were not able to use this agency in the direction and/or negotiation of the future of these relationships, as they were constrained by low relationship power and external contextual and immigration-related factors.

Although some women and girls engage in prostitution or transaction-based relationships, there is a tendency in some existing literature dealing with various forms of exchange-based relationships to portray women and girls as the pursuers of men to exchange sex for money and other resources, and the only beneficiaries. On the other hand, men or boys are depicted as merely providers of gifts, material and financial rewards, or as purchasers of sex and not beneficiaries of any sort. The benefits men sometimes derive from these relationships are rarely mentioned (see Meekers and Calves 1997, Muzvidziwa 2001, Luke 2003, Chatterji *et al.* 2004). However, even in a one-off transaction relationship between a sex worker and client, the client receives some sort of benefits. These and similar relationships involve a reciprocal exchange process. For example, whereas migrant women in this study were provided with food, shelter and finances by their partners, in addition to provision of various forms of intimacy, they were full-time housewives providing free labour in the household; such domestic work costed in monetary terms would be quite expensive in present-day South Africa. Drawing from social exchange theory, partners expect to give and receive something of value from the other (Baumeister and Vohs 2004, Sprecher 1998). Therefore we could deduce that migrant women's partners equally have an economic motive for engaging in relationships with undocumented migrant women. They might have interpreted the women's insecurity and other immigration-related disadvantages as the means to acquiring easy and cheap labour and intimacy. The fact that many of these men refused to fulfil their promises related to marriage and the provision of asylum seeker permits that their partners were mainly interested in shows the extent to which men's engagement in these relationships may have been motivated by exploitation of these women's current vulnerabilities created by the immigration context. However, popular discourses regarding such transactional relationships tend to pathologise the woman motivated by money as a prostitute or with loose morals, even though such a woman rarely sees herself as such (Hunter 2002); whilst the man with similar motives and benefiting from women's free labour and other forms of reciprocity is seen simply as a husband or boyfriend.

The benefits or outcomes of exchange relationships involving cohabitation may not be equal, as one party with more resources and power may stand to have an upper hand in influencing the direction of the relationship. This is reflected in this study, some of the participants reporting that they were constantly physically, sexually and emotionally abused by their partners. Participants explained that whenever they acted contrary to their partner's expectations, abuse and violence resulted. This could be read to mean that their partners, who were said to be the major contributors in the relationship, felt that migrant women owed them compliance in return for their substantial investment (food, shelter, and so forth) in them. Indeed a study conducted in the Eastern Cape also found that gender-based violence is common among men involved in such exchange-based relationships (Dunkle *et al.* 2007). This brings out a reversal in such transactional relationships in that they may not only consist of exchanges but may also be linked with issues like partners expectations, the use of power to demand compliance, and the subordination of the partner with low relationship power so as to maintain the relationship or achieve desired goals in the long run.

Women also spoke of such unequal power relations arising from their partners' privileged possession of financial, and especially valued legal, status (citizenship) which allowed such men decision-making power over them (Emerson 1981). Moreover, this functioned to silence women from reporting abuse. Caught in such situations, migrant women seem to have little relationship and decision-making power regarding various aspects of their life (Pulerwitz *et al.* 2000). This includes their sexuality and motherhood, as some were routinely coerced into unprotected sex, while two of the respondents were forced to abort pregnancies. The women explained that their partners cited that the children born would not be true South African and that they did not have the money to take care of extra 'mouths'. Besides this, xenophobic attitudes of police officials also acted as barriers and affected women's agency towards reporting intimate partner violence. Thus, although migrant women used these relationships to negotiate their livelihoods and permanency in South Africa, they were constrained by the immigration system, which placed them as undocumented immigrants, in a subordinate position relative to their partners. This challenges the assumed distinction between the state and the family and shows how the state contributes to so-called 'domestic' violence.

In relation to issues related to love in these exchange-based relationships, it is interesting to note that many of the participants drew on the mythical distinction between love and money and, because of their financial and legal documentation needs, emphasised their lack of love for their men. Jackie's narrative below, and others above, are examples of this discourse:

> He is about 61 and I am now 25 so you can see the difference. So it did not matter that he was old, I needed to live, I needed a solution. The fact that he was going to marry me, I was going to be solid here in South Africa. So it was a great deal because really love was not there to be honest with you, it was a matter of survival ... (Jackie, 25 years, single)

In the narratives it is as if the women were not expecting money exchanges to coexist in a love relationship, yet the two (money and love) are entangled and difficult to separate in relationships, as gifts and exchanges of various kinds serve as expressions of love (Smith 2009). These exchanges occur in all relationships, even in state-sanctioned heterosexual relationships (Palmary 2008b).

Some participants' idea of the split between love and money, however, was enhanced by biblical or religious teachings of love as unconditional and selfless. To them, love served as a foundation for a true marriage or cohabiting relationship, without which it was void. They dismissed the fact that people engage in relationships for a host of other reasons, including, status, companionship, economic security and information, without neccessarily being in love.

What is also striking is that most women eventually gave up on these loveless relationships, despite enormous difficulties associated with being undocumented, xenophobia and crime in general. This shows how powerful the love discourse is as a major factor in a relationship or cohabitation, and how much it meant to them. It also corroborates the argument that women are more likely to remain in relationships with less money where rich intimacy or love exists instead (Smith 2009).

Before most participants left their partners they had to put up with violence for some period of time. The section below looks at what made it possible for them to stay in such relationships, despite their knowledge that they should end them.

Negotiating intimate partner violence for survival

Normally, abused women are expected to seek help in cases of intimate partner violence (Gondolf and Fisher 1998), or leave abusive relationships. However, in situations where women have long-term strategies or goals to achieve before seeking help or ending such relationships, this may turn out differently. Thus, we need to rethink the question of why women stay, and ask rather what makes it possible for them to remain in or leave an abusive relationship. This section examines factors in these women's struggle's to guarantee their permanency in South Africa that constrained their ability to leave.

According to the migrant women in this study, besides anticipated or negative responses from service providers and the fear of deportation, reporting violence was likely to jeopardise migrant women's acquisition of a South African identity book or an asylum seeker permit and other basic needs, which they set as goals in their relationships. Agency for such women did not mean leaving an abusive relationship or putting up some form of resistance but rather meant fulfilling the set goals that motivated them to engage in these relationships in the first place. In spite of their sense that loveless relationships were inappropriate, remaining in these abusive relationships implied sacrificing or trading the self in the present for expected long-term future freedom and security from abuse, as well as other problems associated with being an undocumented immigrant in South Africa.

Related to this was the participant's fear of being shunned and blamed by family members, especially their parents, for coming back home with no money, these having assumed that the women were employed and that those who migrate usually gain better financial status. Thus, indirectly, the obligations placed on women, and the expectations of family members, tied them to their partners in expectation of gaining financial stability and/or continued financial support to remit home.

In addition to the above, the context in which intimate partner violence occured also seemed to influence how women perceived and responded to intimate partner violence. Similarly, Latta and Goodman (2005), in a study conducted among Haitian migrant women, argued that contextual factors influenced migrant women's tolerance of violence. In a context such as South Africa, the existence and reality (rather than imagined as Smith 1989 indicates) of high levels and different types of crime and violence, not only limited to sexual violence, functioned to limit their ability to leave. Indeed, acts of xenophobia from the general public and some officials (ranging from violent crimes, name calling, association with crime, police harassment, neglect and mistreatment) directed generally and/or specifically at migrants, highly corroborated migrant women's fears in South Africa that they are targets of violence (see Misago *et al.* 2009, Sigsworth *et al.* 2008, and Lefko-Everett 2007). Although women's fear of urban violence could also have been reinforced by the lack of a sense of belonging and powerlessness, as Smith (1989) argues, in South Africa or other contexts where urban crime is widespread and targeted at almost anyone these factors may not hold much weight. In the extracts below, women narrate their fear of public violence and how it affected and influenced their negotiation of intimate partner violence:

I lived four years crying, suffering, he would insult me everyday, and I would not go out. I have no other choice … I have no choice. I have no choice. But what can I do, I cannot be with other people I do not know, maybe they have other baggage I do not know … *This is my life. I have to keep with this man instead of being on the street.* I would rather be beaten, suffocated, abused than staying on the street until the right time comes. If I do not have a relationship with him, he cannot help me, I need basic needs for my school, food, transport, and he is the only one who can help me. (Eliana, 40 years, single)

He abused me most of the time, but what could I do really? I had no one, no money to cater for myself, I feared to be on my own, what if I was attacked in a strange place, who would take care of me? ... So the best way was silence ... I had to *seal my mouth in order to have a shelter and to remain safe* or else I would find myself on the street, where people here could even take advantage of me because am a foreigner ... since we are not wanted here ... So I thought to myself, this man might be bad but he keeps me safe from many dangers of the outside world. I vowed to bear with all until I found a suitable way to leave. (Rehema, 32 years, single)

The home is constructed as safer than elsewhere ('the street') yet according to literature it represents a paradox of safety for women as this is where they are routinely assaulted and killed (Pain 1997, Bondi and Rose 2003, Warrington 2001). An example from Rehema's narrative seems to emphasise such fear, but she ironically felt safer in the home than out of it. Staying at home was also employed as a strategy for avoiding public violence and xenophobia among women in a study that explored the gendered nature of xenophobia in South Africa (Sigsworth *et al.* 2008). Private homes may, however, not always be safe from public violence, as these too were targets for xenophobic violence in attacks in South Africa in May 2008.

In the narratives above, women also seem to view intimate partner violence within the home as tolerable as compared to public violence (see Eliana's narrative above), despite the difficulty related to controlling and/or predicting the severity and nature of violence that she would experience from her partner (Pain 1997). However, the women's long-term goals of acquiring an identity book and other survival needs could have influenced their choice, given that they may in one way or another have known the extent to which intimate partner violence affects women. Thus, to them, private violence was seen as preferable to inevitable public violence and the related problems they would face as homeless women. Women's preference for private over public violence, however, was not only influenced by these contextual factors, but combined with their low social economic status, lack of networks, poverty and undocumented status to increase feelings of powerlessness. Thus not only would their partners draw on above immigration-related disadvantages to abuse them, but also migrant women identified strategies of confinement to help them envisage ending the relationship when their status was secure.

Although the above participants blamed intimate partner violence on the social context, this sat alongside essentialist discourses where women noted they were weaker than men and made powerless by gender inequalities and contextual problems. This is evident in the narratives above, where women position themselves as vulnerable to intimate partner violence, unable to survive on their own or escape such abusive relationships. In constructing themselves as such, they seemed to see abuse as inevitable and presented themselves as entirely without agency. Here, they seem to draw on the discourse of global sisterhood of oppression of women that Mohanty criticizes as one which 'freezes them [women] into archetypal victims who defend themselves and men as subjects who perpetrate violence' (1988: 58). Such discourses of universal patriarchy work to disguise women's agency and limit their capacity to act in the face of violence. However, at some points in the narratives above and elsewhere, migrant women shifted identities to indicate that they were stronger and had future plans, including finding a job. This portrays them as active social agents in influencing the future of their lives, as Eliana puts it here: 'I am strong now because my eyes are open ... but throughout ... I am a strong girl fighting for life and grabbing life.' It would, however, seem that in managing competing discourses of migration and essential womanhood, migrant women present themselves with double identities of strong yet vulnerable, and at times as victims and/or active agents. The stronger and/or agent identity would first of all function to portray them as resilient strong women who do not give up easily despite the contextual and immigration related problems. Second, they also might have intended to use the notion of being vulnerable and helpless to justify why they took up cohabitation as a strategy for survival, given that as a means of livelihood it carries with it strong moral stigma among women in some societies. Finally, they may have had in mind the benefit vulnerability can provide, especially among service providers, who tend to target such categories of women for humanitarian and/or other assistance in South Africa.

Conclusion

This chapter has sought to contribute to the understanding of the interface of immigration policies, unequal power relations and contextual-based factors in shaping migrant women's experiences of and responses towards intimate partner violence as well as strategies they employed for survival in South Africa. Indirectly, the state functioned to fuel intimate partner violence among migrant women through policies related to immigration legislation that are aimed at policing and deporting undocumented migrants in South Africa and that limit access to some essential services in the absence of legal documentation. Migrant women's choice of cohabitation as a means of exchange for legal documentation and the resultant intimate partner violence attest to this.

Although such exchange-based cohabitation, motivated by a desire to secure legal documentation, could be equated to or has similarities with transactional relationships, the nature of migrant women's relationships is quite different, given that there was neither a predetermined mode of payment from both parties as normally articulated in transactional sex, nor were these short-term relationships but long-term stable cohabitation. In addition, although economic factors were a motive in migrant women's engagement in exchange-based relationships with local South African men, as they are in most transactional sex relationships, this was coupled with a combination of discriminatory immigration policies that influenced their choice of such a strategy. It is thus important to note that the transactional sex literature does not adequately explain migrant women's relationships and their motives for engaging with local men.

The discussion also shows that not only women benefit economically or otherwise from transaction-like relationships but men indirectly do so also, especially in a cohabitation relationship through reciprocity from their partners in terms of household chores that would otherwise need to be paid for, and other forms of intimacy. However, differing expectations and misuse of power in such relationships may at times result in violence in a bid to enforce compliance when one partner is more dependent than the other.

In addition to this, it is worth noting that some migrant women may not necessarily be drawn into relationships for love but with the aim of acquiring citizenship as a means of negotiating access to rights they are not accorded in the host state. However, the discourse of love as a foundation of a 'proper relationship' still remained an important aspect for these participants given that, with all the limitations associated with being undocumented and poor, migrant women typically still left relationships in which they had no love for their partners.

Finally, this chapter also highlights important aspects related to migrant women's agency, noting that this is contextually based. In responding to intimate partner violence for example, migrant women did not follow the normative recommended responses of reporting or leaving abusive relationships but instead identified strategies they felt worked for them given their vulnerabilities and needs at that time. However, this agency was also sometimes constrained by a combination of their undocumented status, contextual factors like xenophobia, low relationship power, and migrant women's own idealised notion of being vulnerable in the context of migration.

Notes

[1] This refers to foreign women in South Africa who have been given refugee or asylum status and those who are undocumented. Although the majority were from Zimbabwe, others were from Burundi, Rwanda, Kenya, Swaziland, Nigeria, Congo and Eritrea. Most were unemployed and with low levels of education.

[2] South African immigration law requires that undocumented persons (those who enter and/or live in the country without legal documents) are detected and deported if found in the country. It directs organs of state to ensure that beneficiaries of services provide proof of status or citizenship (Immigration Act, 2002).

[3] As at the third quarter of 2009; www.statssa.gov.za\keyindicators/keyindicators.asp.

[4] This is a section 22 permit that a person (foreigner seeking protection) is issued with while they await a decision on their application for asylum. It acknowledges that someone has lodged an asylum claim but does not mean they are granted refugee status.

[5] In the interviews women explained that they would leave their partners as soon as they got these documents from them and establish a life of their own. But in the short term they also needed the men to provide them with food, shelter and medical treatment for their daily survival, as well as money to remit home to their families.

6   Among the entitlements they expected were gainful employment that would ensure income and the ability to move back and forth to their home country with ease as compared to a situation when they are not allowed to return home if they had acquired a refugee or asylum seeker permit.

7   Statement by Dr Nkosazana Dlamini Zuma, Minister of Home Affairs, on the occasion of the Debate on the Budget for the Department of Home Affairs, National Assembly: Friday 26 June 2009.

8   These include moving with the foreign man to his country, acquisition of citizenship through marriage, and/or being able to secure access to European countries where women could find work if relationships did not work out.

CHAPTER 11

Re-housing trouble: post-disaster reconstruction and exclusionary strategies in Venezuela

Isabel Rodríguez Mora

Introduction

In December 1999 massive floods and mudslides affected Venezuela. Destruction of homes and massive displacement of population were amongst the most significant impacts of the disaster. In order to provide temporary refuge to those displaced, shelters were established throughout the country, while a variety of relief programmes were implemented to address their needs and demands. Psychosocial interventions figured prominently amongst the relief programmes for the victims of the disaster. These were implemented, by national and international organisations, in order to deal with the traumatic impact of the disaster, and were usually targeted at those deemed most vulnerable, such as children and women.

In this chapter I analyse how these psychosocial interventions engaged strategies of social containment and exclusion that operated at the intersection between class and gender, including how these worked to restore and reassert the social order that had been temporarily shattered by the disaster. For this analysis I have drawn from my participation as volunteer and researcher in a variety of psychosocial interventions following the disaster in Venezuela. In particular, I refer to UNICEF's intervention in the shelter established in Fuerte Tiuna, a military compound in the capital, Caracas. The operational coordinator of the project described it as providing children with a space of 'primary mental health attention, through the application of tools to facilitate their emotional and social recovery' (Martínez 2000, author's translation from original in Spanish). It was developed through play sessions that volunteers carried out with children two or three times a week and had the support of professional and military personnel of the Fort. At the time of the disaster, I was engaged in my PhD project (Rodríguez Mora 2003) focused on the disciplinary and political implications of psychosocial interventions in emergencies. The critical perspective that had framed my research became thus the background from which I, as researcher and co-intervener, was able to interrogate the practices and discourses that constituted interventions implemented in Venezuela.

I will examine how UNICEF's intervention, while following the 'humanitarian imperative' and its will of impartiality, was inevitably embedded in Venezuelan social and political dynamics. In this context, the psychological framework with its assumptions of a universal rational subject operated as a gendered disciplinary apparatus that promoted the invisibility of people's social exclusion, and later, with the introduction of a psychosocial component, supported their identification as the problem and their exclusion through a model of sanity based on rationality, hierarchy and order. Following this, re-housing those displaced became an opportunity for the restitution of the social distances that had been temporarily disrupted by the disaster.

Disaster in a divided society

On 15 December 1999 there occurred the biggest natural disaster in Venezuela's recent history. Following unusually intense and continuous rain, floods and mudslides caused thousands of deaths, widespread destruction and the massive displacement of people. The coastal state of Vargas, neighbouring the capital Caracas, was the most affected of all, and catastrophic damage was caused in the rest of the country (CEPAL and PNUD 2000).

The disaster coincided with the day set for a national referendum to approve the new Bolivarian Constitution, a crucial measure to consolidate and deepen the radical changes promoted by Hugo Chávez since his ascension to power, and signalled by rife uncertainty and intense social and political polarisation. Live TV and radio coverage of the events made the whole country an immediate witness of the victims' predicament, and within hours of the disaster massive acts of solidarity were displayed around the country.

While the general solidarity that immediately followed the disaster (with volunteers sometimes surpassing in number those sheltered in some refuges) placed a hiatus in the deep political divisions that shaped the country at the time, the polarisation significantly imprinted the rescue and relief operations and configured the disaster as a terrain where the political and social confrontation was to be played out.

The immediate homelessness of thousands of inhabitants of Vargas and Caracas, and their displacement to surrounding cities, were amongst the most significant impacts of the disaster. By 17 January there were 280 shelters nationally, populated by more than 70,000 people (CEPAL and PNUD 2000) not including those who had found refuge in the home of family and friends.

The differential impact of the disaster mapped onto the profound social divisions that configure Venezuelan society. Those in the shelters came from the most deprived areas of Vargas and Caracas, and had to rely on state provisions and the promise of a definitive resettlement in the future. Living in the shelters, however, entailed more than taking refuge in state-sponsored facilities: it placed those homeless (*damnificados*) in a position of policy availability that made them targets of relief and rehabilitation programmes from an array of institutions. Meanwhile, well-off people found temporary shelter with family or friends or rented new accommodation and remained – on account of the independence afforded by their means – outside the scope of relief agencies.

As Jodelet (2001) has pointed out, 'exclusion always induces a specific organisation of interpersonal or inter-group relationships of material or symbolic form' (53). The location in (and out) of shelters hence reflected the division of cities into *barrios* and *urbanizaciones* (urbanised areas of middle- and upper-class dwellers) that not only marks topological distances constitutive of the dynamics of exclusion/inclusion, but also functions to restrict people's access to well-being as well as their collective entitlement to public life (Rodríguez Mora 1996).

Shelters and the temporary breakdown of social distances

After the initial weeks of the disaster, and following Chávez's orders, all *damnificados* were transferred to military installations, where the soldier's quarters were vacated and adapted to receive them. These military shelters provided a specific form of visibility to people's poverty; produced an (albeit temporary) space of contact between the middle class and the affected population; and located those displaced under the institutional gaze and discipline of the military.

Despite constituting the condition of a majority of Venezuelans, poverty had remained segregated in social, economic and spatial terms. The distance that separates the wealthy and the poor in Venezuela can be estimated by the astonishment that people's poverty elicited in those in charge of their attention in the shelters. This character of the destitute as unknown (and what professionals saw as their anomie) emerged in the account of interveners: 'I have been a teacher since a long time ago, I mean, for 20 years [...] and I thought that I knew all possible levels of children [...] And when I arrived here, the first thing I said was "I didn't know these ones"' (Montes 2000, author's translation from original in Spanish).

For relief organisations, shelters provided accessible settings and a stable population for the implementation of a variety of projects, including psychosocial attention to children's trauma, health and education (although excluding housing, central for people's permanence in the shelter). At the same time, they turned the sheltered population into an immediate object of governmental policies regarding the disaster while placing them within a male-dominated fraternity-like institution organised through the exercise of mutual control and the competition for hierarchy. The direct impact of the presidential mandate (and corresponding military compliance) over those in shelters was revealed, for example, when following Chávez's impromptu initiative during a televised address to the nation, these were renamed as *dignificados* (the dignified ones) and this neologism was hence officially adopted in documents, identity cards and the daily talk of government officials.

I will discuss how under these conditions of contact with the sheltered population, psychosocial interventions deployed gender-based exclusionary strategies that re-established the social distances constitutive of Venezuelan society, concluding with the definite resettlement of *damnificados*.

Psychosocial interventions and the othering of the poor

Psychosocial interventions, aimed at dealing with the traumatic aftermath of the disaster, were considered an integral part of the relief effort. Universities, public and private institutions, and local and international NGOs took part, carrying out a variety of activities such as individual counselling, group debriefing and the gathering and systematisation of testimonies. In what follows, I will analyse how psychosocial interventions provided a framework within which people in shelters were 'othered' (Fine 1998), that is: were fixed by discourses and practices within stable categories that solidify social divisions in Venezuela. This 'othering', while embedded in the psy-disciplines, engaged with other gender-based strategies of social containment and exclusion that reproduce social order in Venezuela. Recourse to such discourses does not presuppose deliberate intentionality in the actions and words of participants, but assumes rather that they derive their significance and impact from the circumstances in which they are embedded so that their meanings and implication can be considered as surpassing the actor's own understanding of their acts (Kelly 2000).

Constructing the psychosocial subject

UNICEF's psychosocial intervention in Venezuela was implemented within two distinctive frames of references. Initially, a normative framework that drew upon a popularised version of PTSD (post-traumatic stress disorder) was employed to refer to objects, processes and subjects of the intervention in terms of the 'psychoaffective'. During this stage, UNICEF retained the trauma model, although rejected one-to-one treatment of children. This entailed asserting a causal-temporal relationship whereby the external destruction of the 'outside' social-physical world by the disaster translated as psychological disorder in the 'internal' psychological space of the individual children.

Presupposing that social reality and subjects constitute separate, stable and fixed entities abstracted from history, this representation of the 'psychoaffective' constructed a series of polarities (outside/inside; past/present; social/biological; rationality/emotionality) that while reproducing an individualistic notion of the rational or logocentric subject (Gergen 1990, Sampson 1989) tended to individualise and pathologise traumatised subjects. This subject, essentialised as a self-contained individual, became thus the basis for a psychological form of explanation and action that looks for 'underlying fixed qualities that operate independently of social relations' (Parker 1997: 293). The focus on universal trauma symptoms that seem to emerge from the disembodied minds of individual children and the attention to the individual trauma story constructed as a clinical case imply the existence of a fixed casual determinism underlying the notion of 'psychoaffective'.

These minds, focus of the intervention, were separated from (unspecified) bodies which have been left out of sight. Unbound from biology, this rational, stable, contained and public subject of the intervention is moulded on the masculine, which is, thus, universalised.

This understanding of the subject is furthered as well by focusing on children and displacing family and communities, described in the project as 'environmental factors' for their development (UNICEF n.d.). Supported by a tradition of psychology within which children's development is represented as their transition from biological to social beings, the selection of children – while asserting the opposition biological–social – would appear to recognise them as sites for the 'uncontaminated' expression of the traumatic impact. This biological identity (and the latent reference to the evolutionary within it) placed the possibility of social 'recovery' in 'rescuing' children from their families and in facilitating thereafter the unfolding of their 'natural' potential. Individual progress and social progress find here a single condition of possibility.

The division of instrumental and emotional work constitutes another way in which UNICEF's intervention is gendered. Women/mothers (assumed to be children's main carers) were assigned therapeutic roles to be exercised through different forms of play, while the public instrumental role was implicitly assigned to the male/father. Confined to traditional roles in the private and in relation to the care of children and family, women were fixed and homogenised and represented 'as natural creatures, beyond culture and society, compelled to remain in the private domestic sphere by their natural maternal instinct' (Rose 1999: 360).

'Empowerment', in this context, was constructed as the acquisition and development of competence in the promotion of children's well-being and family-support skills. Such positioning of women in a world of emotion that has been identified as stereotypically feminine entailed their devaluation *vis-à-vis* the (male) unitary rational subject and this issue is of significance in the positioning of psychological experts in the intervention, as will be discussed in the following sections.

A second stage of the intervention appeared to emerge following the contact of project personnel with people living in the shelter. In this context, a 'psychosocial' discourse was elaborated to account for the interaction between the traumatic impact of the disaster and the effects of long-standing poverty and exclusion of those in the shelter. The emergence of this 'psychosocial' component entailed a shift from children's interiority to their social condition and the inclusion of social experts and new group activities.

During this stage of the intervention, a new discourse describes the population as affected by 'regular emergencies' and 'structural crisis', which stood as oxymorons for the tension between the unexpected and the anticipated character of the disaster. Continuity between people's past and present was presented as provided by their condition of extreme poverty and destitution, which contradicted the traumatic rupture between past and present.

In the extremely polarised social and political situation of Venezuela, UNICEF's project in Fuerte Tiuna provided a context in which the discourse on trauma intersected with the one on social suffering and exclusion to produce categories and relations that justified the 'deservingness' (or not) of the affected population. These categories were not pre-existent to the interaction, but appeared as part of a discourse that simultaneously produced and enacted institutional relations (Burman 1996).

Critical references to the social dynamics of exclusion/inclusion can be found within this discourse on the 'psychosocial'. However, UNICEF's restricted scope of action, the demands for short-term projects with immediate results as well as the availability of those in the shelters (and the inaccessibility and invisibility of those outside) resulted in an understanding of poverty as a problem located within the poor. This identification between the source of the problem and the site of the problem constructed the issue of exclusion as pertaining solely to those in the pole of exclusion, rather than to Venezuelan society as a whole.

In so far as the fundamental marker for people's identity and location – their exclusion – remained fundamentally unchanged after the disaster, this discourse disputed the production of rupture associated with trauma. In contrast, such dislocation was vindicated in regards to the middle class, whose social position was constructed as truly worsened as a result of the disaster. Within this discourse, the *barrios* of Caracas were represented as the site of the structural crisis. Vargas – particularly its middle-class areas – was constructed as the site of the emergency. The traumatic rupture and displacement was presented as taking place between the urbanised Vargas (or the middle-class Caracas) and the destitution caused by the mudslides. On the other hand, as inhabitants of the *barrios* of Vargas and Caracas would have essentially remained located within the same exclusion, informality and poverty, no real rupture was recognised between their lives before and after the disaster.

In terms of psychological processes, the history of prolonged suffering amongst those living in shelters was described as placing a hiatus on the normative impact of the disaster as described by reference to trauma. The reference to *damnificados* as exceptional in comparison to the standards of the (white, rational, educated, male) middle class implied an homogenisation of the poor and, with it, the denial of the multiple power dynamics that are constitutive of their social positioning. This severance of those in shelters from the dynamics that placed them there spared interveners and (in general, the middle class) any challenge about their participation in the power dynamics, and thus left them free to practise a psychological discipline that has been 'scientifically' purified.

The sheltered population as problematic: some gender cues

The representation of the subjects and the notions at work at the core of the trauma theory implied a gendered construction of normality. The androcentric subject is at the core of the idealisation of the middle class striving to succeed within a life prefigured as linear continuity in the direction of progress. This identification of the middle class as the norm hence supported a theorisation and practice upon those in the shelters as exceptions to normal psychological processes and fostered a shift from the problematisation of the impact of the disaster to that of the sheltered population.

Women, in this framework, remained unspecified (and thus devalued) within the poor, massed amongst those whose continuous experience of powerlessness and oppression (although recognised) was granted a protective psychological role for those who suffer it. This understanding seemed to reflect what Lerner (1980) designated as the 'belief in a just world' according to which the more it is believed that a punishment inflicted upon subjects is strong and prolonged 'the less people are inclined to assess positively the victim' (in Jodelet 2001: 57).

People's behaviour was frequently explained by reference to the 'psychology of poverty', according to which poverty is not only a socio-economic condition but more fundamentally a 'culture' that constitutes a psychological problem. This culture, characterised by apathy, incapacity to postpone gratification, indifference towards the future and external locus of control is to be found 'in weak people, deficiently educated, untrained, ugly, always at the border of disease, clumsy and ethnically or culturally different' (Ardila 1990: 404).

While poverty and exclusion placed those in shelters as the quintessential collective – in the absence of a 'psychology of richness' – the shelter as a space of implementation imposed programmatic limits to theorisations and interventions in the structural. For interveners working solely with the population in the shelters, the term 'psychosocial' came thus to identify people in the shelter as bearers of an aggregate of 'psychological' and 'social' problems.

The problematisation of the sheltered population was also gendered through the reassertion of the public/private divide; the feminisation of the poor and the devaluation of women by their association with biology. Those in shelters were presented as passive and dependent subjects subordinated by a paternal relationship with the state/provider. The laziness, dependency and disorder of *damnificados* were contrasted with the diligence, initiative and determination of the middle class and the military. This opposition was particularly evident in press reports about the disaster in which images of people in shelters lying on mattresses – evidence of their unwillingness to contribute to their own well-being – were set against those of the middle class, generally portrayed in action, accompanied by stories attesting to their entrepreneurial character, industry and drive. In comments about people's responsibility for the reconstruction of their lives, a Red Cross representative likened them to children while highlighting the need to avert any expectation concerning the state as provider amongst those affected: '[We have to tell them] that not everything is going to come from father god [papa dios] the government, but that they have to generate or manage their contribution for the survival that awaits them' (Gómez 2000, author's translation from original in Spanish).

At the same time, the fast employment programme managed by the military tended to reinforce the traditional gender division of labour. A 'family salary' was paid – despite the difficulty of identifying traditional family units and the predominance of single-women headed households – and men were assigned odd jobs around the Fort while women were usually allocated to 'private' spaces in tasks such as the cooking and cleaning.

The location of the poor in the opposition rational/biological tended to feminise *damnificados*, who were described as driven by their sexual needs and desires and unable to show continence, which was presented as an exercise of the rational capacity over the instinctual. Such lack of control and discipline suggests their location in a lower evolutionary stage as compared to the middle class. As one key military personnel (see later) put it: 'I don't want to be catastrophic, but people live sort of ... in a very primitive state, with the exception of a few families, but most live like ... animals. They procreate, have reactions, fight for their territory, for the food, and they don't internalise really the situation' (Zerpa 2000a, author's translation from original in Spanish).

The mind/body polarity has at its core the association of the devalued term with the feminine and the exaltation of rationality and transcendence which are presented as masculine traits. According to Shildrik and Price (1999), this devaluation of the body and its association with 'unthinking physicality' marks another set of linkages: 'to black people, to working class people, to animals, and to slaves' (2).

In this way, the construction of the population as passive and impulsive, biological, childlike, deficiently evolved, dependent from a father-like state and displaced to a domestic space that has been devalued seems to invite regulation. At the same time, this need to control and discipline functions to erode people's autonomy while reinforcing their exclusion as citizens with a legitimate political voice and a warranted public space entitled to influence the actions and decision of the state and society at large.

Military, psychologists and the control of the unruly

Within shelters, people's daily lives were subjected to the permanent, direct and systematic surveillance by the military. Practitioners implementing UNICEF interventions adjusted their work to the structures and rules established in the shelters and were in permanent liaison with military personnel.

The practice of (mostly female) psychologists was identified as taking place through a mediatorial role that linked issues of femininity and authority. However, this hinge generated unstable positions to the extent that the 'scientific' credentials of psychologists were balanced against their femininity to promote a cure that required both rationality and order and access (and proximity) to the poor.

While this seems to have worked in the daily functioning of the intervention, the presence of Colonel Haydee Zerpa, a high-ranking military woman and head of the Psychology service of the army, appeared central in this negotiation of masculine and feminine traits:

> I say that it was a luck for us that we were in the team, not for being women, but because, besides [...] I was the only military woman that was there, besides the lieutenant, I think there weren't any more and we were both psychologists, and we could, being military, impose ourselves, let's put it this way, to the military, as with the [male] captain here [...] to enter with the part of psychology, because it's not easy, with the rigid thinking of the military, the discipline, to accept that we invaded them and we are going to put order, and let us do this. You know, there is always a certain resistance. [...] And that is not habitual, because they have a very vertical structure, like two plus two is four, and we were going to change the terms of things. (Zerpa 2000b, author's translation from the original in Spanish)

The viability of the intervention is thus presented as resulting from the engagement of the feminity of the (military) psychologist with the masculinity of the (non-psychologist) military, as through her role as interpreter of the *damnificados*' world and its presentation to the military in terms made possible by her positioning. At the same time, Colonel Zerpa established a maternal-like relationship with some children in the shelter, which was positively presented as a valued form of caring and the exercise of adult responsibility.

Zerpa's simultaneous condition as military, woman and psychologist provoked what Burman (1990) has described as a 'disjunction' between gender and professional status (11). Being highly ranked in the military placed her in a position of power and command over other military (men and women); meanwhile, her position as a woman and psychologist located her in a stereotypically feminine position, closer to the subordinated groups that constitute the *damnificados*.

Within UNICEF, psychologists were identified as functioning simultaneously as judges of normality and intermediaries between institutions and the sheltered population. This capacity to detect pathology and prescribe appropriate treatment was, for instance, identified by two children when I asked what the role of psychologist was:

> **Child 1**: To ask if one is sick, if a child is sick ...
> **Child 2:** If he has the head like a mango ...
> (Rodríguez Mora 2003, author's translation from the original in Spanish)

While being sick and suffering (mental) deformity (having 'the head like a mango') were identified as conditions meriting the intervention of psychologists, their mission was linked to the re-establishment of order and proper behaviour amongst children.

Interestingly, this ordering role of psychologists overlapped with the positioning of the military by some of UNICEF's project personnel, for whom the issue of order turned their participation into a relevant condition for the psychosocial processes mobilised by the intervention. So when I asked, 'What is the role of the military here?', I was told:

> A: They put order, put order in the shelters. They are also in the process of implementation, but more in the psychological area [...] It has been interesting, because the military have put order, and the order ... the imposed order is bad, isn't it? Because it's from above ... but the order that the military have imposed finally helps to solve problems of people living together ... well, we must incorporate all key actors and agree ... we need to know what mothers need, we need to know what are the needs of fathers, what are the needs of the family. People behave in one way individually and in other ways when they are in groups. (Rivero 2000, author's translation from original in Spanish)

In this way, hierarchical structure inherent to military order was incorporated into the model of sanity promoted by the intervention, which was thus placed in the intersection between the military order and a psychological rationality through which interventions are configured as projects of moral reforms on the standards of the middle class.

Re-housing and the restoration of social distances

A few days after the disaster, the government announced its intention of 'transforming adversity into opportunity' by using the relocation of those left homeless to diminish the urban congestion in Caracas, while 'reducing the population in marginal areas' (Salmerón and Chiappe 1999). Announcements about relocations to the axis Apure-Orinco, a band of territory in the South of Venezuela, were followed by news about the prospective establishment of new agricultural areas and small industrial developments that would provide employment for those relocated. The latter were urged to prepare for working the land, despite their urban origins and lack of farming knowledge or experience. Those plans were met with dismay by their intended beneficiaries. In a press report titled 'Dignified in perfect formation' people's rejection of the relocation plans is documented in the words of one of the *damnificados*: 'The military are very wrong if they believe that they are going to send us where they want and put us to plant black beans' (Aguirre 2000).

Meanwhile, middle-class groups were engaged in negotiations with the government to organise their resettlement within the capital, as reported in another journal:

> This group is made up by professionals and employees, who mostly maintain their jobs in Caracas, and therefore they can hardly be relocated in other areas of the country. In this case [...] an inventory is being made of existing houses to assess means of financial access which will have, in any case, exceptional norms. (Hernández 1999)

For government planners, re-housing *damnificados* entailed moving gender-neutral agents of production. This gender neutrality involved the denial of the private/body (marked as feminine) and the assertion of a (masculine) subject constructed as a disembodied rational agent. Nonetheless, such position as agents seems to contradict the way in which *damnificados* had been feminised as well as their exclusion from the decision-making processes surrounding the relocation.

The resettlement of those in shelters was carried out in an abrupt, imposed and mostly forced manner. Weisenfeld and Amaro (2007) described the process in these terms:

> The damnificados did not even have the chance to participate in choosing the region, settlement, type of housing or neighbours of their new habitat [...] and these settlements were, mostly, distant from their previous place of residence and were assigned to people that were strangers amongst them. (5)

The resettlements, located more than 500 km from Caracas (in the states of Barinas, Trujillo and Zulia) were organised as grids of between a hundred and two hundred identical houses, with a surface of less than forty-five square meters each; they were handed over unfinished and lacked water, a drainage system, toilets and kitchens. Resettlements were built in scarcely urbanised, isolated areas, distant from schools, hospital or police stations and very poorly served by transport. These developments can be considered a case of what Skotte (2004) has labelled 'tents in concrete': housing that reproduces shelters, condemning its population to a life of permanent impermanence. Those houses, decided and built without the participation of their intended inhabitants, stand in stark contrast to the *barrios* of origin of the population, which are the result of self-construction over many years in a process through which inhabitants 'construct and strengthen themselves and their communities and develop affective links with their environment and their neighbours' (Weisenfeld 1994: 4). In this context the building of a house is integral to the building of the community, which thus gives the house physical-environmental, psychological and social dimensions. In this sense, the houses, surrounding environment, communities and the houses' inhabitants constitute a single reality (García, Giuliani and Wiesenfeld 1994).

The relocation sites, in isolated locations 'out of sight, out of mind', furthered the stigmatisation and marginalisation of those displaced by the disaster. For those resettled there, the exclusion and discrimination from the local population as well as by governmental institutions was identified as the most negative experience since the disaster, as expressed by one of the resettled women: 'when you say you are a *damnificado*, the people from Barinas believe that one is a criminal, a thief' (Wiesenfeld and Amaro 2007: 14).

If houses can be considered as embodiments of social relationships, those in the resettlements signified the powerlessness of their inhabitants, their dislocation from the surrounding world and their distance from the instances of decision making, far from the promise of dignification and its implied sense of their personal and social worth.

Rather than creating a platform for social and personal recovery (Skotte 2004), these settlements reinforce the original social exclusion of their inhabitants and reproduce the social confinement and precariousness of the *barrio*. However, lacking participation and decision making, these new settlements have failed to stimulate the consolidation of homes; that is, of places of residence invested with affective and symbolic meaning, as their previous houses had for the *damnificados* (Weisenfeld and Amaro 2007).

The re-housing implemented by the government addressed a subject existing only in the public sphere and in relation to production sites. Houses, thus, were conceived of as residences for these (public) productive agents, rather than as sites for social relationships. This displacement of the private renders women invisible and constructs inhabitants of resettlements as unattached subjects, housing functioning as a form of dormitory for the workforce.

Conclusion

The massive displacement of inhabitants of the *barrios* in Vargas and Caracas as a result of the disaster in 1999 raised middle-class fears for what was considered their invasion of cities, their dislocation from the periphery and with it the disruption of the social arrangements that maintained deep structural divisions in Venezuela.

Under these circumstances, psychosocial interventions to address the trauma of those displaced became a context in which the exclusion was materially and symbolically reproduced, as the discourses and praxis of psychology intersected with the demands for order and hierarchy of the military shelters.

While several strategies of containment were displayed in the context of the psychosocial intervention, they had at their base the dismissal of those in shelters as true psychological victims of the disaster. The visibility afforded by the shelter of people's poverty and exclusion and the corresponding invisibility of the beneficiaries of such processes was reflected in discourse that 'othered' the poor. Furthermore, as those in the shelters did not fulfil the intervener's expectations regarding gratitude, austerity, docility and sexual constraint, psychological explanations were used to reassert the boundaries of exclusions that prescribe and proscribe spaces that those coming from '*barrios*' could legitimately occupy, that is, their place as subjects and citizens.

Gender-based strategies of exclusion resulting from the tensions and polarities that structure psychology (and that are integral to the patriarchal origins of the discipline) are reflected in the privileging of the (masculine) rational and the dismissal of the (feminine) irrational that is ascribed to the population.

While the government proclaimed its aim of 'dignifying' those displaced by the disaster, the resettlement in remote locations, away from their communities of origin, seemed to further their social and economic estrangement; rather than promoting community, this form of spatial separation reinforced 'the disintegration of locally grounded forms of togetherness and shared, communal living' (Bauman 1998: 21).

The indignity expressed by *damnificados* reflected their rejection of their newly established confinement and of the barriers it imposed for the emergence of a social solidarity that has as a fundamental condition effective contact with the other.

CHAPTER 12

An arm hanging in mid-air: a discussion on immigrant men and impossible relationships in Greece

Stavros N. Psaroudakis

Introduction

This text is part of my effort to articulate something on a subject that is very difficult even to define: the barriers constraining the interpersonal lives of male refugees and immigrants in Greece – a category to be specified further later on. My intention is to address the relationships rendered impossible for them, due to their devalued status. The term 'impossible' here is meant to confer a variety of meanings; impossible might mean 'very uncommon', 'severely deprecated', 'very hard to expect or imagine' – because of this deprecation – or 'unattainable' ... With this text, I attempt a first commentary, not a full discussion or argumentation, on the interpersonal side of the social relationship between male immigrants and Greeks. What follows is divided into two parts: in the first I discuss these issues stimulated by my personal work (as a psychologist working with asylum seekers) and extra-work (in the frame of the immigrant movement). My impasses and the aporias of producing a coherent account are outlined after this, and they are what lead me finally to discuss the issue indirectly, so to speak, on the basis of somebody else's account, a video artist's one. Excerpts of a dialogue with an artist who has created a relevant video piece are discussed in the second part.

12.1 Source: From the video Weast, *courtesy of Thanasis Tatavlalis*

Let me first try to become more clear with regard to my subject matter here: one could incontestably give gloomy answers to 'simple' questions such as: 'Is it common that male refugees date Greeks?', 'Are male refugees seen as desirable short- or long-time partners among the Greeks?', 'Do mixed relationships, no matter how frequently they occur, bring about xenophobic responses?', 'Is there discrimination, inequality in these matters?' There are indeed real issues which allow these questions to generate 'commonsensical' answers in the Greek context. However, the way to proceed further from them is not commonsensical at all. Indeed, the lack of a critical register to situate points on the complex reality addressed by questions such as the above is a crucial point I want to make with this text.

The 'new immigration' state of Greece, which received hundreds of thousands of Albanians and former USSR and Eastern bloc citizens in the 1990s, has seen in this decade the coming of many thousands of refugees from Afghanistan, Pakistan, Bangladesh, Iraq, the Maghreb and the sub-Saharan Africa countries. A great number of these 'new-comers', who consist disproportionately of young males, try to escape to Europe primarily from Western Greece ports. An equally great number of them, though, stay and try to survive the status of a '*sans papiers*' in Greece. At the time of writing (summer/autumn 2009) they have to resist and survive an extreme deterioration of immigration policies, and what seems a diffuse, reinvigorated anti-immigrant consensus. Even children and pregnant women from war-zones are being pushed-back ('*refouled*') to Turkey or detained in old military bases, which the Greek state wants to turn into refugee camps (see, for these, Human Rights Watch 2009). A new law, in effect since June 2009, makes it impossible for refugees to appeal against a rejection of their political asylum application (Amnesty International 2009). It also allows the deportation of any immigrant who is accused – not convicted – of committing a misdemeanour. What is more, para-state extreme-right groups have, rather, been allowed to cooperate with the police forces in the various operations of the 'cleansing' of Athens centre from undocumented immigrants (see Hellenic League of Human Rights 2009, for an overview of the immigrant repression in the summer of 2009 see Z-Magazine, 2009).

These changes for the worse consolidate the segregation lines I would like to discuss, but do not help me to locate my perspective on this text on any of the available registers of critique of this inhuman regime. Refugees and immigrants are to be found at the intersections of various forms of extreme precarity and devalued social positions. This also reflects the way they are perceived and treated interpersonally and sexually by the Greek majority. It is especially in these terms that discrimination – a term virtually absent in Greek public discourses – is so ubiquitous that it ends up unremarked upon and becomes naturalised. This diffuse status of discrimination is what makes some relationships deserve the title of 'impossible' but also what makes it difficult to discuss it in concrete terms.

Despite this difficulty, in this text I am not targeting some status of the invisibility of immigrants and their relationships that are condemned (I do not 'shed light' on things one just does not see or hear about). I believe what I point towards is a real discriminatory *absence* of relationships. This absence is striking for the ones willing to remark it, though – as an absence – it has the quality of something hard to spot and intangible, which is only betokened by furtive signs, non-conveyed desires and undemonstrated feelings, and is channelled into endless talks of frustrated ventures. The many difficulties male immigrants and refugees face in pursuing a full interpersonal and sexual life of their choice, no matter how they conceive this, is what inspires this text. My experience in the immigrant and anti-racist movement, and my discussions with immigrant friends and comrades, have made me see this as a solid reality, as a real issue. I am aware that the knowledge one can claim to have of little-spoken desires and unaccomplished relationships can only serve as the basis for fragile arguments and strange discussions. This is, knowingly, an odd text.

Small talk after the detention space: moments of silence and aporia

In my first attempt to write something on the issue, about a year ago, my departure point was the space of detention – all too emblematic for precarious immigration in Greece. In other words, my idea was to produce an account of my then-recent one-year-long NGO psychological work with young – 'unaccompanied minors' – refugees detained in the Thessaloniki police detention spaces (prison cells in police headquarters buildings). From my direct exchanges with young immigrants, no matter how scattered they were, I thought I could go on to discuss in more general terms the barriers young male immigrants have to overcome in Greece to enjoy fuller lives, along the lines of a critique of the poverty of integration discourses. This proved difficult, and I will not dwell on this much, but I will not omit it either.

A psychologist paying visits to detained immigrants was and still is an exceptional state of visibility and care for detainees in Greece, who are more often than not denied fundamental rights, such as legal assistance – access in that space was a privilege that my NGO had worked hard to win. That this was a privilege was one of the few certain things in that vague and more or less novel (in a Greek context) field of psychological work. I perceived this as an opportunity, and a kind of obligation to make the most of it for the young detainees who found themselves confined in those horrible premises.

Strangely enough, though, and importantly for this chapter, the part of the job I remember as the most disheartening one would always come after the detention space, so to speak. Time and time again during my visits the police personnel would inform me of some detainees who were 'likely to be released today', as they would have it; more to the point, availability on my part to accompany them during their first hours out might confirm or bring forward their release, which was still being negotiated and examined by police officers. After some paperwork had been signed, I would find myself 'out there', in the industrial area where the police headquarters are located, provisionally accompanying two, three, four or five 'unaccompanied minors' – males from Afghanistan and Iraq primarily in their teens (on the situation of 'unaccompanied minors' in Greece (see Human Rights Watch 2008).

Later, on the bus towards the city centre where the NGO's offices were located, I remember invariably thinking that the scenery should have a 'shock value' for the just-released detainees. I remember wondering what the young immigrants were thinking of it all. If any of them spoke any English or Greek, some words would be exchanged, smiles, some laughs also, brought on by the misunderstandings. The crowded bus context could be noisy or silent, but our strange dialogues would always attract attention.

But there were also moments of rupture in the discussions, when silence would fall for a split second and become telling. This often would be when some beautiful girl would get on or off the bus. The young immigrants would almost invariably catch a glimpse of her and cease talking. Following them, I would also do so. I believe the silence on both parts emanated from a common perception of what we were doing there: I had to play the NGO psychologist, who is more than willing to assist his 'beneficiaries' in taking care of their most urgent survival and travel needs and helping them to make the most difficult decisions on the basis of what they have been through. They in turn had to play the beneficiaries who, on the very moment of their release from prison, wanted chiefly to make the most of the privilege of having someone professional there to help them – extremely few detainees in Greece enjoy this right.

With all these issues to discuss, what was the use of me explaining to them that the possibility to hang out with Greeks – girls or boys – and have intimate relationships with them was very slight? How could I do so when this was not a right I could work towards safeguarding? What was the point of them discussing this with me? They already knew all this and the barriers they would meet. We both knew that these barriers were and would be crucial in shaping their lives. All these important issues, which might reasonably inform not only discussion between adolescents and a psy-expert, but any discussion of human solidarity and care, were silenced, and had a self-explainable quality.

In attempting to elaborate on this working experience of mine with the young asylum seekers from a perspective that would not neglect these moments of silence and those that remained untold, but assign them the importance and gravity they had for us when we experienced them, I became aware of how hard it is to integrate such a view on desire and sexuality in any of the discussions available on the Greek immigration regime.

Aporias of *mainstream immigration discourses* vis-à-vis *male immigrants' desires*

Integration politics and discourses do not allow much space for these matters – nor much ground for researchers to build on. A recent study (Baldwin-Edwards 2009) on 'indices of integration' in Athens (where more than 50 per cent of all immigrants in Greece reside), dealt briefly, at the end of the chapter on 'social and cultural integration', with the issue of marriages among Greeks and Albanians, only to state that there are no available data. If there are no data on the marriages of Greeks with Albanians, whom the official mass media discourse portrays as the community 'best integrated' in Greece,[1] one can know very few things about the more recent mass of immigrants and refugees from Afghanistan, Pakistan, Bangladesh, Somalia, Nigeria – and anticipate even less.

'Sexual freedom' is one of the fundamental liberties protected by Greek law, and formally this applies to immigrants and refugees in the Greek territory. Greece's record is very poor in the 'freedom from' clauses (rape, forced prostitution etc.; concerning this see, for instance, Amnesty International 2007). Still, what might be somehow more relevant for my discussion here is that the 'free to' dimensions of sexual freedom (the freedom one has to have the sexual life one desires rather than just be spared the attentions of whoever one detests) are almost totally hollow, given the derogatory, provisional and precarious socio-economic positions that both male and female 'new-comers' *sans papiers* are institutionally condemned to. Laws and legalistic discourses of sexual freedom, of course, are not expected to conceive this cruel lack of choice and self-fulfilment, not even along the lines of the freedom from discrimination (see, for instance, The European Commission against Racism and Intolerance [ECRI] 2009 for how these issues are totally absent).

The issue is that one may also spot this lack in the pro-immigrant discourses which are expected to address them, so that mainstream public discourses could be counter-acted. In the latter, migrant 'masculinities' oscillate within the all-too-familiar polarity – from the female sexual politics and the articulation of masculinities in other contexts – of *normalised absence* and *pathologised presence* (a term coined by Phoenix 1987, discussed in Burman 2008 and Burman and Chantler 2005). Schematically put, male immigrants in Greece do *not* enter mainstream discourses as sexual persons in their own right: they either fall short of the stereotypes of desirability (they are socially rendered asexual) and thus remain sexually invisible; or they are treated as one-dimensionally, excessively or pathologically sexual (as in the case of male prostitutes or sex-crime offenders). In the case of male workers from Afghanistan, Bangladesh, Pakistan or India, one might here recognise a local variant of the sexualisation of racism that Gargi Bhattacharyya writes of in *Dangerous Brown Men* (2008): 'a different sexualisation from that of the mythically phallic black man' (21), a process which is much more of a disciplinary asexualisation.[2]

In all cases, this polarity stands for a calculated *terra incognita* within and around immigrant men's lives in Greece; there is a constant discursive policing of (in)visibility and boundaries in effect around 'mixed' relationships and marriages, marginal family formations, sexual frustration, loneliness, queer sexualities, devalued sexual and partnership practices, fantasies. Those issues are selectively unaddressed by discourses from both the Right and the Left. Consideration of the chances male immigrants have to enjoy full interpersonal, family, erotic, sexual lives in Greece is either anathema or relegated to a question of luxury (as issues the society 'is not ready to discuss' broadly), and, by remaining unaddressed, they are also deemed in effect unthinkable. Thus, these aspects of immigrant life become *in absentio* discursively and socially fully regularised, which means scored with almost insurmountable lines of segregation and forbidden relations (even in ideological terms 'diversity' is not really 'celebrated' in Greece).

To summarise so far, even 'centre-right' newspapers can critically point out that in Greece, '[I]n every sphere, there is a sense that it's not really urgent to solve migrants' problems' ('Are Greeks Racist?' 2009). The gross lack of any facilitative basic institutional regime and the adverse social milieu male immigrants and refugees of the new immigration 'tide' have to overcome to pursue a fulfilling interpersonal or sexual life falls certainly into a broadly shared blind spot, to say the least.

A discussion with Thanasis Tatavlalis on the Weast *video: context and background*

Given the lack of a frame to situate my thoughts and experiences on these questions, it would be very difficult for me to come up with a coherent account of this voiceless sphere of male immigrant life. So I have adopted a different take on the issue, elaborating on someone else's 'coherent account', so to speak. Though this does

12.2 Source: From the video Weast, *courtesy of Thanasis Tatavlalis*

not include direct testimonies of immigrants, as said, everything I write here is also the product of many discussions with my immigrant friends and comrades. I recorded a short interview – or rather a dialogue – with the director of a short digital film I came across through my research on new media artists in Greece – which is my current work. The video entitled *Weast*[3] features in an unsettling way much of what I would like to address.[4]

This approach – the interview – is obviously much more indirect and mediated than other ways of addressing and researching the issue. Furthermore, the fact that I draw so much from a video art piece to discuss a social relationship can certainly drift me towards the treacherous grounds of aesthetising the social relationship(s) involved. This is reinforced by the fairy-tale-like elementary plot, which is, however, what renders the video scathing or violent, in the ways discussed in the interview. I have to admit this danger, and only state that, of course, a short film/video art piece, as an allegorical 'slice' of what looks like an 'impossible' relationship for newcomer male immigrants in Greece, can instigate, but not substitute for, processes of social critique and argumentation on the social conditions of this 'impossibility'.

Furthermore, although there is no simplistic moral in the video, or my approach, a further major risk lies in providing one more account that boils down (even with its political incorrectness) to a sympathetic message for the problems immigrants 'have', problems that should be somehow administered (for a discussion see Marvakis, Parsanoglou and Tsianos 2006). I have to recognise this as a necessary risk: what I try to do here is to problematise a social (non-) relationship, not to frame it as a problem. On the contrary, my aim is to show the poverty of regulation discourses.

The fact that immigrants from Pakistan, Bangladesh and Afghanistan gathered in the centre of Athens' 'quasi ghetto' (which for a good part is cheap and convenient for those seeking small, provisional, legal or illegal ways to earn a living until they find a way out of Greece) clearly created a novel *double visibility* of immigration: the double visibility of skin-colour difference and that of the concentrated presence/residence within or in the proximity of traditional urban zones of power, consumption and tourism. These characteristics differentiate to some extent the new immigrants from those, mostly Albanians, USSR Greek 'repatriates' or Bulgarians, who came in the previous two decades and sooner or later after their arrival dispersed in residential urban or rural areas. What is of interest here is that recent immigration has made for a new 'surface' of difference and Otherness, which seems easier to represent – or exploit – with artistic means, and this is eagerly done by young artists or amateurs involved in anti-racist politics.

Thanasis Tatavlalis, my conversational partner and director of *Weast*, is a 28-year-old well-off young Greek artist. Thanasis has studied, in his own words, 'incompletely various stuff', including cinema. He has worked abroad as a crew member in film productions. He has done six short films, and a documentary. He has also done painting, music and sculpture.

I will give here a basic story line of the video in question, to contextualise the questions of the discussion: a young Greek woman dressed like a strange *femme fatale* meets in the street a Bangladeshi immigrant, and they start walking together. They stop by a street vendor and she buys him a pair of old-fashioned sneakers, which he wears immediately. They keep walking and she gives him a funny, shiny suit to wear. They talk of something (the video is silent/without sound), she hugs him by the shoulder. His new shoes start to fall apart. He throws them away.

What follows is the interview.

A discussion with Thanasis Tatavlalis[5] (my interventions are in italics)

What has been your concept and your intention in making this video?

I had no intention of making an immigration-related video, although the school I had been attending recently was at Omonoia square, and there I could observe many people among the 'dead-stock', many immigrants among them … I do not mean this in a moralistic sense; whatever one thinks about it, I think that there are people among the 'dead-stock' in the centre of Athens, people in very difficult situations, with no one to help or speak to them […] My idea precedes the big fuss of the recent period about these people [immigrants] in the squares and the streets … The video is not about these people while they are making the news […]

What about the person that appeared in your video?

He was the tenth one I approached, and the only one who
accepted my suggestion and cooperated until the end. His
name is Dulal, he is Bangladeshi. I would promise everyone
I met 50 Euros for his participation. [...] He was the only
one who listened to the end and agreed. I do not believe he
did it for the money. Although I cannot claim to have got to
know him as a person, he was strangely available. And in
the end, I had to persuade him to accept the money [...]

*So, you find Dulal ... tell me about his 'strange availability',
as you termed it before ...*

He was very mellow ... He told me he spoke Greek, but
after that he kept nodding without speaking. When we
started shooting, I understood that he did not speak Greek
at all; at some points he missed completely my instruction;
then, at other points, he seemed to understand perfectly
well. One more thing was that he did not at all insist on the
money after the shooting was over – he had not asked for
the money in advance. Not that he did not want the money,
but he was not in a hurry to take it, so to speak ... When I
mentioned the money, he was more like 'do not rush things,
let's first have the job done right'. I don't know if he did it
for money, or for art, but I think he understood or found
intriguing the subject and the way we treated him ...

*Do you think that he thought there was a positive message
for immigrants?*

I could tell you yes, or at least this is what I would like to be
the case ... At any case, his strange availability made it hard
for me to understand what he was thinking. He might just
as well have liked Yuli, he might have just been attracted
by her.

*Yuli appears in the video as a beautiful blonde young
woman; she seemed as a kind of a young femme fatale, a
theatrical version of female sexual stereotypes, with the
stockings, the red high heels, austere makeup ... And then*

there was some kind of eroticism in the way the interaction was set and in the way the whole thing developed ... The scenario brings together those two people, plus the illusory atmosphere ...

[...] I am not sure if Dulal had perfectly understood in the beginning what he was supposed to do and who he was supposed to interact with. The other woman in the crew – also a beautiful young woman – exchanged telephone numbers with Dulal. But he did not try to contact her after the shooting, and neither did he respond to her calls. Actually he did not answer my calls as well and this is why we cannot find him now [to discuss the film's score, which could be a song of Dulal's choice]. I mean, perhaps he found intriguing and alluring the possibility of meeting, interacting, getting to know a woman like Yuli in the beginning, but after he understood that this was a strictly professional thing he held back, he did not seek any further contact...

This is also a perspective, I mean there is a widespread image of the immigrant in the centre of Athens at least, as lonely or isolated from the Greeks, and this is even more so in the case of immigrants from Pakistan or Bangladesh, where skin colour and perceived appearance differences do have an effect of segregation ...

I think that in Greece there is about 80 per cent male migration from these countries and this makes it inevitable that many of these male immigrants will seek or would like to relate with Greek women ... But it seems that this is something difficult and rare; I actually have not seen people from those countries, to the extent I can recognise them as such from their physical features, walking in the street with the company of some Greek girl ...

Yes, I think this is the case, there is this discrepancy between the sexes of people coming to Greece, though it is hard to know exactly, since of course many of them are 'undocumented'. What I meant with immigrants being solitary is that they may have relatives here, or friends and people from their region in their country of origin, and hang

12.3 Source: From the video Weast, *courtesy of Thanasis Tatavlalis*

out with them, but in terms of sexual relationships, I do not know, I can remember an Eleftherotypia[6] *article on the visits immigrants from Pakistan pay* en masse *every Sunday to prostitutes in the areas of Athens where the brothels are* ...

Yes, Metaxourgeio, Fylis ...

Yes, so I am asking if you think that the interaction and hanging out together with a Greek woman was among Dulal's motives for participating in the movie, and if in some sense the fact that in the process it became clear to him that this would be a 'professional' and ephemeral thing made him feel somehow fooled or betrayed ... perhaps I am going too far with all this speculation ...?

Well, I can only tell you that his attitude after the shooting was uniquely grateful, indebted, not for the money, but for the company, but this contradicts somehow with the fact that he did not respond to our calls, he did not cooperate further [...]

In any case, due to the language barriers, or due to the fact that this was a weird or unexpected situation, there was a kind of feeling of implicit and explicit exchange, of giving and taking ...

Yes, there was such a feeling ....

I was thinking how this situation, this encounter, between Dulal, an immigrant from Bangladesh, and Yuli, could have happened in real life. I mean, since it is Yuli who approaches Dulal in the movie, why would she do that, with what intentions of interpersonal relating, so to speak? I have already regarded the possibility of him approaching her as very hard to imagine ...

Yes, I agree completely ...

So ... in today's Greece, Yuli, as a caricature or an exaggerated image of a 'sexy', 'desirable' Greek woman approaching a Bangladeshi immigrant worker, [can] only [be] imagined as seeking 'selfishly' some new interpersonal or sexual experience. The violence of the video in my opinion lies in that it exposes how many – other – forms of relationships are unimaginable, to the point that the encounter itself seems impossible, a fairy-tale ...

I have thought about this and I have done some research and observations ... Young males from Bangladesh and Pakistan, a great number of them, earn a living by working as male prostitutes in Athens. They are preferred, I think, by older Greek men for their 'exotic' colour of skin ... I do not know of any women picking boys and young men for the same reason ... I think it is highly improbable that Greek women do this with boys and men from these countries ... On the other hand, I know that Yuli, who is a conscious person, so to speak, would seek to talk and hang out with Dulal for instance, even out of the context of any project. Perhaps many Greek women would do this as well, for humanistic reasons, to put it this way, I do not know, stop an immigrant in the street and talk, walk with him. But I guess they are reluctant to do this, since they think, perhaps reasonably, that something of a non-mutual, asymmetrical interest will develop; in other words, that they would then have to deal with some persistence on his part, him being enamoured, and perhaps to refute his desire, which is very likely that he will develop, given the scarce chances of immigrants from these countries to date Greek girls. In some other context, in some company of people, for instance, I am sure that many Greek girls would of course be very much interested to learn about the life of any immigrant and refugee, but that's another thing, isn't it? I think all these describe some common perceptions, lines of reasoning and ways of relating. I should also tell you that my idea of direction was that Yuli should behave in a strict, aloof and authoritative manner towards Dulal, and the idea behind her dress and makeup was to confer this kind of attitude. But she failed to do so, she looks caring and really interested in what Dulal tells her.

Yes, despite the fact that the suit for instance she gave him is rather embarrassing, it looks like she cares for him, even if in some 'twisted' way. But these moments perhaps attenuate the feeling one gets, or I got, of the great gap, the wall between the people and their worlds. And the oddness of the encounter. In some sense, it is what makes it not just fictional but mythical ...

I agree with you, and I am thinking of keeping all these images, where Yuli seems caring, in the final cut. There is also a moment where Yuli hugs Dulal's shoulders for a while, while walking. After some moments, I asked Dulal to take his suit off, but he did not understand my instruction, and he raised his arm and tried to hug her as well; upon seeing this I told him not to, so his arm hung in mid-air for some time, until he put it back in his pocket. This mistake of direction is perhaps what the whole video is about.

Conclusion

My interest in Tatavlalis' film rests exactly on the fact that it is a video I can easily assume would be perceived as disturbing by most of the Greek public. It is an anti-racist film, though it risks not looking like one, since seemingly it does not 'celebrate diversity' or 'respect'. For the most part the refugee protagonist is presented in an apparently humiliating way and Tatavlalis told me that he met with some angry reactions from some bystanders for that while shooting, who were angry about what seemed to be 'mistreatment of an immigrant' (Thanasis thought of these reactions as a positive index of social sensibilities in the Greek metropolis – though we both agreed that one should examine it also in the frame of them). *Weast* is scathing, I believe, exactly because, despite this 'humiliation', it still looks like a utopian anti-racist video for the Greek context. Somehow, for the viewer, the conditions of the encounter between Dulal and Yuli are, I think, easily put in parenthesis, and what is celebrated is their relationship. What it all boils down to is the encounter and the attitudes of the persons involved: Dulal's acting, and the whole atmosphere, in the end make him appear absolutely dignified: he looks like someone who has won for himself company, confidence and visibility without caring much for people's reactions and without negotiating anything in return for that. Yuli, on the other hand, looks equally 'conspiring' against naturalised invisibility and segregation. In the end, my positive apprehension of the film lies mainly in my idea that, if presented to some average neighbourhood Greek audience – in some of the public screenings solidarity groups do, for instance – it could put clichéd argumentations out of place and move them productively one step further.

Apart from the discussion with Thanasis, however, the discussion on the video, as much as my overall treatment of the issue in this odd text, has, I believe, made clear that one can be left with more impossibilities than possibilities while trying to discuss a solid barrier. At this point, my contribution can only be a commentary. There are of course fundamental assumptions in this text that will have to be inconclusively dealt with in this brief discussion.

My topic here was male immigrants and refugees as people who want or would like to have relationships with Greeks, but who trip up on or founder between settled dividing lines and deprecations. The situation with immigrant and refugee women is a sad reality of sexual stereotyping, violence and devaluation, which is both similar and different to that of men. The socio-economic status of the refugee or immigrant intersects with the regimes of racialised, aged and gendered relationships in the Greek context and within immigrant networks of communities, and here I have only attempted to comment on some consequences of young men's complex polyhedron of social devaluation.

Immigrant men's potentials for self-determined interpersonal and sexual and erotic lives depend on and intersect with sexual 'orientation', and my apparent focus on heterosexual relationships of course imposes limitations on the range of my account. My aim here was to indicate or register one of the many 'impossible' gendered relationships for immigrants and refugees in the Greek context. What might be also said with certainty is that gay, lesbian and queer desires and identities amplify these dividing lines, given that homophobia is a highly and openly tolerated attitude in Greece, despite the existence of an active LGBQT movement and a rich 'gay scene' in Athens.[7] The points I want to make here revolves mainly around the 'possible' desires and the 'impossible' bonds between immigrant men and Greek women, and I gained momentum for writing this text from the video which deals with such a relationship. In all, I had to both observe and assume heterosexual desires on the side of male immigrants and refugees, in order to render concrete the dividing lines segregating immigrant sexual desire, and not slide into abstractions. Still, I believe that the limits on which the desire and potential for relationships of immigrants and refugees, irrespective of their sexual orientations, crash against have a common source. This is, of course, the globally devalued status of immigrants and refugees. In this sense I think this commentary on impossibilities also carries fundamental relevance for the homoerotic and queer side of immigrant masculinities as well, although it does not address them directly.

I have tried to expose through different angles some complex, as much as harsh, restrictions which are produced by and affect Greek society by and large, and which for the time being seem solid and insurmountable. I have to conclude with what has been my intention and political emotion, so to speak, while writing this text in the summer of 2009, a summer of repression. If some months or a year ago it made sense to join the struggle for 'integration' in the sense of less dividing lines, the rise of a wide anti-immigrant consensus really made it imperative to note that these dividing lines should not be there and that they have cruel effects on real people.

Notes

1   A kind of reversal in discriminatory discourses has been clearly taking place lately in Greece: the until-recently vilified Albanians – 50 per cent of all immigrants in Greece – appear in public, mass media, discourses now as the 'good', integrated immigrants. 'Superfluous' Muslims from Asia and Africa are now pointed to as 'the problem', among them Pakistanis as well, who have been for years the favourite examples of 'good immigrants'.

2   Bhattacharyya writes:

> The proclamation of openness and innovation is an important element of how advanced capitalism bills itself in the War on Terror. For this reason, the deployment of a disciplinary sexualisation cannot easily be reduced to ideas of heterosexual citizenship. In an era where enemies of the West are portrayed as lacking the ability to gain pleasure from even the most straightforward of heterosexual relations, western culture is presented as tolerant and attentive to more diverse methods of showing love and experiencing pleasure. The alleged sexual dysfunction that is attributed to extremists and terrorists becomes contrasted with the supposedly healthy attitude to sexuality that characterises free societies.

Bhattacharyya's account refers to a different ideological matrix than the one in which I believe immigrant asexualisation is inscribed in Greece. Sexualised racism in Greece cannot and does not need to use the War on Terror ideology, whose pervasion of Greek society was rather limited anyway. However, homologies do exist, since of course the war on illegal immigration and anti-immigrant ideologies of all sorts have been, in Greece as well, legitimised by ideas of cultural inferiority in terms of gender-relations 'backwardness' as well. What is more, I draw a parallel with Bhattacharyya's argument on the non-exclusively heterosexual reach of this process in the discussion part of this text.

3   The video participated at the local – Thessaloniki – AZA short film festival (September, 2009) http://www.azafestival.com/.

4   The interview transcript includes many points of Thanasis' ideas on the artistic side of the video, as well as on the conditions of making it etc. Due to length limitations I had to omit them, and keep only the parts that are relevant for this discussion.

5   The interview with Thanasis Tatavlalis was conducted in June 2009. We did of course talk in Greek, and this is my translation of excerpts of the discussion. For this chapter I also tried to interview the people acting in the video, Yuli Tassiou and Dulal. As explained in the interview, Thanasis lost contact with Dulal – and he did not ask his full name. I managed to conduct a short interview through email with Yuli, but it was difficult to meet her in person, for during the summer period she tours around Greece with a theatre company. Since the two interviews were clearly incommensurate in terms of the time that my conversants could afford to elaborate on their ideas, I decided not to include her account in this text. Of course, the absence of her and Dulal's accounts compromises my account severely – but I hope the interview is still interesting and useful for the reasons I describe in the main body of text.

6   'Eleftherotypia' (Freedom of Press) is a special case of 'progressive' newspaper in Greece, being social-democratic in its politics, voicing liberal and at times 'radical' perspectives in most human-rights/minorities issues, and adopting 'patriotic' positions and populist attitudes at the same time.

7   Greek law is severely discriminatory against LGBQT rights; for a discussion in English by a lesbian advocacy group see http://www.sapphogr.net/dikaiwma/eg/index.html.

Bibliography

(In Greek publications authors' names have been transliterated and the titles have been translated into English.)

Abu-Lughod, L. (1990), 'The romance of resistance: tracing transformations of power through Bedouin women', *American Ethnologist*, vol. 17, no. 1: 41–55.

Aguirre, M. (2001), 'Dignified in perfect formation', *El Universal*, 23 January.

Agustín, L. (2005), 'At home on the street: questioning the desire to help and save', in E. Bernstein and L. Schaffner (eds), *Regulating Sex: The Politics of Intimacy and Identity*, Routledge, New York.

Ahearn, L. (2001), 'Language and agency', *Annual Review of Anthropology*, vol. 30: 109–37.

Ahmed, S. (1999), 'Home and away: narratives of migration and estrangement', *International Journal of Cultural Studies*, vol. 2, no. 3: 329–47.

Ahmed, S. (2002), 'Affective economies', keynote presentation at Lancaster University, September.

Allen, H. (1987), *Justice Unbalanced: Gender, Psychiatry and Judicial Decisions*, Open University Press, Milton Keynes.

Althaus, F. A. (1997), 'Female circumcision: rite of passage or violation of rights?', *International Family Planning Perspectives*, vol. 23, no. 3: 130–3.

Amnesty International (2007), *Greece: Uphold the Rights of Women and Girls Trafficked for Sexual Exploitation*, Public Statement of 12 June, available at www.amnesty.org/en/library/info/EUR25/002/2007.

Amnesty International (2009), *Greece: Proposed Changes to Asylum Procedures Flagrantly Violate International Law*, Public Statement of 15 May 2009, www.amnestyusa.org/document.php?id=ENGEU R250052009&lang=e.

Andall, J. (ed.) (2003), *Gender and Ethnicity in Contemporary Europe*, Berg, Oxford.

Anderson, B. (2000), *Doing the Dirty Work? The Global Politics of Domestic Labour*, Zed Books, New York.

Anderson, B. and A. Phizacklea (1997), *Migrant Domestic Workers. A European Perspective*. Report for the Equal Opportunities Unit, DGV, Commission of the European Communities.

Anderson, B. and J. O'Connell Davidson (2003), *Is Trafficking in Human Beings Demand Driven? A Multi-Country Pilot Study*, International Organization for Migration, Geneva.

Andrews, M., S. Sclater, C. Squire and M. Tamboukou (2000), *Lines of Narrative: Psychosocial Perspectives*, Routledge, London.

Anthias, F. and G. Lazarides (eds) (2000), *Women on the Move: Gender and Migration in Southern Europe*, Berg, Oxford.

Anthias, F. and N. Yuval-Davis (1989), *Woman – Nation – State*, Macmillan, London.

Anthias, F. and N. Yuval-Davis (1992), *Racialized Boundaries: Race, Gender, Nation, Colour and Class in the Antiracist Struggle*, Routledge, London and New York.

Ardila, R. (1990), 'Psicologia social de la pobreza', in J. Whittaker (ed.), *La psicología social en el mundo de hoy*, Trillas, Mexico.

Are Greeks Racist? (2009), *Editorial Athens Plus*, 25 September.

Arendt, H. (1973), *The Origins of Totalitarianism*, Harcourt Brace, New York.

Arnfred, S. (2005), *Re-thinking Sexuality in Africa*, Nordiska Afrikainstitutet, Uppsala.

Arnott, J. (2004), 'SWEAT submission to the South African Law Reform Commission on Trafficking Legislation', www.sweat.org.za/index. php?option=com_content&task=view&id=62&Itemid=28.

Aromaa, K. (2005), 'Trafficking in human beings: uniform definitions for better measuring and for effective counter-measures', paper presented at the ISPAC *International Conference on Measuring Human Trafficking – Complexities and Pitfalls*, Courmayeur, Mont Blanc, Italy, 2–4 December.

Bakare-Yusuf, B. (2003), 'Beyond determinism: the phenomenology of African female existence', *Feminist Africa: Changing Cultures*, vol. 2.

Baldwin-Edwards, E. (2009), *Integration of Immigrants in Athens: Indices of Development and Statistics*, www.mmo.gr/pdf/publications/ mmo_working_papers/Migrants_in_Greece_Report_Grk.pdf.

Batsleer, J., E. Burman *et al.* (2002), *Domestic Violence and Minoritisation: Supporting Women to Independence,* Manchester, Women's Studies Centre and Manchester Metropolitan University, Manchester.

Bauman, Z. (1998), *Globalization: The Human Consequences*, Polity, Cambridge.

Baumeister, R. F. and K. D. Vohs (2004), 'Sexual economics: sex as female resource for social exchange in heterosexual interactions', *Personality and Social Psychology Review*, vol. 8, no. 4: 339–63.

Bennett, C. (2008), *Relocation, Relocation: The Impact of Internal Relocation on Women Asylum Seekers*, Asylum Aid, London.

Berger, J. (1980), *About Looking*, Writers and Readers Publishing Cooperative Limited, London.

Bernstein, E. and L. Schaffner (eds) (2005), *Regulating Sex: The Politics of Intimacy and Identity*, Routledge, New York.

Bhabha, H. (1994 [2004]), *The Location of Culture*, Routledge, London.

Bhabha, J. (2004), 'Demography and rights: women, children and access to asylum', *International Journal of Refugee Law*, vol. 16, no. 2: 227–43.

Bhabha, J. (2006), 'Border rights and rites: generalizations, stereotypes and gendered migration', in S. Van Walsum and T. Spijkerboer (eds), *Women and Immigration Law: New Variations on Classical Feminist Themes*, Routledge-Cavendish, London.

Bhabha, J. (2007), 'The gendered fallout of war', unpublished manuscript.

Bhattacharyya, G. (2008), *Dangerous Brown Men: Exploiting Sex, Violence and Feminism in the 'War on Terror'*, Zed Books, London.

Billig, M., S. Condor, D. Edwards, M. Gane, D. Middleton and A. Radley (1988), *Ideological Dilemmas: A Social Psychology of Everyday Thinking*, Sage, London.

Black, R., J. Crush, S. Peberdy, S. Ammassari, L. McLean Hilker, S. Mouillesseaux, C. Pooley and R. Rajkotia (2004), *Migration and Development in Africa: An Overview*, Idasa, Pretoria.

Bögner, D., J. Herlihy and C. Brewin (2007), 'Impact of sexual violence on disclosure during Home Office interviews', *British Journal of Psychiatry*, vol. 191: 75–81.

Bondi, L. and D. Rose (2003), 'Constructing gender, constructing the urban: a review of Anglo-American feminist urban geography', *Gender, Place and Culture*, vol. 10, no. 3: 229–45.

Bourdillon, M. (2006), 'Children and work: a review of current literature and debates', *Development and Change*, vol. 37, no. 6: 1201–26.

Braidotti, R. (2005), 'A critical cartography of feminist post-modernism', *European Journal of Women's Studies*, vol. 20, no. 47: 169–80.

Brennan, D. (2004), *What's Love Got to Do With It: Transnational Desires and Sex Tourism in Dominican Republic*, Duke University Press, Durham.

Brown, J. (2005), 'Evaluating surveys of transparent governance', in UNDESA (United Nations Department of Economic and Social Affairs), *6th Global Forum on Reinventing Government: Towards Participatory and Transparent Governance*, Seoul, Republic of Korea, 24–27 May, United Nations, New York.

Bruin, R. and K. Wouters (2003), 'Terrorism and the non-derogability of non-refoulement', *International Journal of Refugee Law*, vol. 15, no. 1: 5–29.

Bui, H. N. and M. Morash (1999), 'Domestic violence in the Vietnamese immigrant community: an exploratory study', *Violence Against Women*, vol. 5, no. 7: 769–95.

Burman, E. (1990), 'Introduction', in E. Burman (ed.), *Feminist and Psychological Practice*, Sage, London.

Burman, E. (1996), 'Psychology discourse practice: from regulation to resistance', in E. Burman, G. Aitken, P. Alldred, R. Allwood, T. Billington, B. Goldberg, A. Gordo-Lopez, C. Heenan, D. Marks and S. Warner (1996), *Psychology Discourse Practice: From Regulation to Resistance*, Taylor & Francis, London.

Burman, E. (1997), 'Differentiating and de-developing critical social psychology', in T. Ibanez and L. Iniguez (eds), *Critical Social Psychology*, Sage, London.

Burman, E. (2008a), 'Beyond "women vs. children" or "womenandchildren": engendering childhood and reformulating motherhood', *International Journal of Children's Rights*, vol. 16, no. 2: 177–94.

Burman, E. (2008b), *Developments: Child, Image, Nation*, Taylor & Francis, London.

Burman, E. (in press), 'Between justice and pathologisation: juxtapositions of epistemic and material violence in transnational migration and domestic violence research', in J. Shostack and G. Shostack (eds), *Violence, Democracy and the Rights of People*, Routledge, London.

Burman, E. and I. Parker (eds) (1993), *Discourse Analytic Research*, Routledge, London, text available on www.discourseunit.com.

Burman, E. and K. Chantler (2005), 'Domestic violence and minoritisation: legal and policy barriers facing minoritised women leaving violent relationships', *International Journal of Law and Psychiatry*, vol. 28, no. 1: 59–74.

Burman, E. and M. Maclure (2005), 'Deconstruction as a method of research: stories from the field', in B. Somekh and C. Lewin (eds), *Research Methods in the Social Sciences*, Sage, London.

Burman, E., G. Aitken, A. Alldred, R. Allwood, T. Billington, B. Goldberg, A. Gordo Lopez, C. Heenan, D. Marks and S. Warner (1996), *Psychology Discourse Practice: From Regulation to Resistance*. Taylor & Francis, London.

Burman, E., S. Smailes and K. Chantler (2004), '"Culture" as a barrier to domestic violence services for minoritised women', *Critical Social Policy*, vol. 24, no. 3: 358–84.

Burr, V. (1995), *An Introduction to Social Constructionism*, Routledge, London.

Butler, J. (1990), *Gender Trouble*, New York and London; Routledge.

Calavita, K. (2006), Gender, migration and law: crossing borders and bridging disciplines, *International Migration Review*, vol. 40, no. 1: 104–32.

Ceneda, S. and C. Palmer (2006), '*"Lip Service" or Implementation? The Home Office Gender Guidance and Women's Asylum Claims in the UK*', Asylum Aid, London.

CEPAL and PNUD (2000), *Los efectos socioeconómicos de las inundaciones y deslizamientos en Venezuela en 1999* (LC/MEX/ L.421), CEPAL/PNUD, Caracas.

Chant, S. (ed.) (1992), *Gender and Migration in Developing Countries*, Belhaven Press, London.

Chantler, K. (2006), 'Independence, dependency and interdependence: struggles and resistances of minoritized women within and on leaving violent relationships', *Feminist Review*, vol. 82: 27–49.

Chantler, K. (2007), 'Border crossings: nationhood, gender, culture and violence', *International Journal of Critical Psychology*, vol. 20: 138–66.

Chantler, K., E. Burman, J. Batsleer and C. Bashir (2001), *Attempted Suicide and Self-Harm (South Asian Women)*, Manchester Metropolitan University and Manchester, Salford and Trafford Health Action Zone, Manchester.

Chantler, K., G. Gangoli and M. Hester (2009), 'Forced marriage in the UK: religious, cultural, economic or state violence?', *Critical Social Policy*, vol. 29, no. 4: 587–612.

Chapkis, W. (2005), 'Soft glove, punishing fist: the Trafficking Victims Protection Act of 2000', in E. Bernstein and L. Schaffner (eds), *Regulating Sex: The Politics of Intimacy and Identity*, Routledge, New York.

Chatterji, M., N. Murray, D. London and P. Anglewicz (2004), *The Factors Influencing Transactional Sex among Young Men and Women in 12 Sub-Saharan African Countries*, USAID, Washington.

Christopoulos, D. (2004), 'Adventures of Greek nationality: who has (not) the "qualifications" to be a Greek?', *Theseis*, no. 87: 59–88.

Cohen, S. (2006), *Standing on the Shoulders of Fascism: From Immigration Controls to the Strong State*, Trentham Books, Stoke-on-Trent.

Collins, P. (2000), *Black Feminist Thought: Knowledge, Consciousness, and the Politics of Empowerment*, Routledge (2nd edn), New York.

Consortium for Refugees and Migrants in South Africa (CORMSA) (2009), *Protecting Refugees, Asylum Seekers and Immigrants in South Africa*, Consortium for Refugees and Migrants in South Africa, Johannesburg.

Crush, J. and V. Williams (2005), 'International migration and development dynamics and challenges in South and Southern Africa', paper presented at the United Nations expert group meeting on International Migration and Development, New York.

Curt, B. (2001), *Textuality and Tectonics: Troubling Social and Psychological Science*, Open University Press, Buckingham.

Cwinkel, J. (2005), 'Contentious issues in research on trafficked women working in the sex industry: study, design, ethics, and methodology', *Journal of Sex Research*, vol. 42, no. 4: 306–16.

De la Hunt, L. and W. Kerfoot (2008), 'Due process in asylum determination in South Africa from a practitioner's perspective', in J. Handmaker, L. De La Hunt and J. Klaaren (eds), *Advancing Refugee Protection in South Africa*, Berghahn Books, New York.

Delany, A. (2005), *Situation Analysis on the Commercial Exploitation of Children and Child Trafficking: KwaZulu-Natal, Johannesburg*, report for the Programme toward the Elimination of the Worst Forms of Child Labour by the Community Agency for Social Enquiry, November.

Department of Health (2006), *Memo: Access to Comprehensive HIV and AIDS Care, Including Antiretroviral Treatment*, Department of Health, Pretoria.

Department of Home Affairs (1998), 'Refugees Act: No. 130 of 1998', *Government Gazette*, Pretoria.

Department of Home Affairs (2000), 'Refugee Regulations No. R 366', *Government Gazette*, Pretoria.

Department of Home Affairs (2002), 'Immigration Act No. 13', *Government Gazette*, Pretoria.

Dickenson, S. (2004), *Sex in the City: Mapping Commercial Sex across London*, The POPPY Project, London.

Dittmore, M. (2005), 'Trafficking in Lives', in K. Kempadoo (ed), *Trafficking and Prostitution Reconsidered: New Perspectives on Migration, Sex Work and Human Rights*, Paradigm, Boulder.

Dodson, B. (1998), *Women on the Move: Gender and Cross-Border Migration to South Africa*, Migration Policy Series No. 9, Kingston, Southern African Migration Project, Cape Town, Idasa.

Doezema, J. (1988), 'Forced to choose: beyond the voluntary v. forced prostitution dichotomy', in J. Doezema and K. Kempadoo (eds), *Global Sex Workers: Rights, Resistance, Redefinition*, Routledge, New York.

Doezema, J. (2000), 'Lost women or loose women: the re-emergence of the myth of "white slavery" in contemporary discourses of "trafficking in women"', *Gender Issues*, vol. 18, no. 1: 23–50.

Doezema, J. (2002), *Who Gets to Choose? Coercion, Consent and the UN Trafficking Protocol*, www.walnet.org/csis/papers/doezema-choose.html.

Dousia, G. (1999), 'Rights have gender', in *Deltio Thyellis, Special Issue: Rights in the "New Era"*, no. 13.

Du Mont, J. and D. Parnis (1999), 'Judging women: the pernicious effects of rape mythology', *Canadian Woman Studies*, vol. 19, no. 1/2: 102–9.

Du Toit, D., L. Hunzinger, R. Marks and T. Raviv (2005), *Programme of Assistance to the South African Government to Prevent, React to*

Human Trafficking and Provide Support to the Victims of the Crime, draft report to the National Prosecuting Authority and the EU Delegation South Africa, June.

Duffield, M. (2001), *Global Governance and the New Wars*, Zed Books, London.

Dunkle, K. L., R. Jewkes, M. Nduna, N. Jama, J. Levin, Y. Sikweyiya and M. P. Koss (2007), 'Transactional sex with casual and main partners among young South African men in the rural Eastern Cape: prevalence, predictors, and associations with gender-based violence', *Social Science & Medicine*, vol. 65, no. 6: 1235–48.

Emerson, R. M. (1981), 'Social exchange theory', in M. Rosenberg and R. H. Turner (eds), *Social Psychology: Sociological Perspectives*, Basic Books, New York.

Enloe, C. (1990), '"Womenandchildren": making sense of the Persian Gulf crisis', *The Village Voice*, vol. 25, no. 9.

Erez, E. (2000), 'Immigration, culture conflict and domestic violence/woman battering', *Crime Prevention Community Safety*, vol. 2, no. 1: 27–36.

The European Commission against Racism and Intolerance (ECRI) (2009), Directorate General of Human Rights and Legal Affairs, Council of Europe.

Evans, J. and P. Hall (1999), 'What is visual culture', in J. Evans and P. Hall (eds), *Visual Culture: The Reader*, Sage Publications, London.

Fekete, L. (2006), 'Enlightened fundamentalism? Immigration, feminism and the Right', *Race and Class*, vol. 48, no. 1: 1–22.

Fine, M. (1998), 'Working the hyphens: reinventing self and other in qualitative research', in N. Denzin and Y. Lincoln (eds), *The Landscape of Qualitative Research: Theories and Issues*, Sage, London.

Fornah (2006), Fornah v. Secretary of State for the Home Department, www.homeoffice.gov.uk/rds/pdfs08/hosb1108.pdf.

Foucault, M. (1980), *Power/Knowledge: Selected Interviews and Other Writings 1972–1977*, ed. C. Gordon, Harvester Wheatsheaf, New York.

Foucault, M. (1994), 'Governmentality', in J. D. Faubion (ed.), *Power: The Essential Works of Foucault 1954–1984, Volume 3,* London, Penguin Books.

Frello, B. (2008), 'Towards a discursive analytics of movement: on the making and unmaking of movement as an object of knowledge', *Mobilities*, vol. 3, no. 1: 25–50.

Gangoli, G. and K. Chantler (2009), 'Protecting the victims of forced marriage: is age a protective factor?', *Feminist Legal Studies,* vol. 17, no. 3: 267–88.

Garcia, I., F. Giuliani and E. Wiesenfeld (1994), 'El Lugar de la Teoria en Psicologia Social Comunitaria: Comunidad y Sentido de Comunidad', in M. Montero (ed.), *Psicologia Social Comunitaria*, Guadalajara, Universidad de Guadalajara, pp. 75–101.

Gasa, N. (2007), 'Feminisms, motherisms, patriarchies and women's voices', in N. Gasa, (ed.), *Women in South African History: Basus'Iimbokodo,*

Bawel'Imilambo / They Remove Boulders and Cross Rivers, HSRC Press, Cape Town.

Gedalof, I. (2007), 'Unhomely homes: women, family and belonging in UK discourses of migration and asylum', *Journal of Ethnic and Migration Studies*, vol. 33, no. 1: 77–94.

Gergen, K. (1990), 'Social understanding and the inscription of self', in J. W. Stigler, R. A. Shweder and G. Herdt (eds), *Cultural Psychology: Essays in Comparative Human Development*, Cambridge University Press, New York.

Gettleman, J. (2007), 'Rape epidemic raises trauma of Congo War', *New York Times*. 17 October, www.nytimes.com/2007/10/07/world/africa/07congo.html?_r=1&oref=slogin.

Giles, W. and J. Hyndman (2004), *Sites of Violence: Gender and Conflict Zones*, University of California Press, California.

Giles-Vernick, Tamara (2001), 'Lives, histories, and sites of recollection', in Luise White, Stephan F. Miescher and David William Cohen (eds) *African Words, African Voices*, Bloomington, Indiana University Press, pp. 194–213.

Glarnetatzis, N. (2001), 'Taking a look at the anti-racist movement in Greece', in A. Marvakis, D. Parsanoglou and M. Pavlou (eds), *Migrants in Greece*, Ellinika Grammata, Athens.

Global Commission on International Migration (GCIM) (2005), *Migration in an Interconnected World: Report of Global Commission on International Migration*, Glocal Commisison on International Migration, Geneva, www.gcim.org/attachements/gcim-complete-report-2005.pdf.

Goldstein, D. M. (2002), 'Desconfianza and problems of representation in urban ethnography', *Anthropological Quarterly*, vol. 75, no. 3: 485–517.

Gómez, R. (2000), Interview, Fuerte Tiuna, 23 February.

Gondolf, E. and E. Fisher (1988), *Battered Women as Survivors: An Alternative to Treating Learned Helplessness*, Lexington Books, New York.

Gorham, D. (1978), 'The "maiden tribute of modern Babylon" re-examined: child prostitution and the idea of childhood in late-Victorian England', *Victorian Studies*, vol. 21, no. 3: 353–79.

Gould, C. and N. Fick (2008), *Selling Sex in Cape Town: Sex Work and Human Trafficking in a South African City*, Institute for Security Studies, Pretoria.

Gouws, A. (ed.) (2005), *(Un)thinking Citizenship: Feminist Debates in Contemporary South Africa*, UCT Press, Cape Town.

Gready, P. and J. Ensor (2005), *Reinventing Development? Translating Rights-Based Approaches from Theory into Practice*, Zed Books, London.

Greatbatch, J. (1989), 'The gender difference: feminist critiques of refugee discourse', *International Journal of Refugee Law*, vol. 1, no. 4: 518–27.

Halkias, A. (2004), *The Empty Cradle of Democracy: Sex, Abortion and Nationalism in Modern Greece*, Duke University Press, Durham.

Hall, S. (1997), 'The work of representation', in S. Hall (ed.), *Representation: Cultural Representations and Signifying Practices*, Sage Publications, London.

Hamilton, P. (1997), 'Representing the social: France and Frenchness in post-war humanist photography', in S. Hall (ed.), *Representation: Cultural Representations and Signifying Practices*, Sage Publications, London.

Hanmer, J. and C. Itzin (eds) (2000), *Home Truths About Domestic Violence*, Routledge, London.

Haraway, D. (1991), *Simians, Cyborgs and Women: The Reinvention of Nature*, Free Association Books, London.

Harding, S. (1987), *Feminist Methodology: Social Science Issues*, Indiana University Press, Bloomington.

Hellenic League for Human Rights (2009), *The Asylum Crisis and the Rise of Racist Violence and Xenophobia in Greece*, www.hlhr.gr/press/ Statement%20asylum%20and%20racist%20violence%20in%20 Greece%20EN.pdf.

Henriques, J., W. Hollway, C. Urwin, V. Couze and V. Walkerdine (1984), *Changing the Subject: Psychology, Social Regulation and Subjectivity*, Routledge, New York.

Henschel, B. (2003), *The Assessment of Commercial Sexual Exploitation of Children: A Review of Methodologies*, UNICEF.

Hernández, T. (1999), 'Catástrofe natural: Solución al reto habitacional – Ejecutivo dispone de 5.500 viviendas', *El Universal*, 21 December.

Herzfeld, M. (2007), 'Small-mindedness writ large: on the migrations and manners of prejudice', *Journal of Ethnic and Migration Studies*, vol. 33, no. 2: 255–74.

Hester, M., K. Chantler, G. Gangoli, J. Devgon, S. Sharma and A. Singleton (2008), 'Forced marriage: the risk factors and the effect of raising the minimum age for a sponsor, and of leave to enter the UK as a spouse or fiancé(e)', www.nursing.manchester.ac.uk/learning/staff/ kchantler/FM_RESEARCH_SUMMARY_08.pdf.

Hirsch, M. (1999), 'Introduction: familial looking', in M. Hirsch (ed.), *The Familial Gaze*, University Press of New England, Hanover.

Hirschowitz, R., S. Worku and M. Orkin (2000), *Quantitative Research Findings on Rape in South Africa*, Statistics South Africa, Pretoria.

Hogan, D. and E. Marandola (2005), 'Towards an interdisciplinary conceptualization of vulnerability', *Population, Space and Place*, vol. 11, no. 6: 455–71.

Home Office (2006), *Gender Issues in Asylum Claims*, London, Home Office.

hooks, bell (1994), 'In our glory: photography and black life', in D. Willis (ed.), *Picturing Us: African American Identity in Photography*, The New Press, New York.

Howarth, D. and Y. Stavrakakis (2000), 'Introducing discourse theory and political analysis', in D. Howarth, A. Norval and Y. Stavrakakis (eds), *Discourse Theory and Political Analysis: Identities, Hegemonies and Social Change*, Manchester University Press, Manchester.

Hughes, D. (2001), 'The "Natasha" trade: transnational sex trafficking', *National Institute of Justice Journal*, January: 9–15.

Human Rights Watch (2008), *Left to Survive: Systematic Failure to Protect Unaccompanied Migrant Children in Greece*, www.hrw.org/en/reports/2008/12/22/left-survive.

Human Rights Watch (2009a), 'South Africa', *World Report 2009*, Human Rights Watch, New York.

Human Rights Watch (2009b), 'Greece – halt crackdown, arrests of migrants: moving detained migrants to north raises fears of "pushbacks" to Turkey', Public Statement 27 July 2009, www.hrw.org/en/news/2009/07/27/greece-halt-crackdown-arrests-migrants.

Hunter, M. (2002), 'The materiality of everyday sex: thinking beyond "prostitution"', *African Studies*, vol. 61, no. 1: 99–120.

Immigration Appelate Authority (2000), *Asylum Gender Guidelines*, Immigration Appelate Authority, London.

Indra, D. (1999), *Engendering Forced Migration: Theory and Practice*, Berghahn Books, London.

International Alert (2005), 'Women's bodies as a battleground: sexual violence against women and girls during the war in the Democratic Republic of Congo, South Kivu (1996–2003)', www.international-alert.org/pdf/sexual_violence_congo_english.pdf.

International Crisis Group (2008), *DR Congo*, www.crisisgroup.org/home/index.cfm?id=1174&l=1.

International Helsinki Federation for Human Rights (IHF) (2003), 'Anti-terrorism measures, security and human rights: developments in Europe, Central Asia and North America in the aftermath of September 11, April 2003, at 17', see www.ihf-hr.org/documents/doc_summary.php?sec_id=58&d_id=4082.

International Organization for Migration (2009), *Annual Report: International Organization for Migration*, Geneva.

Jackson, N. (2006), 'International organizations, security dichotomies and the trafficking of persons and narcotics in post-Soviet Central Asia: a critique of the securitization framework', *Security Dialogue*, vol. 37, no. 3: 299–317.

Jacobsen, K. and L. Landau (2003a), 'Researching refugees: some methodological and ethical considerations in social science and forced migration', *Forced Migration Working Paper Series* (2), www.migration. org.za.

Jacobsen, K. and L. Landau (2003b), 'The dual imperative in refugee research: some methodological and ethical considerations in social science research on forced migration', *Disasters*, vol. 27, no. 3: 95–116.

Jamal, A. (2009), 'Gendered Islam and modernity in the nation-space: women's modernism in the Jamaat-e-Islami of Pakistan', *Feminist Review*, vol. 91: 9–28.

Jewkes, R. and N. Abrahams (2002), 'The epidemiology of rape and sexual coercion in South Africa: an overview', *Social Science & Medicine*, vol. 55, no. 7: 1231–44.

Jewkes, R. K., C. Vundule, F. Maforah and E. Jordaan (2001), 'Relationship dynamics and teenage pregnancy in South Africa', *Social Science & Medicine*, vol. 52, no. 5: 733–44.

Jodelet, D. (2001), 'Os processos psicossocias da exclusao', in B. Sawaia (ed.), *As Artimanhas da exclusao. Analise psicossocial e etica da desigualdade social*, Petropolis, Vozes.

Jolly, S. with H. Reeves (2005), 'Gender and Migration', www.bridge.ids.ac.uk/reports/cep-mig-or.doc.

Kambouri, E. (2007), *Every-day Life of Women Migrants from Albania and Ukraine*, Gutenberg, Athens.

Kambouri, H. (2008), 'Feminine jobs/masculine becomings: gender and identity in the discourse of Albanian domestic workers in Greece', *European Journal of Women's Studies*, vol. 15, no. 1: 7–22.

Kapur, R. (2002), 'The tragedy of victimization rhetoric: resurrecting the "native" subject in international/post-colonial feminist legal politics', *Harvard Human Rights Journal*, vol. 15, no. 1: 1–38.

Kapur, R. (2005), 'Cross-border movements and the law: renegotiating the boundaries of difference', in K. Kempadoo (ed.), *Trafficking and Prostitution Reconsidered: New Perspectives on Migration, Sex Work and Human Rights*, Paradigm, Boulder.

Kasimati, K. and L. Mousourou (2007), *Gender and Migration: Theoretical References and Empirical Research*, Gutenberg, Athens.

Kelly, K. (2000), 'Action research, performance and critical hermeneutics', *Annual Review of Critical Psychology*, vol. 2: 89–108.

Kempadoo, K. (ed.) (2005), *Trafficking and Prostitution Reconsidered: New Perspectives on Migration, Sex Work and Human Rights*, Paradigm, Boulder.

Khan, S. (2003), 'Zina and the moral regulation of Pakistani women', *Feminist Review*, vol. 75, no. 1: 75–100.

Kiwanuka, M. (2008), 'The effect of migration on urban migrant women's perceptions of domestic violence', unpublished thesis, University of the Witwatersrand, Johannesburg, South Africa.

Kneebone, S. (2005), 'Women within the refugee construct: "exclusionary inclusion" in policy and practice – the Australian experience', *International Journal of Refugee Law*, vol. 17, no. 1: 7–42.

Laczo, F. and M. Gramegna (2003), 'Developing better indicators of human trafficking', *Brown Journal of World Affairs*, vol. X, no. 1: 179–94.

Landau, L. B. (2006), 'Transplants and transients: idioms of belonging and dislocation in inner-city Johannesburg', *African Studies Review*, vol. 49, no. 2: 125–45.

Landau. L. B. (2008), 'Reconsidering inclusion in Africa's cities of shifting sands: Johannesburg, South Africa', *Forced Migration Studies Programme Working Paper*, Forced Migration Studies Programme, Johannesburg.

Landau, L. B. and T. Monson (2008), 'Displacement, estrangement and sovereignty: reconfiguring state power in urban South Africa', *Government and Opposition*, vol. 43, no. 2: 315–36.

Latta, R. E. and L. A. Goodman (2005), 'Considering the interplay of cultural context and service provision in intimate partner violence: the case of Haitian immigrant women', *Violence Against Women*, vol. 11, no. 11: 1441–64.

LaViolette, N. (2007), 'Gender-related refugee claims: expanding the scope of the Canadian guidelines', *International Journal of Refugee Law*, vol. 19, no. 2: 169–214.

Lefko-Everett, K. (2007), 'Voices from the margins: migrant women's experiences in Southern Africa', *Migration Policy Series*, no. 46, Southern African Migration Project, Cape Town and Kingston.

Lerner, M. J. (1980), *The Belief in a Just World: A Fundamental Delusion*, Plenum Press, New York.

Lewis, G. (2006), 'Imaginaries of Europe: technologies of gender, economies of power', *European Journal of Women's Studies*, vol. 13, no. 2: 87–102.

Lifongo, M. (2009), 'Control mechanisms in human trafficking', *Eye on Trafficking*, vol. 20: 4–5.

Loescher, D. and J. Scanlan (1986), *Calculated Kindness: Refugees and America's Half-open Door, 1945 to the Present*, Free Press, New York.

Longfield, K., A. Glick, M. Waithaka and J. Berman (2002), 'Cross-generational relationships in Kenya: couples' motivations, risk perception for STIs/HIV and condom use', *Working Paper No. 52*, PSI Research Division, Washington.

Lonsway, K. and L. Fitzgerald (1994), 'Rape myths: in review', *Psychology of Women Quarterly*, vol. 18, no. 2: 133–64.

Lopes, D. (2005a), *Situation Analysis on the Commercial Sexual Exploitation of Children and Child Trafficking: Mpumalanga*, Johannesburg: Report for the Programme toward the Elimination of the Worst Forms of Child Labour by the Community Agency for Social Enquiry, November.

Lopes, D. (2005b), *Situation Analysis on the Commercial Exploitation of Children and Child Trafficking: Limpopo*, Johannesburg: Report for the Programme toward the Elimination of the Worst Forms of Child Labour by the Community Agency for Social Enquiry, November.

LSE (2005), *LSE Identity Project Report*, http://is2.lse.ac.uk/IDcard/identitysummary.pdf.

LSE (2006), *House of Commons Select Committee on Science and Technology Inquiry into 'Scientific Advice, Risk and Evidence:*

How Government Handles Them' with Particular Reference to the Technologies Supporting the Government's Proposals for Identity Cards, London School of Economics and Political Science Identity Project Team.

Luke, N. (2003), 'Age and economic asymmetries in the sexual relationships of adolescent girls in sub-Saharan Africa', *Studies in Family Planning*, vol. 34, no. 2: 67–86.

Macklin, A. (1995), 'Refugee women and the imperative of categories', *Human Rights Quarterly*, vol. 17, no. 2: 213–77.

Macklin, A. (2004), 'A comparative analysis of the Canadian, US and Australian directives on gender persecution and refugee status', in D. Indra (ed.), *Engendering Forced Migration: Theory and Practice*, Berghahn Books, New York.

Mahalingam, R. and J. Lei (2005), 'Culture, essentialism, immigration and representations of gender', *Theory & Psychology*, vol. 15, no. 6: 839–60.

Malkki, L. (1992), 'National Geographic: the rooting of peoples and the territorialisation of national identity among scholars and refugees', *Cultural Anthropology*, vol. 7, no. 1: 24–44.

Martens, J., M. Pieczkowski and B. Van Vuuren-Smyth (2003), *Seduction, Sale and Slavery: Trafficking in Women and Children for Sexual Exploitation in Southern Africa*, International Organization for Migration, Pretoria.

Martínez, D. (2000), Interview, Fuerte Tiuna, 24 February.

Marvakis, A., D. Parsanoglou and V. Tsianos (2006), 'And yet they move! ... The revolution of hopes and the autonomy of migrants', *Synchrona Themata*, no. 92.

Mathews, S., N. Abrahams, L. Martin, L. Vetten, L. van der Merwe and R. Jewkes (2004), 'Every six hours a woman is killed by her intimate partner: a national study of female homicide in South Africa', *MRC Policy Brief*, no. 5.

Meekers, D. and A. Calvés (1997), '"Main" girlfriends, girlfriends, marriage and money: the social context of HIV risk behaviour in sub-Saharan Africa', *Health Transition Review*, Supplement to vol. 7: 361–75.

Menjivar, C. and O. Salcido (2002), 'Immigrant women and domestic violence: common experiences in different countries', *Gender and Society*, vol. 16, no. 6: 898–20.

Meth, P. (2004), 'Using diaries to understand women's responses to crime and violence', *Environment and Urbanization*, vol. 16, no. 2: 153–64.

Misago, J. P., L. B. Landau and T. Monson (2009), *Towards Tolerance, Law, and Dignity: Addressing Violence against Foreign Nationals in South Africa*, International Organization for Migration, Johannesburg.

Mohanty, C. Talpade (1988), 'Under Western eyes: feminist scholarship and colonial discourses', in J. Alexander and C. Mohanty (eds), *Feminist Genealogies, Colonial Legacies, Democratic Futures*, Routledge, New York, pp. 51–80.

Mohanty, C. (1994), 'Under Western eyes: feminist scholarship and colonial discourses', in P. Williams and L. Chrisman (eds), *Colonial Discourse and Postcolonial Theory*, Harvester Wheatsheaf, New York.

Mojab, S. (1998), '"Muslim" women and "western" feminists: the debate on particulars and universals', *Monthly Review*, vol. 50, no. 7: 19–30.

Montes, I. (2000), Interview, Fuerte Tiuna, 13 April.

Morokvasic, M. (2007), 'Migration, gender and empowerment', in I. Lenz, C. Ullrich and B. Fersch (eds), *Gender Orders Unbound: Globalization, Restructuring and Reciprocity*, Barbara Budrich, Opladen.

Morokvasic, M., U. Erel and K. Shinozaki (eds) (2003), *Crossing Borders and Shifting Boundaries – Vol. I: Gender on the Move*, Leske and Budrich, Opladen.

Motsemme, N. (2004), 'The mute always speak: on women's silences at the Truth and Reconciliation Commission', *Current Sociology*, vol. 52, no. 5: 909–32.

Murray, A. (1998), 'Debt-bondage and trafficking: don't believe the hype', in K. Kempadoo and J. Doezema (eds), *Global Sex Workers: Rights, Resistance, Redefinition*, Routledge, New York.

Muzvidziwa, N. V. (2001), 'Marriage as a survival strategy: the case of Masvingo, Zimbabwe', *Zambezia*, vol. xxviii, no. ii: 147–65.

Neocosmos, M. (2006), *From Foreign Natives to Native Foreigners: Explaining Xenophobia in Post-Apartheid South Africa*, Council for the Development of Social Science Research in Africa (CODESRIA), Monograph Series, Dakar.

OAU (1961), *Convention Governing Specific Aspects of Refugee Problems in Africa*, OAU, Addis Ababa.

Oxford, C. (2005), 'Protectors and victims in the gender regime of asylum', *National Women's Studies Association Journal*, vol. 17, no. 3: 18–38.

Pain, R. H. (1997), 'Social geographies of women's fear of crime', *Transactions of the Institute of British Geographers*, vol. 22, no. 2: 231–44.

Palmary, I. (2003), 'Nationalism and asylum: implications for women', *Agenda*, vol. 55: 5–14.

Palmary, I. (2005), 'The possibility of a reflexive gaze: the relevance of feminist debates on reflexivity, representation and situated knowledges for psychology', in P. Kiguwa and T. Schaeffer (eds), *The Gender of Psychology*, UCT Press, Cape Town.

Palmary, I. (2006), 'Gender, nationalism and ethnic difference: feminist politics and political psychology', *Feminism & Psychology*, vol. 16, no. 1: 44–51.

Palmary, I. (2008a), *For Better Implementation of Children's Rights in South Africa*, UNICEF, Pretoria.

Palmary, I. (2008b), 'Poor girls: child migrants, sexuality and poverty in South Africa', a paper presented at the BPS Psychology of Women Section Annual Conference, Windsor, England.

Parker, I. (1992), *Discourse Dynamics*, Routledge, London (full text available on www.discourseunit.com).

Parker, I. (2003), *Critical Discursive Psychology*, Sage, London.

Parker, I. (2007), *Revolution in Psychology: Alienation to Emancipation*, Pluto, London.

Parker, I. and the Bolton Discourse Network (1999), *Critical Textwork*, Open University Press, Buckingham.

Parpart, J. (1995), 'Deconstructing the development "expert": gender, development and the "vulnerable groups"', in M. Marchand and J. Parpart (eds), *Feminism/Postmodernism/Development*, Routledge, London.

Parrenas, R. (2001), *Servants of Globalization: Women, Migration and Domestic Work*, Stanford University Press, Stanford.

Parsanoglou, D. and J. Tsiamoglou (2008), 'National report: the case of Greece', in Mediterranean Institute of Gender Studies (MIGS) – University of Nicosia, *Integration of Female Migrant Domestic Workers: Strategies for Employment and Civic Participation*, Nicosia, University of Nicosia Press.

Pavlou, M. (2007), '"Greece, Greece, we are your children!" Macropolitical challenges of migration for the state and society', in X. Kontiadis and Th. Paptheodorou (eds), *Transformation of Migration Policy*, Papazisisis, Athens.

Pettman, J. J. (1996), 'Boundary politics: women, nationalism and danger', in M. Maynard and J. Purvis (eds), *New Frontiers in Women's Studies: Knowledge, Identity and Nationalism*, Taylor & Francis, London.

Phoenix, A. (1987), 'Theories of gender and black families', in G. Weiner and M. Arnot (eds), *Gender Under Scrutiny*, Hutchinson, London.

Phoenix, A. and P. Pattynama (eds) (2006), 'Editorial: intersectionality', *European Journal of Women's Studies*, Special Issue, vol. 13, no. 3: 187–92.

Pillay, A. (2001), 'Violence against women in the aftermath', in S. Meintjies, A. Pillay and M. Turshen (eds), *The Aftermath: Women in Post-conflict Transformation*, Zed Books, London.

Psarra, A. (2009), 'For an important female work', Newspaper *AVGI*, 22 February.

Pulerwitz, J., S. L. Gortmaker and W. Dejong (2000), 'Measuring sexual relationship power in HIV/STD research', *Sex Roles*, vol. 42, no. 7: 637–60.

Raj, A. and J. Silverman (2002), 'Violence against women: the roles of culture, context, and legal immigrant status on intimate partner violence', *Violence Against Women*, vol. 8, no. 3: 367–98.

Rao, V., G. Gupta, M. Loshkin and J. Smarajit (2001), *Sex Workers and the Cost of Safe Sex: The Compensating Differential for Condom Use in Calcutta*, www.worldbank.org/aidsecon/papers/sexworkers_safesex2.pdf.

Raymond, J., J. D'Cunha and S. Dzuhayatiin (2002), *A Comparative Study of Women Trafficked in the Migration Process: Patterns Profiles and Health Consequences of Sexual Exploitation in Five Countries*, Coalition Against Trafficking in Women, http://action.web.ca/home/catw/attach/CATW%20Comparative%20Study%202002.pdf.

Razack, S. (1995), 'Domestic violence as gender persecution: policing the borders of nation, race, and gender', *Canadian Journal of Women and the Law*, vol. 8: 45–88.

Razack, S. (2004), 'Imperilled Muslim women, dangerous Muslim men and civilised Europeans: legal and social responses to forced marriages', *Feminist Legal Studies*, vol. 12, no. 2: 129–74.

Riley, D. (1988), *Am I that Name? Feminism and the Category of 'Women' in History*, Macmillan, London.

Rivero, C. (2000), Interview, Fuerte Tiuna, 14 February.

Rodríguez Mora, I. (1996), '"En defensa del orden ..."': Análisis psicosocial de propuestas autoritarias frente al prolema de la delincuencia común en Venezuela', in M. Lozada (coord), *Democracia, espacio público y vida cotidiana. ¿La cuestión de lo político o la política en cuestión?*, Facículo 7, Caracas.

Rodríguez Mora, I. (2003), 'Psychosocial interventions in emergencies: theoretical models and their ethical and political implications in the Venezuelan context – the case of UNICEF, unpublished PhD dissertation, University of Cambridge.

Rose, G. (1999), 'Women and everyday spaces', in J. Price and M. Shildrick (eds), *Feminist Theory and the Body: A Reader*, Edinburgh University Press, Edinburgh.

Sakellis, I. and N. Spyropoulou (2007), 'Employing immigrant women from Albania and Ukraine in domestic services in Greece', *The Greek Review of Social Research*, vol. 124, no. C: 71–93.

Salmerón, V. and G. Chiappe (1999), 'Gobierno inicia traslado de refugiados al interior del país', *El Universal*, 21 December.

Sampson, E. (1989), 'The deconstruction of the self', in J. Shotter and K. Gergen (eds), *Texts of Identity*, Sage, London.

Sanghera, J. (2005), 'Unpacking the trafficking discourse', in K. Kempadoo (ed.), *Trafficking and Prostitution Reconsidered: New Perspectives on Migration, Sex Work and Human Rights*, Paradigm, Boulder.

Save the Children, UK and Forced Migration Studies Programme (2009), *Regional Seminar on Children Who Cross Borders in Southern Africa*, Save the Children UK, Pretoria.

Scarry, E. (1985), *The Body in Pain: The Making and Unmaking of the World*, Oxford University Press, New York.

Scott, J. (1997), 'The infrapolitics of subordinate groups', in M. Rahnema with V. Bawtree (eds), *The Post-development Reader*, Zed Books, London.

Scott, J. (1998), *Seeing Like a State: How Certain Schemes to Improve the Human Condition Have Failed*, Yale University Press, New Haven.

Seshadri-Crooks, K. (2000), *The Desire for Whiteness: A Lacanian Analysis of Race*, Routledge, New York.

Shepherd, L. (2008), *Gender, Violence and Security*, Zed Books, London.

Shildrick, M. and J. Price (1999), 'Openings on the body: a critical introduction', in J. Price and M. Shildrick (eds), *Feminist Theory and the Body: A Reader*, Edinburgh University Press, Edinburgh.

Shuman, A. and C. Bohmer (2004), 'Representing trauma: political asylum narrative', *Journal of American Folklore*, vol. 119, no. 446: 394–414.

Shuman, A. and C. Bohmer (2007), 'Producing epistemologies of ignorance in the political asylum process', *Identities: Global Studies in Culture and Power*, vol. 14, no. 5: 603–29.

Siddiqui, N., S. Ismail and M. Allen (2008), *Safe to Return? Report of a Transnational Research Project Investigating Pakistani Women's Access to Domestic Violence and Asylum Support Services in the UK and Pakistan*, Women's Studies Research Centre, Manchester Metropolitan University/South Manchester Law Centre, Manchester.

Sigsworth, R., C. Nqwane and A. Pino (2008), *The Gendered Nature of Xenophobia in South Africa*, Centre for the Study of Violence and Reconciliation, Johannesburg.

Sihlwayi, S. (2009), 'Community stabilization can reduce human trafficking', *Eye on Trafficking*, vol. 20: 5.

Silverman, D. (2004), *Qualitative Research: Theory, Method and Practice*, London, Sage.

Silvey, R. (2006), 'Geographies of gender and migration: spacializing social difference', *International Migration Review*, vol. 40, no. 1: 64–81.

Sinha, A. (2001), 'Domestic violence and the U.S. asylum law: eliminating the cultural hook for claims involving gender-related persecution', *New York University Law Review*, vol. 76: 1562–98.

Skotte, H. (2004), 'Tents in concrete? Housing the internally displaced', in *House: Loss, Refuge and Belonging*, Trondheim, Norway.

Slim, H. and P. Thompson, with O. Bennett and N. Cross (1998), 'Ways of listening', in R. Perks and A. Thomson (eds), *An Oral History Reader*, Routledge, London.

Smart, C. (1999), 'A history of ambivalence and conflict in the discursive construction of the "child victim" of sexual abuse', *Social Legal Studies*, vol. 8, no. 3: 391–408.

Smart, C. (2004), 'Equal shares: rights for fathers or recognition for children?', *Critical Social Policy*, vol. 24, no. 4: 484–503.

Smart, C. and S. Sevenhuijsen (eds) (1989), *Child Custody and the Politics of Gender*, Routledge, London.

Smith, J. D. (2009), 'Managing men, marriage and modern love: women's perspectives on intimacy and male infedility in south eastern Nigeria', in J. Cole and T. Lynn (eds), *Love in Africa*, University of Chicago Press, Chicago.

Smith, S. J. (1989), 'Social relations, neighbourhood structure and the fear of crime in Britain', in D. Evan and D. Herbert (eds), *The Geography of Crime*, Routledge, London.

Sontag, S. (1977), *On Photography*, Penguin Books Ltd, London.

South African Law Reform Commission (2006), *Discussion Paper 111: Trafficking in Persons*, Project 131, including the Combating of Trafficking in Persons Bill, South African Law Reform Commission, Pretoria.

Spijkerboer, T. (2000), *Gender and Refugee Status*, Ashgate/Dartmouth, Burlington.

Spivak, G. (1994), 'Can the subaltern speak?', in P. Williams and L. Chrisman (eds), *Colonial Discourse and Post Colonial Theory*, Harvester Wheatsheaf, New York.

Sprecher, S. (1998), 'Social exchange theories and sexuality', *Journal of Sex Research*, vol. 35, no. 1: 32–43.

Stanley, L. and S. Wise (1983), 'Back into the personal: or our attempt to construct feminist research', in G. Bowles and R. D. Klein (eds), *Theories of Women's Studies*, Routledge and Kegan Paul, London.

Stavrakakis, Y. with N. Chrysoloras (2006), '(I can't get no) enjoyment: Lacanian theory and the analysis of nationalism', *Psychoanalysis, Culture and Society*, vol. 11: 144–63.

Steinfatt, T., S. Baker and A. Beesey (2002), 'Measuring the number of trafficked women in Cambodia: Part I of a series', paper presented at a conference titled The Human Rights Challenge of Globalization in Asia–Pacific–US: The Trafficking in Persons, Especially Women and Children, Honolulu, 13–15 November.

Stevens, M. (1993), 'Recognizing gender-specific persecution: a proposal to add gender as a sixth refugee category', *Cornell Journal of Law and Public Policy*, vol. 3: 179–220.

Stiliou, L. (2007), 'Bulgarian migrant women working as live-in caregivers of the elderly: reflections on "domestic" and "public"', paper presented at international workshop on Gender, Work and the Household: Comparative Perspectives, University of the Aegean, Mytilene, 30–31 March 2007.

Summers, C. (1991), 'Intimate colonialism: the imperial production of reproduction in Uganda, 1907–1925', *Signs: Journal of Women in Culture and Society*, vol. 16, no. 4: 787–807.

Sylvester, C. (1998), 'Homeless in international relations? "Women's" place in canonical texts and feminist reimaginings', in A. Phillips (ed.), *Feminism & Politics*, Oxford University Press, Oxford and New York.

Tastsoglou, E. and J. Hadjiconstandi (2003), 'Never outside the labour market, but always outsiders: female migrant workers in Greece', *The Greek Review of Social Research*, Special Issue *Gender and International Migration: Focus on Greece*, vol. 110: 189–220.

Tuepker, A. (2002), 'On the threshold of Africa: OAU and UN definitions in South African asylum practice', *Journal of Refugee Studies*, vol. 15, no. 4: 409–23.

Ueno, C. (2004), *Nationalism and Gender*, Transpacific Press, Melbourne.

UNFPA (2006), *The State of the World Population: A Passage to Hope, Women and International Migration*, UNFPA, New York.

UNHCR (1951), *Convention Relating to the Status of Refugees*. UNHCR, Geneva.

UNHCR (1992), *Handbook on Procedures and Criteria for Determining Refugee Status under the 1951 Convention and the 1967 Protocol Relating to the Status of Refugees*, HCR/IP/4/Rev.1.

UNHCR (2002), *Guidelines on International Protection: Gender-Related Persecution within the Context of Article 1A(2) of the Convention and/or its 1967 Protocol relating to the Status of Refugees*, UNHCR, Geneva.

UNHCR (2006), *The State of the World's Refugees 2006: Human Displacement in the New Millennium*, www.unhcr.org/publ/PUBL/4444afca0.pdf.

UNHCR (2009), *2008 Global Trends: Refugees, Asylum Seekers, Returnees, Internally Displaced and Stateless Peoples*, www.unhcr.org/4a375c426. html.

UNICEF (2005), *Female Genital Mutilation/Cutting: A Statistical Exploration*, UNICEF, New York.

UNICEF (n.d.), *The Long Journey of the Concept of Child Development in UNICEF Emergency Interventions: The Example of Psychosocial Programming*, UNICEF.

United States Department of State (2009), *Trafficking in Persons Report*, United States Department of State, Washington.

Vaiou, D. (2006), *Integration of New Female Migrants in Greek Labor Market and Society and Policies Affecting Integration: State of the Art*, FeMiPol, Working Paper, No. 10, WP 4, www.femipol.uni-frankfurt. de.

Valji, N. (2001), 'Women and the 1951 Refugee Convention: 50 years of seeking visibility', *REFUGE*, vol. 19, no. 5: 25–35.

Valji, N. and L. de la Hunt (1999), *Gender Guidelines for Asylum Determination*, National Consortium on Refugee Affairs, Cape Town.

Valji, N., L. de la Hunt and H. Moffett (2008), 'Protecting the invisible: the status of women refugees in Southern Africa', in J. Handmaker, L. de la Hunt and J. Klaaren (eds), *Advancing Refugee Protection in South Africa*, Berghan Books, New York.

Van Leeuwen, T. and R. Wodak (1999), 'Legitimizing immigration control: a discourse-historical analysis', *Discourse Studies*, vol. 1, no. 1: 83–118.

Van Schalkwyk, S. and Z. Mhlanac (2007), 'Forced marriages: a pan-African reality', *Mail and Guardian*, 23 December 2007, www.mg.co.za/article/2007-12-23-forced-marriages-a-panafrican-reality.

Vanwesenbeeck, I. (2001), 'Another decade of social scientific research on sex work: a review of research 1990–2000', *Annual Review of Sex Research*, vol. 12: 242–89.

Vearey, J. (2008), 'Migration, access to ART, and survivalist livelihood strategies in Johannesburg', *African Journal of AIDS Research*, vol. 7, no. 3: 361–74.

Vearey, J., L. Nunez and I. Palmary (2007), *Assessing Non-citizen Access to ART in Johannesburg*, Forced Migration Studies Programme and Lawyers for Human Rights, Johannesburg.

Vetten, L. (2005), *Addressing Domestic Violence in South Africa: Reflections on Strategy and Practice*, Centre for the Study of Violence and Reconciliation, Johannesburg.

Visweswaran, K. (2004), 'Gendered states: rethinking culture as a site of South Asian human rights work', *Human Rights Quarterly*, vol. 26, no. 2: 483–511.

Vovou, S. (2001), 'A feminist approach to migrant women', in A. Marvakis, D. Parsanoglou and M. Pavlou (eds), *Migrants in Greece*, Athens, Ellinika Grammata.

Walters, W. (2004), 'Secure borders, safe haven, domopolitics', *Citizenship Studies*, vol. 8, no. 3: 237–60.

Warrington, M. (2001), 'I must get out: the geographies of domestic violence', *Transactions of the Institute of British Geographers*, vol. 26, no. 3: 365–82.

Webster, W. (1998), *Imagining Home: Gender, "Race" and National Identity 1945–64*, Routledge, London.

Weekes, A. (2006), 'South African anti-trafficking legislation: a critique of control over women's freedom', *Agenda*, vol. 70.

White, N. R. (1998), 'Marking absences: Holocaust testimony and history', in R. Perks and A. Thomson (eds), *The Oral History Reader*, Routledge, London.

Wiesenfeld, E. (1994), 'The construction of meaning of slum house', paper presented at the XXIII International Congress of Applied Psychology, Madrid.

Wiesenfeld, E. and A. Amaro (2007), 'Cuando mudarse es más que cambiar de vivienda. El significado del realojo para víctimas de inundaciones en Venezuela', in J. Gissi y, D. Sirlopú (eds), *Nuevos asedios a la psique latinoamericana*, Santiago de Chile, Ediciones de la Universidad Católica de Chile.

Wijers, M. (1998), 'Women, labor, and migration: the position of trafficked women and strategies for support', in K. Kempadoo and J. Doezema (eds), *Global Sex Workers: Rights, Resistance, Redefinition*, Routledge, New York.

Young, L. and H. Barrett (2001), 'Adapting visual methods: action research with Kampala street children', *Area*, vol. 33, no. 2: 141–52.

Yuval-Davis, N. (1997 [1998]), *Gender and Nation*, Sage, London.

Yuval-Davis, N. (2006a), 'Intersectionality and feminist politics', *European Journal of Women's Studies*, Special Issue, vol. 13, no. 3: 193–209.

Yuval-Davis, N. (2006b), 'Human/women's rights and feminist transversal politics', in M. Marx Ferree and A. Tripp (eds), *Global Feminisms: Transnational Women's Organizing, Activism, and Human Rights*, New York University Press, New York.

Yuval-Davis, N. and F. Anthias (eds) (1989), *Woman – Nation – State*, Macmillan, London.

Zavos, A. (2008), 'Moving relationships/shifting alliances: constructions of migration in the leftist anti-racist movement in Athens', *Annual Review of Critical Psychology*, Special Issue on Asylum and Migration, vol. 6 (online), www.discourseunit.com/arcp/arcp6/Zavos.pdf.

Zerpa, H. (2000a), Interview, Fuerte Tiuna, 28 June.

Zerpa, H. (2000b), 'Participación del ejército in projectos psicosociales en Fuerte Tiuna', en AVEPSO *Memorias que construyen memorias*, Caracas, 8 August.

Zia, A. S. (2009), 'The reinvention of feminism in Pakistan', *Feminist Review*, vol. 91: 29–46.

Z-Magazine (2009), *Greece Immigrant Repression*, www.zmag.org/znet/viewArticle/22026.

Žižek, S. (2008), *Violence*, Profile Books, London.

About the contributors

Chandré Gould is a senior researcher in the Crime, Justice and Politics Programme of the Institute for Security Studies. She is co-author of *Selling Sex in Cape Town: Sex work and human trafficking in a South African city.*

Sajida Ismail is a practising solicitor, specialising in immigration and asylum law in a not-for-profit Law Centre. Much of her casework concerns issues relating to gender violence and discrimination, and she is co-author of a report which examined domestic violence issues in Pakistani women's asylum cases.

Caroline Wanjiku Kihato is a visiting senior research fellow at the School of Architecture and Planning at the University of the Witwatersrand in Johannesburg. She is working on understanding urban land markets on the continent, and, in collaboration with UN-HABITAT, is developing a guide book on urban land markets for policy makers.

Monica Kiwanuka is a PhD student in the Forced Migration Studies Programme at the University of the Witwatersrand in Johannesburg. Her work is on the dynamics related to gender violence and displacement with particular focus on domestic violence and issues of service delivery in the host countries.

Julie Middleton is a senior programme officer with Freedom House Southern Africa, where she works closely with civil society in Zimbabwe on capacity building and human rights promotion, protection and monitoring programmes. Before coming to

Freedom House, she worked with CIVICUS: World Alliance for Citizen Participation.

Isabel Rodríguez Mora is a Venezuelan social psychologist living in London. She has a PhD from the University of Cambridge and has carried out research on the disciplinary, ethical and political implications of trauma-oriented interventions in emergencies, the discourse and practices of alternative forms of political action and public spaces and democracy.

Stavros N. Psaroudakis is doing PhD psychosocial research on new media art practices in Greece at the Discourse Unit, Manchester Metropolitan University. His research interests revolve around precarious subjectivities, including young artists, scientists and immigrants. He is a fellow of the Greek Scholarships Institution (IKY).

Alexandra Zavos is finishing her PhD on 'The politics of gender and migration in the anti-racist movement in Athens' at Manchester Metropolitan University. She is currently based in Athens and is working as senior researcher for the EU-funded project 'Gender, migration and intercultural interactions in South-East Europe and the Mediterranean: an intersectional approach' (www.gemic.eu).

Index

(Fictitious names of immigrants are presented in inverted commas; e.g. 'Rose')